"Miller has provided us with frontline research in an emerging sector of World Christianity—the indigenous theology of Christians from a Muslim background. World Christianity, Muslim-Christian relations, conversion studies, or missiology—if any of these are your area of interest, this book is for you. If the mission of God in our world or, perhaps, 'frontier theology' is your concern, *Living among the Breakage* is for you. In these pages, Miller engages the theology of the globally emerging churches of Christians from a Muslim background (CMB). He approaches the task from several creative angles: field work amongst Iranian diaspora congregations; analysis of CMB books, poetry, and testimonial literature; and the case study of a semi-covert CMB congregation in the Arabophone Middle East. What Miller has done here is compelling in its creative simplicity. *Living among the Breakage* is a work of contextualization, but a 'contextualization from within': this is a disciplined effort at eliciting, ordering, and analyzing the distinctive (if thoroughly informal and implicit) theology of the growing, sometimes overlooked, CMB churches around the world. Though this is a systematic and analytic piece of research, Miller remains highly attuned to the practical, earthy, and conflicted experience of former Muslims in transition between Church and Mosque, with a foot yet in each world—the 'old' and the 'new.' *Living among the Breakage* is an original work with an exciting sympathy and sensitive realism towards its subjects—people and communities under pressure, struggling to adapt to new realities, contexts, and identities; believers who for all their experience of liminality are making dynamic contributions to the living texture of tomorrow's global Church."

—**Brent Neely**, author; coeditor, with Peter Riddell, of *Islam and the Last Day: Christian Perspectives on Islamic Eschatology* (2014)

"In *Living among the Breakage*, Miller offers his readers an insightful exploration into the dynamics of Muslim conversion to Christianity and a rare look into the processes and products of contextual theologizing produced by some of the newest members in the global body of Christ. This is a must-read for those interested in world Christianity, Christian-Muslim relations, and the ongoing translation of the gospel into a myriad of cultural and religious contexts.

—**J. Scott Bridger**, author of *Christian Exegesis of the Qur'ān* (Pickwick, 2015); Associate Professor of Global Studies & World Religions, Criswell College

"Duane Miller's new work, *Living among the Breakage*, is a must-read for those interested in religious conversion. Miller moves beyond questions of why and how conversion takes place to engage the critical question of how converts and their communities become makers of theology. Bringing into conversation the indigenization theories of Shoki Coe, Robert Schreiter's models of 'God knowledge' and Steven Lukes' understanding of power, Miller creates a rich analytical framework for understanding the forces shaping the impetus, possibility, and results of conversion. Placing this within an understanding of how modernity is shaping the possibilities experienced by Muslims who convert to Christianity makes Miller's work an excellent textbook for students seeking to understand the transformations taking place in religious communities around the world. His chapters describing his fieldwork among different groups of Muslim converts to Christian then become models for the kind of analysis he describes. Miller's work greatly enriches our understanding of conversion generally—Muslim conversion to Christianity specifically—and our ability to grasp the changing religious landscape of the contemporary world."

—**Robert Hunt**, Director of Global Theological Education, Director of the Center for Evangelism and Missional Church Studies, Perkins School of Theology, Southern Methodist University

"On discipleship and the theology of ex-Muslims Dr. Duane has provided a road map for the Northern Church and the Global South (Majority World), as they agonize over the tension of Muslims, ex-Muslims, their theology, and how to disciple them. If there's one book about the world of Islam and ex-Muslims that is to be read, it is *Living among the Breakage*. It's a gold mine!"

—**Tony Weedor**, Desk Director, Africa, Advancing Native Missions

"How do you discern theology-in-the-making, especially among Christian believers from a Muslim background? Miller suggests that the activity together of such a Christian group may yield some insight. He looks at a specific instance of church planting, but sadly concludes that the theology-making there is going nowhere because of a static state of patronage that is being perpetuated among the leadership. Elsewhere Miller looks at conversion and persecution narratives deriving from Christian believers from a Muslim background, discerning within them what he calls 'liberation' and 'wisdom' theologies. Such narratives are widespread. Within a specific, Iranian-originated fellowship, Miller finds an intentional emphasis on 'Persian-ness' with a corresponding hostility to what is perceived as Arabo-Islamic contaminations. Out of his research Miller finds some common theological themes: dissatisfaction with the theory of penal substitution (maybe deriving from an Islamic perspective on the responsibility/accountability of the individual to God); messiness around matters of 'church' (including the importance of baptism, the lack of welcome/family feel in immature churches, and the paucity of strong leadership); and the re-formation of identity in experiences of rapid cultural change, minority status as 'Christian,' persecution, etc. Overall, Miller iterates a suggestion that theology-making among Christian believers from a Muslim background needs to find focus in an understanding/emphasis on God's power (the essential face of a 'Monad' god) as finding envelopment within and best expression through God's love (the essence of 'Trinity'). Miller's search is for precious expressions of Christian hope among the breakage of often poor, struggling communities of believers. It is amazing what he does find there!"

—**Right Reverend Dr. Bill Musk**

LIVING AMONG THE
BREAKAGE

LIVING AMONG THE
BREAKAGE

Contextual Theology-Making
and Ex-Muslim Christians

DUANE ALEXANDER MILLER

PICKWICK *Publications* · Eugene, Oregon

Pickwick Publications
An Imprint of Wipf and Stock Publishers
199 W. 8th Ave., Suite 3
Eugene, OR 97401

www.wipfandstock.com

PAPERBACK ISBN: 978-1-4982-8416-5
HARDCOVER ISBN: 978-1-4982-8418-9
EBOOK ISBN: 978-1-4982-8417-2

Cataloguing-in-Publication data:

Names: Miller, Duane Alexander.

Title: Living among the breakage : contextual theology-making and ex-Muslim Christians / Duane Alexander Miller.

Description: Eugene, OR: Pickwick Publications, 2016.

Identifiers: ISBN 978-1-4982-8416-5 (paperback). | ISBN 978-1-4982-8418-9 (hardcover). | ISBN 978-1-4982-8417-2 (ebook).

Subjects: LCSH: Christianity and other religions—Islam | Islam—Relations—Christianity | Muslims | Christianity—Islamic countries.

Classification: BV2626.3 M55 2016 (print). | BV2626.3 (ebook).

Manufactured in the U.S.A.   09/26/16

This book is dedicated to Blessed Ramon Llull:
currus Israhel et auriga eius

While emotion takes to itself the emotionless
Years of living among the breakage
Of what was believed in as the most reliable—
And therefore the fittest for renunciation.

—T. S. ELIOT, *THE DRY SALVAGES*, PART II

Contents

Preface

Carrying out the research for this book changed my life. I traveled over four continents, slept in the flat of Iranian refugees, sat down for a conversation with an Islamist who openly promoted the execution of apostates, and accompanied a new convert to his first conversation with his mother after coming out as a Christian and being chased from his home.

My perception of my own religion, Christianity, was transformed. I met Christians who believed so sincerely and deeply in the religion revealed by Jesus Christ that they were imprisoned, tortured, and exiled from their homelands. Through these relationships so many passages from the New Testament about persecution came alive to me. These women and men were blessed because they had been persecuted. They had lost their immediate families but had gained a much larger family. But I was also saddened as it became clear to me that many churches are suspicious of Muslims who want to learn about Jesus and his message. How could the church do this?

"Alex," she said, "Your writing is rather . . . journalistic." My doctoral supervisor and I were walking from New College in Edinburgh to George Square where my *viva voce* defense was scheduled. My supervisor, Elizabeth Koepping, was mentioning this as a reservation. It is my hope that my "journalistic style" will open up the fascinating world of these Christian converts from Islam to any educated reader, including the non-specialist.

These men and women have suffered much for the sake of their decision to exercise their inalienable human right to choose, of their own volition, how (and through whom) they will relate to God. It is my hope that this book will draw you into their world, and that, whether Christian, Muslim, or something else, this will be an occasion for questioning and testing your own convictions.

Duane Alexander Miller
March 5, 2016

Acknowledgments

Many of the people and institutions I would like to thank cannot be mentioned by name, and the reasons for this will become clear in the body of the work. My thanks must go first and foremost to my wife, Sharon, to whom I am bound in holy matrimony, "a dignified and commodious sacrament," and who took care of our children during long spells of research and travel. I remain convinced that a virtuous mother raising virtuous children makes a greater contribution to society and the Kingdom of God than do academics who write theses, articles, books, and conference papers. I lack the virtue and patience to be a stay-at-home dad, so I have settled for this inferior vocation.

My gratitude goes to my friends and colleagues as well, scattered throughout the world though they may be: Azar Ajaj, Bryson and May Arthur, Ajit and Avneet Baid, Scott Bridger, Sophie Cartwright, Tony Clapham, Richard Davis, Kamal Farah, Lottie Hayes, Ayazhan Kazhygerey, Stephen Louy, Brent Neely, Kirk and Annie Sandvig, Scott and Miriam Seely, Marina Shelly Havach, Philip Sumpter, Ray Register, and Matt and Mave Walter. I wish to thank also my family—all the Babiaks, Boteros, Millers, and Pittmans. And of course my supervisor, Elizabeth Koepping, who told me, "Alex, writing your thesis is the pickiest thing you'll ever do."

I also am thankful for friends in Edinburgh: for the hospitality of the Old Kirk in Pilton, and my friend the Rev. Tony Foreman, and also the ministries of Old Saint Paul's Episcopal Church and the Catholic Chaplaincy of Saint Albert the Great at George Square.

Nazareth of Galilee
The Feast Day of St Luke the Evangelist, 2013

Abbreviations

CMB	Christian from a Muslim background
CPM	Church-planting movement
CT	*Christianity Today*
CTQ	*Concordia Theological Quarterly*
EMQ	*Evangelical Missions Quarterly*
IBMR	*International Bulletin of Missionary Research*
IC	Iranian Christian
IJFM	*International Journal of Frontier Missiology*
IM	Insider movement
LWP	*Lausanne World Pulse*
MBB	Muslim-background believer
MBC	Muslim-background congregation
MIR	*Missiology: an International Review*
MF	*Mission Frontiers*
MW	*Muslim World/Moslem World*
SFM	*Saint Francis Magazine*

A NOTE REGARDING ARABIC AND THE QUR'AN

Throughout this work I have opted to use the figure '3' to denote the Arabic letter 'ع' (3*iin*), except in words already in common circulation, like *Iraq* or *Omar*. Likewise I have used the figure 'x' to denote the letter 'خ' (*xiin*). Finally, as is becoming more common among Muslims in the Anglophone world, I sometimes use the singular feminine noun *Muslima* to refer to a female Muslim. As to the Qur'an, I have mostly use Pickthall and Yusuf Ali, both in the public domain, *al humdu lillah*. At times I have opted for my own translation from the common text of the Uthmanic recension.

A Brief Introduction

I have chosen these verses from Eliot to begin this book because he understood modernity.[1] He contributed to its formation and was also one of its fiercest critics. In these words of Eliot I see so many themes that surface and resurface in the modern world: breakage—a sense that a whole that once existed is no longer tenable, for the West that whole was Christendom which, for all it failings, "provided both a social-structural and a cognitive unity that was lost, probably irretrievably, upon its dissolution at the beginning of the modern age."[2] Thus, modernity entails the renunciation of "what was believed in as the most reliable." Christendom, for all its faults, made sense to Muslims, who walked in the *sunna* of their Prophet who unapologetically folded empire and piety into one, single, indivisible movement.

In this reading, the modern human is like the Hebrew in the days of the Judges: "In those days there was no king in Israel; everyone did what was right in his own eyes."[3] Since there was no transcendent order it became apparent that humanity had to produce its own order, and the so-called Enlightenment promised a new world order based on reason. But then Western Europe, the focal point of the new humanity and the triumph of reason descended into the violence and degradation of two world wars. Reason and education, it seemed, could not construct the New Atlantis of which Sir Francis Bacon dreamed.

In the Muslim world the authority of the "the most reliable" has also been subject to "renunciation" and "breakage." Peter Berger describes how religious institutions in the West in the twentieth century underwent a process of delegitimation, meaning "a weakening of the values and assumptions on which a political order is based."[4] Something analogous has happened in much of the Muslim world and this breakage, renunciation, and delegitimation have powerfully affected the options that Muslims have before them.

1. Excerpt from "The Dry Salvages" from *Four Quartets* by T. S. Eliot. Copyright 1941 by T. S. Eliot, renewed in 1969 by Esme Valerie Eliot. Reprinted by permission of Houghton Mifflin Harcourt. All rights reserved.

2. Berger, *Modernity*, 171.

3. Judg 21:25

4. Berger, *Modernity*, 159.

In this book, how some Muslims have rejected the *diin* of Islam for the *religio* of Christianity will be explored. And the modern world is a context in which such questioning is viable. The authority or *power* of the old structures has been eroded; new options and choices are placed before people. Some people make choices that previously would have been unthinkable— whether that be the Baptist lady in Oklahoma who converts to Buddhism or the Muslim sheikh in Mecca who converts to Christianity. Furthermore, modernity is characterized by rapid social change. In such a context it is often the case that "[t]he old sign system can no longer account for the problems with which the culture has to deal, or the loyalties it demands and the codes it prescribes are no longer acceptable to the members of the culture."[5]

Modernity not only presents a space wherein questions *may* be asked, but has created a space wherein choices *must* be made. This is what Berger calls the heretical imperative, by which he means that we are forced to choose or create our own sense of meaning, purpose and value. Some experience this as freedom, but for others it is oppressive, like Eliot's "emotionless years of living among the breakage."

The old paradigm of Christendom that situated all of humanity in a transcendental divine plan is gone. But what of Islam? Historically, Islam has strongly asserted that there is a transcendental order, it has been revealed to us (in great detail), and that humanity can and must live according to it, and that the use of power—whether coercive or otherwise—is licit to enforce said order.

Modernity entails, for better and worse, greater freedom to choose, and sometimes the obligation to choose (Berger's heretical imperative), even if one does not really desire that freedom. "*Modernity pluralizes both institutions and plausibility structures.*"[6] But even in this context of breakage and fragmentation—whether in terms of identity or relationships or the authority of social / religious / political institutions—many people have a felt need, an inner desire, to identify an overarching order for life and meaning. A number of Muslims have furthermore concluded that the order proposed by Islam, as they know it, is deficient. So they turn away from what they regard as wrong and old, to something that is right and new. In this book, these are the converts from Islam to Christianity. And in relation to "the breakage of what was one believed in as the most reliable," let us ask, do they try to assemble a new order, a new vision of God and humanity and society? That is to say, do ex-Muslim Christians formulate their own theologies? And if so, what are their contents, origins, and ends?

5. Schreiter, *Local Theologies*, 71–72.
6. Berger, *Heretical Imperative*, 17, italics in original.

1

Theology-Making and Power

REASON FOR THIS RESEARCH

During my early days in the Middle East, while studying Arabic, I met a few Christians who were converts from Islam and became aware of the challenges they faced. I wanted to learn more about converts from Islam to Christianity.

In the latter half of the twentieth century an unprecedented number of known conversions from Islam to Christianity have occurred. This book asks, do these converts engage in the activity of making their own theologies? And if so, what sort of theologies are they making, and what knowledge about God are they proposing and indeed assuming?

This leads to further questions: what are the various forms that "God knowledge" might take? Theology-making is a process; if it is taking place some model of what that looks like will also be needed. Theology-making, if it is occurring at all, is taking place within a set of contexts—what are they? There is also the question of *who:* are only certain persons qualified to be theology-makers? And a final question is *why? If* these believers are making theology, then what are their goals?

In trying to answer the research question, and those that it entails, it is necessary to examine some aspects of the contexts in which these converts might be making theology.

But returning to my initial interest in Christian converts from Islam, I tried to research the topic, and found that there is a great deal of material in the field of missiology which seeks to specify *how* to make Muslims into followers of Christ and what such converts *should* look like. In 2008 I interviewed an Anglican priest living in Egypt who knew some Christians from a Muslim background (CMBs), and I asked him about their theology—what sort of theology do they produce? He responded that they do not produce theology; rather they are worried about things like family life and work and how to remain safe in the midst of an Islamic society. As I continued to read and research I realized that the Anglican priest and I had been thinking about theology in terms of our own Western tradition wherein theology is often systematized, communicated/discussed through books and journals, taught and learned at seminaries/universities, and wherein the goal of the theology-making task is grasping certain knowledge. This was something of an epiphany for me.

The missiologists I had read were doing (applied) theology *about/for* ex-Muslim Christians. But in reading the material written by actual converts and in meeting and spending time with them, I started to suspect that they might be intensely involved in the process of making their own theology. The Anglican priest was correct that CMBs are not publishing systematic theological texts. But they *are* asking questions, and they *are* identifying problems and challenges, which often emerge from their own specific contexts. This work is an effort to explore both the questions they are asking, the means whereby they are proposing and evaluating possible solutions, and the conclusions, if any, they are coming to. It is an attempt to test my initial hypothesis.

RESEARCH METHODOLOGY

Apart from archival/textual collection of material, I did research in two main ways, quantitative and qualitative, although the division between those is not rigid.

For chapter 3 a brief questionnaire was circulated to numerous people with experience in ministry to Muslims and/or Christian ministry within an Islamic context. This does not claim to be a random, quantitative survey though. Some of the respondents I knew myself, and others were contacts of two colleagues, who wish to remain anonymous and helped to gather this information. Regarding the contacts I knew personally, I had met them in various ways, including during my time studying Arabic in the Middle East and theology in the USA, through churches that I had attended or where I knew someone, and through research/publication networks for people with a common interest in Christianity in the Muslim world. Additional details on that questionnaire will be described in the body of that chapter.

Fieldwork: Locations and Languages

As with the questionnaire, the selection of the places where I carried out my fieldwork was largely dictated by where I could gain access. I wanted to do research in at least one place where apostasy from Islam could lead to persecution. I speak Arabic so the logical scope of that was somewhere in the Arab world, as using a translator has several drawbacks. Having lived in the Arab world for several years I was familiar with the region's cultural and religious contours, and having done fieldwork among a minority population there meant that I was not new to the challenges involved.[1] Because of security and ethical issues it is not possible to go into greater detail about precisely how and where the research was done. Suffice to say that a well-connected indigenous colleague of mine and I were discussing research interests and he connected me with Andraus (chapter 4). Interviews were carried out in either Arabic or English, according to the preference of the person being interviewed.

In relation to the Iranian congregations in the USA and the UK, this was also determined largely by pragmatic circumstances. On several occasions I was invited or encouraged to visit Iranian Christian (IC) communities in other places, but restraints related to finance and travel made that impossible. Traveling to Iran to research an illegal activity (apostasy) was not possible: personal safety apart, the Iranian government would hardly grant a visa for such research. As I do not speak Farsi, interacting with Anglophone ICs in the Diaspora was a welcome option. On the few occasions when I did interact with a new arrival from Iran one of the Anglophone ICs would translate for me, but this happened rarely.

The study of CMBs is very much unresearched. When a study of a community is produced, there are very few existing studies of other communities to which it can be compared. In relation to the topic of theology-making, there is *one* unpublished doctoral thesis which cannot be circulated for security reasons. Therefore I felt that given the constraints of time, money and travel, it would be helpful to find communities that are quite different from each other. ICs in the Diaspora and Arabophone Christians in the Middle East seemed to meet those criteria.

As to Arabs CMBs in the Diaspora, I did meet and interview a number of them individually. They do not exist in sufficient numbers to form their own Muslim-background congregations and so attend conventional Arabophone or Anglophone congregations.

Interviews and Participation

A key source of information was interviews. Interviews ranged between 20 and 90 minutes. Each started with a notification of my institutional

---

1. Miller, "Church in Jordan," 134–53.

affiliation, that I would not use specific place or person names and an offer to share the eventual results of my research.

I recorded answers in a notepad, though sometimes a digital voice recorder was used. I noted early on that having a voice recorder made most people feel uneasy, especially ex-Muslims, whereas me taking hand-written notes did not. So I determined that a notepad was preferable, even though "individuals who rely exclusively upon memory and notes always stand the chance of being charged with incompleteness or bias."[2] It was not uncommon for interviews to be followed up by additional meetings, phone calls, or email correspondence. Most interviews were done with Muslim-background believers and ministry leaders working with such individuals. I also kept a journal of the process and memories which came to me at the time of research or at the time of transcription, which formed an additional resource—the "headlines" or "headnotes"—which shape how the written or recorded notes are construed and interpreted.[3] Usually, within a few days of the final interview, I would go back over my notes and add any clarifications or observations that after reflection seemed interesting or important. Then I would transcribe them to a Word document for future access. In all, about 100 interviews were carried out in nine sites.[4]

While interviews were a main source of my information, I also observed some of their religious events, like seminars, prayer meetings, evangelistic activities, and church services. I stayed in people's houses overnight, ate with them, and went with them to meetings and Sunday worship. This is not uncommon for ethnographic fieldwork which ". . . focuses on the everyday, and on otherwise unheard, or muted, voices."[5] I never paid money to any of my informants, but when we would meet over a meal, I would offer to pay for that.

If asked, I clarified that I was not a member of the clergy. I explained my interest in studying and understanding their community, with phrases like, "I'm curious to learn more about Iranian Christians" or "I'm doing research on Christians who used to be Muslims." For the layperson these explanations were readily accepted, and I suspect that is because I had first been vetted by a church leader. Church leaders often requested more detail, and I was open in discussing the details of the *questions* I was investigating,

---

2. Georges and Jones, "Studying People," 144.

3. Cohen, "Method," 449–69; Ottenberg, "Fieldnotes," 139–60.

4. Because the names and locations are sensitive, I have decided not to include them in the book or an appendix.

5. Armbruster and Laerke, "Taking Sides," 23.

but avoided discussing preliminary findings so as to not influence their answers.

Reflexivity: How Did They Perceive Me?

"Fieldwork involving other people is one of the most intensively personal kinds of scholarly research I know. Everything about the fieldworker influences the information collected."[6] Because of this, I also had to ask the questions, how was I viewed by the people I was researching? And, how did I perceive them?

I was an outsider because I wasn't Persian/Arab, and I did not belong to their denomination/church. However, I was an insider for the Arabs, because I was a fellow Christian, who, with them, spoke Arabic, had lived in the Middle East, and was familiar with their world. As someone who has written a few articles on the history of Protestant missions in Middle East, I also was fairly knowledgeable about the history of the Middle East and the different peoples, areas, religions and political realities there. At first in both the Middle East and in the USA I was greeted with suspicion and distance, but eventually the gatekeepers in those two places, who were church leaders, decided they could trust me.

In relation to the ICs, I quickly found that they had mixed feelings about the Arabic language. On the one hand they seemed impressed that I had learned a difficult language, but on the other hand I found that they have negative associations with the language as being imposed on them from the outside, as was Islam. As an American Christian, they did not associate me with that negativity though.

In relation to the Arabophone Christians, I was neither from their denomination nor did I live in either of those areas. On the other hand, at the time of my field research, I was affiliated with a Christian educational institute they were aware of, though in a different area in the Middle East. Again, I was not an insider, but I was close enough to the insider to be able to carry out research and be trusted. My extensive knowledge of the topic and the experiences, writings, and history of other converts, I feel, earned the respect and trust of the communities being researched. All in all, I felt accepted and trusted by the people I spoke with, but was not an indigenous researcher, and thus did not have to face the many challenges associated with such a project. While few of my interviewees ever met my wife or children, I felt my status as a married man with children also was beneficial in establishing a good relationship.

6. Jackson, *Fieldwork*, 16.

As I reflect on the field-research, I find it difficult to conceive of a non-Christian being given access to these Arab and Persian communities. Commonality of basic doctrines and concepts—especially the centrality of Jesus Christ in understanding the will and personality of God—created a space wherein the interviewees felt they had a freedom to "be themselves" and not be defensive, which I suspect would have been the case had they been speaking with a non-religious secular person or a Muslim. I suspect that such research carried out by a person who did not share some general Christian beliefs would have led to interviews becoming contests of worldviews.

Reflexivity: How Did I Perceive Them?

How did I see my informants? Their drive and willingness to engage in a stressful and sometimes-dangerous task with little or no compensation led me to respect them. Like many fellow members of Generation X in North America, I was raised with no religion at all, not even nominal. I was, for instance, unaware that Easter or Christmas had any religious meaning at all until my teens. In my teens, while living in Puebla, México, I started to attend a small evangelical church that met in the garage of one of the church ladies. At first my mother attended but even after she stopped, I continued to attend. Eventually, I decided to become a Christian and made a confession of faith one Sunday morning. While I would today disagree with some theological teachings of that church, I feel it is this experience which helps me to appreciate and respect the gravity of religious conversion, and also to be non-judgmental towards individuals and communities whose religious articulations are not very sophisticated or nuanced. Some of the believers I met were like that, but fewer than I would have suspected.

I come to a similar conclusion as Kathryn Kraft, who likewise did case studies among MBBs: "I suggest that defining researchers as insiders or as outsiders is largely a futile endeavor and, therefore, researching the 'other' also draws an unnecessary artificial line between researcher and researched."[7]

Ethics and Security

In relation to fieldwork among a sensitive population there are also ethical considerations that must be taken into account, and this was done in

---

7. Kraft, "Community and Identity," 69.

accordance with the regulations of the institution supervising the research. "[O]ne largely unacknowledged problem is the issue of security breaches arising from researchers' confidentiality lapses, [and] other problems relate to the impact of the researchers' presence on the people and communities being studied."[8] Different respondents requested different levels of anonymity in relation to person and place names, or none at all, which is not uncommon in fieldwork.

Nonetheless, maximal caution has been used, and especially so for my research in the Middle East, where conversion from Islam to Christianity is considered taboo and deviant. Not being able to discuss details related to specific historical, political, legal, demographic and cultural data detracted from the specificity of the study. But given the precautions of the institution and the safety of the group studied, the only other option would be to eliminate fieldwork. I was reminded of this when realizing I could not even extend the customary thanks to the educational facilities/libraries I had used as that might reveal the specific research sites.

Given the sensitivity of this research, a further ethical question is: who benefits from it? In the previous paragraph I outlined the precautions taken to preserve the safety and wellbeing of the groups studied. But beyond that, "it is clear to most researchers that subjects comply due to some tacit belief that a common good will be the result of the research."[9] What potential benefit did the interviewees see in this research for themselves? In general, I genuinely felt that the converts and those working with them wanted their stories to be told. They were, with a few exceptions like brand-new believers, aware that significant numbers of Muslims are converting each year. I understood that they perceived a careful, critical, scholarly (and secure) study of their communities would be welcomed, as they had never had access to such a work before. Even when I mentioned that my findings could include critical observations of the converts, their life and thought, and their congregations, they accepted this. I felt this was validated after one of the Arab leaders emailed me asking how to reference a draft of my thesis in *his* dissertation.

Another aspect important to evaluating a project involving casework, suggested by Cassell, is the quality of the interaction between the researcher and the researched.[10] I feel like our relations were characterized by honesty, and when asked questions I did not try to avoid answering them. When asked if I am a Christian, to which I replied that I am, the next question

8. Jacobsen and Landau, "Dual Imperative," 187.

9. Whittaker, "Ethics," 531.

10. Cassell, "Ethical Principles," 28–41.

would often be, what kind of Christian, to which I would reply, "Anglican," which might lead to the question, "what does that mean?" So proceeded the initial questions and answers, negotiating a common platform. When asked about my work I replied that I teach and am working on a doctoral degree; asked to summarize the topic of my research I would normally respond with "Muslims who become Christians" and leave it at that, unless the person had additional questions.

Some members of my research pool had recently fled from Iran, and they were mostly single, young men. They seemed happy to have someone interested in their stories and lives. Having an American scholar doing research under the aegis of a well-known university, taking notes about their lives, represented to them a welcome reversal of roles—they were the ones with the resource (knowledge) I needed. One refugee and his brother in particular told me I must stay with them when I was visiting their city in the UK, which I did. "[T]he results of fieldwork entail more than the objects produced and presented to others to document and describe in retrospect an individual's completed fieldwork adventure,"[11] and as a result of my fieldwork, I have maintained contact with a number of my informants.

By the standard of the quality of the relation formed, and by the (eventual) eagerness of my informants to share their stories (with maximal guarantees of anonymity in place), it is ethical to publish the research within the parameters discussed above.

Names of Places and People

In almost all cases someone would ask that a specific location-name not be used, so even if most people being interviewed felt comfortable with me using a specific city-name, if one or two people did not, I honored their request. So in chapter 6, even city names in the USA and the UK are replaced by generic names.

Regarding the Middle East research (chapter 4), I cannot disclose the names of any specific locations, so certain historical and political realities must be spoken of in vague terms, so as not to compromise the security of the individuals and churches involved. It is sufficient to clarify that during a period of very strong European influence missionaries were permitted to work in Juduur and Kitma. Evangelizing Muslims in the then-Ottoman Empire was frowned upon by the European political actors because the conversion of a Muslim might well cause political tension, if not rioting and even loss of life. The context of the local Christians is one of centuries

---

11. Georges and Jones, "Studying People," 136.

during which trying to convert Muslims[12] was a dangerous and/or forbidden activity. Sometimes missions and European political influence worked closely together, but sometimes they butted heads. "To say that missionaries were agents of colonialism, full stop, is a crude over-simplification."[13] All that can be said is that Juduur and Kitma (chapter 4) were once part of the Ottoman Empire.

The use of fictitious names for people and places was an ethical requisite for the publication of the research. "In choosing one good, we may find ourselves in conflict with another good. We can find ourselves in tragic situations in which every choice to act, honoring one good, violates another one";[14] in this book the good of greater historical and political detail has sometimes opposed the good of a maximal standard related to the security of the communities studied. When the two goods were in conflict, the latter has been privileged throughout.

WHO ARE THEOLOGY-MAKERS?

Returning to the initial questions posed in this chapter, it is necessary to find a way of speaking about theology-making that is structured enough to yield insight, but flexible enough to address the fact that many ex-Muslim Christians find themselves in a very different context than the academic and ecclesiastical contexts wherein much of Western academic theology is being made.

My Anglican colleague in Egypt who said that converts are not writing theology was correct within bounds, if one understands theology as a professional, specialized activity, done by specialists according to the norms of university education. According to this, Christians from a Muslim background by and large are not making theology. But historically, in reference to Christian theology-making, which is our sphere of interest here, this approach to theology-making, and thus theology-makers, is the exception and not the norm. A historical approach may be helpful here. Insofar as we accept that the New Testament and later patristic writings are "theology" or "theological texts," we can work our way backwards to what or who a theology-maker is. The authors of these texts were thinking Christians,

12. The phrase "Muslim evangelism" in this thesis refers only to efforts of Christians to evangelize Muslims. The efforts of Muslims to call people (including "lax" Muslims) to Islam is called *da3wa*.

13. Makdisi, *Artillery of Heaven*, 9–10. Makdisi's study is related to Ottoman Lebanon. His observations hold valid for the areas studied here.

14. Mattingly, "Vulnerable Ethics," 463.

addressing issues faced by their churches. They were responding to conflicts within the churches (expressed in many of the Pauline and Ignatian letters, 1 Clement, the Nicene Creed, the Definition of Chalcedon), criticisms directed at the churches from gentiles and Jews (as in Justin Martyr), political realities that deeply impacted the churches (Luke, Acts to some extent, and the *City of God*), and persecution (the martyrdoms of Polycarp, Perpetua and her companions). Yet none of these writings came from "professional" theologians. Their professions were often intimately related to the church, though that may or may not have been their source of income, and in composing these works they were acting as pastors, catechists, bishops, missionaries and defenders of the faith (apologists). Their writings grew from that experience and in this they were, from their own point of view, not trying to enunciate something novel, but rather to act as representatives of a larger community, whether a diocese or the church catholic.[15] Their authority to speak on behalf of that church may have been attached to a specific title (like apostle or bishop), but this was not necessarily the case. Moreover, when they composed and communicated their God-knowledge or, rather, the God-knowledge of their community, they did not hesitate to draw on the piety and practice of the community. And so the Nicene Creed incorporates elements of older baptismal confessions, Paul quotes hymns of unknown provenance in his epistles, and Irenaeus can compose a catalog of heresies as well as liturgical hymns.

Historically we can then identify the locus of theology-making: some sort of leader or another, in some form endorsed by her community, speaking on behalf of the church and the faith, while drawing on the piety, prayers, and practices already existing within her community of worship. Furthermore, the endorsement of the community need not be academic, or related to a specific title (bishop, pastor), though it may be. Endorsement can also come in the form of sharing—that a book or article or prayer has been shared with the world (distribution) is one form of endorsement.

In sum, the communities of believers are the theology-makers, though often specific members of said communities will be the spokespersons and/or disseminators of the theology. With this clarification having been made, we can examine some different models of theology-making.

---

15. Bevans, *Models.*

WHAT IS THEOLOGY-MAKING?

An American, Evangelical Model: Directed Contextualization

> *The gospel of Jesus Christ must be attractively presented into the context of any given group of people. This is a process which involves great sensitivity.* –Phil Parshall[16]

A first possibility is indicated by the word *contextualization*, which is a topic of great interest (and controversy) among the evangelical community (if heavily influenced by American voices).

The term "contextualization" was introduced around 1973 by Shoki Coe but it did not gain popularity with evangelicals for several years because it was connected with the World Council of Churches, an organization that was seen as suspect by many evangelicals. Another factor was that missionaries were wary of engaging in too much adaptation, seeing that as a gateway to syncretism.[17]

However, articles like Paul Hiebert's "Critical Contextualization" and books like *The Gospel and Islam*[18] and Parshall's groundbreaking *New Paths in Muslim Evangelism: Evangelical Approaches to Contextualization*, enabled the concept, or at least the word, to gain greater acceptance. By the 1990s most evangelicals understood "contextualization" to be something the missionary did to or for others, though there was (and is) vigorous debate about how far the missionary could go in "contextualizing" the Gospel for the Muslim audience.[19]

One influential explanatory metaphor is mentioned in the foreword to Parshall's book: Christian missionaries are to communicate the seed of the

---

16. Parshall, *New Paths*, 31.

17. "Religious mixing." In the social sciences it is commonly used to simply describe religious mixing (Shaw and Stewart, "Syncretism," 1–26). In evangelical circles it is generally seen to be dangerous and to be avoided in that it will compromise the "essence" of the Christian message. For instance, "Syncretism represents the blending of differing, even contradictory, beliefs into a new belief system that loses the unique essence of the original beliefs" (Campbell, "Releasing," 170 n3).

18. Edited by Don McCurry. Interestingly, one contributor, Tabor, an evangelical scholar, sees contextualization as the prerogative of the local church whereas Hiebert wavers between theology-for and theology-by. In any case, his influential article is concerned narrowly with contextualizing pre-Christian *rituals*.

19. For instance Shaw, "Power and Glory"; Woodberry, "Common Pillars"; Dutch, "Muslims"; Massey, "Amazing Diversity"; Gilliland, "The Word"; Talman, "Contextualization"; Arab World Ministries, "Appropriate Limits"; McNeal, "Muslim Women"; Oksnevad, "Discipleship"; Abu Daoud, "Observations"; Bourne, "Summary"; Herald, "Making Sense"; William, "Inside/Outside," etc.

gospel while removing the cultural hull. Removing the cultural (Western) hull is central to the process of "contextualization." Two points should be noted about this "American" form of "contextualization." First, the primary agents of "contextualization" here are foreign missionaries, and secondly, they are engaged in evangelism and church planting. Such "contextualization" understands the missionary or evangelist as the primary agent, which is substantially different from the original use of the term by Shoki Coe. Since this form of contextualization is done *for* the community being evangelized, it is reasonable to call this *directed contextualization*.

There is an ongoing and vigorous debate among evangelical missionaries and ministers working within an Islamic setting regarding the limits of directed contextualization.[20] Syncretism for them is something to be avoided, so the goal is (directed) contextualization without syncretism. For instance, the question arises whether missionaries should allow MBBs to recite the *shahada*—there is no deity but Allah and Muhammad is the messenger of Allah—or if it is appropriate for a missionary to call himself a Muslim for the sake of securing converts. The argument in favor of the latter is that the word, grammatically speaking, simply means "one who submits [to God]"; the argument against that as commonly understood such a label is a deceit.

Directed contextualization implies a model of theology-making carried out by foreign (whether foreign nationals or nationals from a totally different class, caste or ethnic group) agents done *for* those who are to receive the message about Jesus. The research question here, though, is not concerned with theology done *for* ex-Muslim Christians, but rather to investigate their *own* theology.

An Ecumenical Model: Shoki Coe and Organic Contextualization

The term "contextualization" was first introduced by Shoki Coe, a Taiwanese pastor and educator, in the context of his work with the educational fund of the World Council of Churches. Coe understood contextualization as the next step, after indigenization, in developing a true theology that is *by* and *from* the younger churches. On a practical level this was needed because importing Western models of theological education had led to a financial

20. Wolfe, "Insider Movements," and Sleeman, "Origins," both contain genealogies (that is, the history of the development of the concept) related to the debate about contextualization and related topics like C-scale and Insider Movements. The C-scale was an attempt to evaluate how "contextualized" different "Christ-centered communities" are, and was first proposed in John Travis, "Spectrum," 407–8. I have not found it to be of any use in my research.

situation of dependence that is not viable in the long term for most institutions outside of the West.[21] And on an ecclesiastical level it was necessary because the previous step (indigenization), while a necessary one, was not and could not be the final goal for the local church:

> Indigenous, indigeneity, and indigenization all derive from a nature metaphor, that is, of the soil, or taking root in the soil. It is only right that the younger churches, in search of their own identity, should take seriously their own cultural milieu. However, because of the static nature of the metaphor, indigenization tends to be used in the sense of responding to the Gospel in terms of traditional culture. Therefore, it is in danger of being past-oriented.[22]

The language surrounding indigenization is closely related to the ordering of the church, specifically in terms of pastors, priests and other leaders being indigenous: "Indigenisation was more about ecclesiological form than theological substance."[23] So while indigenization implied that the key leaders would not be foreigners, the deeper structures and grammar of the local church,[24] were largely inherited. While the contextualizing community may change surface things like dress or decorations within a church, in Coe's theory, said community is also able to transform and alter the "deep structures" of the church's life. In Coe's situation, the churches in Taiwan had inherited the European seminary tradition, and the question of how to educate and form the future leaders of the church can hardly be said to be peripheral or superficial—indeed, it goes to the very heart of the question of the church's future viability and touches on every aspect of the church's life.

For Coe, even if all the teachers were indigenous, the seminary structure itself, while perhaps viable in other contexts, was not viable in the way it had been inherited in Taiwan. So Coe desired to move beyond that model, and proposed what he saw as a substantially different way of thinking about theological education, which is nothing less than the dialectic between contextuality (a term largely forgotten today) and contextualization:

---

21. Coe, "Education," 8.

22. Coe, "Renewal," 240.

23. Stanley, "Inculturation," 22.

24. The words "local church" are being used here for the sake of brevity. Historically, in evangelical Christianity a church is a group of people that baptizes, celebrates Communion, and engages in reading and teaching the Bible. While not wanting to propose any strict definition of "local church," all the foregoing is indicated by the use of the term. The level of locality—town, city, country, diocese—is variable and dynamic.

> By contextuality we mean that wrestling with God's world in such a way as to discern the particularity of this historic moment; and by contextualization we mean the wrestling with God's word in such a way that the power of the incarnation, which is the divine form of contextualization, can enable us to follow His steps to contextualize.[25]

According to Coe then, there is a method for contextualization. Contextualization is not *anything* the local church does, even if its leadership is indigenous. A genuine process of contextualization first requires the act of the community in discerning its contextuality—which is to say that the community, with recognized voices who can formulate the mind of the community, critically evaluates itself and the world and discerns what God is doing in the world at the moment. Coe is also clear that in evaluating its contextuality the local church should not be restricted to reflecting on "theological" topics only, but is also capable of addressing social justice and political issues. If the local church does not engage in this first step, then it cannot actually engage in the process of contextualization, as Coe sees it. Furthermore, if the local church is not in fact accurate in its reading of its contextuality, of "that critical assessment of what makes the context really significant in the light of the *Missio Dei*,"[26] then it will not be able to engage in the process of contextualization on a genuine level.

The degree of latitude a local church has in reading its own contextuality and determining its own path forward is both limited and empowered by its leadership structure. A congregation that is part of a diocese will take this into account in reading its contextuality. A diocese that is part of a national church would also take this into account. The reality of regional or national or international structures of church governance can limit the options open to a local church in engaging in contextualization. But those structures can also make possible activities and missions and options that a lone congregation would not have the resources to accomplish. Contextualization can take place simultaneously at multiple levels—the congregation, the regional association or diocese, the national council, and the global. Moreover, there is no guarantee that all of these moments of contextualization will necessarily point to the same way forward. The term "local church" can thus be used to refer not only to a congregation or something larger, but in this book it generally refers to specific congregations.

Contextualization presupposes an earlier, critical assessment of the church's contextuality. But once that critical assessment has taken place,

25. Coe, "Renewal," 7.
26. Coe, "Education," 241.

then the local church is able to "wrestle with God's Word," as he put it, and from this "dialectic" engage in the process of contextualization. The process sees the local church critically evaluating its own situation and needs, and discerning how it can participate in God's activity in redeeming and transforming the world. The local church then, drawing on its own resources, most notably Scripture, but also its liturgy, history, sister churches, and cultural wealth, is able to propose a possible path to address the needs revealed by its evaluation of its own contextuality. The church then can try out its hypothesis in its own life, and evaluate its success or failure. If the theology-makers stop at the point of discerning contextuality and identifying challenges or problems, but do not take steps to somehow propose a possible solution or course of action, then they would appear *not* to be engaging in genuine, authentic contextualization. Furthermore, it is possible for a local church to err during this double-wrestle. The local church may misread its own contextuality, or propose an inauthentic form of contextualization. Coe's theory of contextualization is not relativistic, and he does believe that a community of theology-makers (for our purposes) can indeed incorrectly evaluate God's desire for the world in their own contextuality (the World of God), and he also is aware that they can misread and/or misapply the meaning and message of the Word of God. Thus there must be room for the possibility of an inauthentic or incorrect contextualization.[27] Sometimes there are multiple, conflicting voices within a given community.

Note that the concepts of evangelistic mission or planting churches do not arise at all, even marginally, in either of the two key articles (1973, 1974) in which Coe formulated these views. Significantly, it is presupposed that the agents of this process of contextualization would be the local, indigenous church. Coe's discourse was taking place partly in response to the perceived failures of Western churches—and is certainly not asking them to actually *do* the contextualizing. The tone is rather that Western churches should remain an important part of the conversation as local churches carry out this work, doing theology *with them*, not *for them*, and thus preserving both the locality and catholicity of the endeavor:

> True catholicity could not possibly be a colourless uniformity, but must be a rich fullness of truth and grace, which unfolds and manifests itself as we take the diversified contexts in time and space, where we are set, and respond faithfully as the Incarnate Word did on our behalf, once and for all.[28]

27. From a traditional Christian point of view one might read the Arian controversy or the birth of Mormonism in this light.

28. Coe, "Renewal," 242–3.

Coe was keenly aware of how helpful conversation with and input from other churches could be. Indeed, the World Council of Churches, which made possible the work that he and his colleagues did, was dedicated to the concept of the churches of the world being in discussion with one another.

But what then is the role of the foreigner/outsider in the process of contextualization—if, as mentioned before, she can be part of that process, but not its principal agent? Indeed, sometimes foreign agents are able to identify weaknesses in the lives of a local church to which the local church might be initially blind. So an Arab Christian might note how consumerist many American Christians are, and an American Christian might ask questions about how healthy it is to have authoritarian church leaders in the Arab world. This is an important role, and it means that a foreign agent is raising a question or issue and suggesting it for further contemplation. But that is where it ends, if the local church decides that this is not a topic of interest to them. In the ecumenical model of contextualization, if there is a place for the foreigner, this is it: to do theology *with*, to ask questions *with*, and then respect the agency and power of the local church which will then determine whether or not to pursue the question.

The model of contextualization proposed by Coe in the ecumenical context of the WCC will be called *organic contextualization* throughout this work. The specification is necessary to differentiate it from *directed* contextualization.

Notwithstanding the strengths of Coe's theory, there are also some difficulties. The fact that "local church" means different things to differing people has already been mentioned. Another question surfaces: what happens when there are differences in opinion regarding the reading of the contextuality of the local church and/or the proposed ways of addressing that contextuality, which is to say contextualization itself? Within a congregation it is possible that women and men, or young and old, or wealthy and poor, read the *missio dei* differently. Coe never addresses this issue in his rather sparse writings. The local church is, in practice, never a homogenous body, and within a local church there are always different voices and interests. What is a key area of interest for one person or group within a local church may not be important to another group, or perhaps the groups have differing visions for how to address a certain issue. The best that can be done is to pay specific attention to different voices, not trying to force them all into one mold or pattern, and I have tried to do this within the context of my fieldwork.

In spite of these limitations, Coe's work remains the best theoretical framework available for this study. I concur with Coleman and Verster, who, after surveying the many possible definitions of contextualization proposed since the 1970s, that Coe's original theory, while older, is "the most complete."[29]

For the sake of illustrating how the American version of contextualization (directed) and the WCC version of contextualization (organic) function, some examples will be helpful.

Two Examples of Directed Contextualization

The first example is a harmony of the Gospels written in classical Arabic titled *Siirat al Masiih bi Lisaan 3arabi Fasiih* (or in English, *The Life of the Messiah in a Classical Arabic Tongue*). This harmony of the Gospels was translated/composed by two scholars, one American and one non-Christian Palestinian, who desired to present the teachings and life of Jesus to Muslims in a manner that they would understand and accept. Multiple steps were taken to make this occur. First, this is one book, so the traditional four gospels have been folded into one.[30] This is more amenable to how Muslims understand the meaning of the word *injiil* as it occurs in the Qur'an, where it is portrayed as a single body of teachings given to Jesus by God. Second, each chapter is given a name much like the names of the surahs of the Qur'an. For example, *Al Kalima* (The Word) which is a rendition of the opening verses of John 1, *Al Midhwad* (The Manger), *Al Sab3iin* (The Seventy), *Al 3arsh* (The Throne), *Al Xubz* (The Bread), and so on. Finally, the verbs and nouns and sentence structure used throughout imitate Qur'anic language. The project is a fascinating one and warrants further research,[31] and is a good example of directed contextualization in relation to Christian mission to Muslims. However, it does not have its origin in the local church, therefore it is *directed*. Had the Palestinian been a Christian, and thus potentially a theology-making representative of some local church, this project could also have possibly been considered to be organic contextualization. The indigenous agent was not qualified to be a theology-maker for the local churches, and the fruit of his labor was not at all welcomed by the local churches.

29. Coleman and Verster, "Gospel among Muslims," 102. For examples of other possible approaches see, among others, Hesselgrave, "Authentic and Relevant," and Kraft, "Dynamic Equivalence."

30. The *Diatessaron* of Tatian, an early harmony, was not used as a template.

31. One of the individuals involved in this project is now deceased, the other (the American) no longer classifies himself as a Christian and in an interview (2010) told me he regrets the entire the endeavor.

Another instance of directed contextualization is a method for plant-ing home churches consisting both of local Western Christians and Muslim disciples of Christ, some of whom might call themselves Christians, while others may not, according to their preference or conscience. This church-planting strategy is being used in several cities in the USA, though its long-term success (or failure) has yet to be determined. The program begins with several teachings on the nature of Islam, the Qur'an, the Prophet, and customs found in many Islamic societies around the world. After that basic education, a group of people from a local church (or churches) then agree to meet at someone's home on a regular basis for a meal which is followed by a liturgical prayer where men and women are separated, portions of the Bible are read, and a "contextualized" version of the Apostles' Creed may be used as a confession of faith/*shahada*. These people are committed to meeting Muslims in their neighborhoods and intentionally speak with them and get to know them and form a friendship with them. At the meals, the food is all *hallal* and neither pork nor alcohol are ever served. The idea is that Muslims invited to participate in this sort of community will feel more comfortable than they would if invited to church on a Sunday morning, which is not an unreasonable notion. Furthermore, from the point of view of discretion for the Muslim who wants to know more about the Christian faith, having din-ner with friends attracts much less attention than visiting an actual church building. Eventually, the goal is that as a Muslim-background congregation is established, organic contextualization done by the former Muslims not their facilitators, would then also become possible.

In conclusion regarding the term contextualization, it is used in two rather very different ways. The original coining of the term represented the next step beyond indigenization and was to be carried out primarily by the local church, here called organic contextualization. Organic contextu-alization takes place when believers form their own questions, determine their own methods for addressing those questions or issues, posit possible answers/solutions, try out those possible solutions, and then evaluate the success or failure of the experiment. Organic contextualization, in this globalized world, may well be carried out in conversation with other (non-indigenous) Christians and churches. But the questions, framework, and solutions come from the indigenous church. It is *theology by, theology from*, and *theology with*. Organic contextualization is a lengthy process and can take decades or perhaps centuries. Furthermore, contextuality and contex-tualization may be discerned/carried out incorrectly.

The second meaning of the term refers to a missionary method whereby the Christian message is stripped of its "Western trappings" and alleges to be a more robust form of the cultural adaptation that Christian missionaries from Paul to Augustine of Canterbury to Ramon Llull to Temple Gairdner have employed, and in this work it will be referred to as directed contextualization.[32]

Beyond the two versions of contextualization explored here, there is a third important concept which must be examined with the goal of discerning to what extent it may be helpful in addressing the research question. That concept is inculturation.

A Roman Catholic Approach: Inculturation

After Vatican II profound changes in the Catholic approach to mission took place. In an effort to explain these changes, the head of the Society of Jesus, Pedro Arrupe, helped to popularize the term *inculturation*. His famous 1977 definition follows:

> Inculturation is the Incarnation of the Christian life and the Christian message into a certain culture, to be precise in such a way that this experience is not only expressed in forms of the culture concerned (this would be only a superficial adaptation), but so that it becomes the principle of a new inspiration, at the same time guide and uniting power, changing and creating this culture anew. Inculturation so stands at the beginning of a new creation.[33]

Inculturation is like organic contextualization in many ways: they both see the incarnation as a doctrinal foundation for their way of doing theology.[34] They are both dynamic methods/relationships that seek to allow for non-Western Christianities to exercise their own agency and power while in conversation with Western churches, both as a global and historical reality.[35] Both claim that it must be the indigenous agents of the church who carry out the fullness of the process. Both have a high estimate of their novelty: contextualization claims to be a new way of doing theology, and inculturation implies that "the whole of Church history and the history of theology

---

32. For a brief article on Llull see Bridger, "Raymond Lull," 1–25.

33. Quoted in Maier, "Inculturation," 505.

34. See Coe, "Education," 7.

35. In the context wherein Coe was working he and his WCC colleagues were concerned with creating a space where in the "younger churches" had a voice that was not seen as inferior or subordinate to the voices of the well established churches of the developed world. That having been said, contextualization and inculturation theory can be used to analyze and understand those "older" churches as well.

must be rewritten"[36]—no small task. Both claim the prerogative of not only altering superficial forms, but aim at the "deep structures of the faith" in its relation to culture.[37] Finally, both contextualization and inculturation, as processes, envision a fuller understanding of fundamental theological realities like God, Christ, and the church, as many churches bring their God-given, contextualized, inculturated, insights into the catholicity of the church. As Peter Schineller puts it, "The mission of inculturation is one key part of that search for the fullness of Christ, a fullness that will only come at the end."[38]

What then is the difference? The definition of inculturation given by Aylward Shorter is " . . . the creative and dynamic relationship between the Christian message and a culture or cultures."[39] He clarifies later, "we really are speaking of a dialogue between a . . . Christianized culture of the missionary and the hitherto un-Christianized culture to which he comes."[40] Shorter, like Schineller, was a missionary in Africa. Given their background and area of mission, it was helpful for them to think about the relation between two cultures, that of the missionary, and that of the missionized. Shorter understands that there is no such thing as the Christian faith apart from specific instantiations of it in given cultures (*pace* some evangelicals it appears, and their "seed and kernel" analogy for directed contextualization). Inculturation seeks to move beyond the older model, wherein "Armed with the myth of the superiority of Western European culture, [missionaries] simply transplanted western Christianity to American and African soil, showing little respect, and often disdain, for traditional local cultures."[41] Rather, "The quest for inculturation is a quest for a secure and integrated identity, motivated by a concern to find ways of being both authentically Christian and authentically Chinese, Indian, African, or whatever."[42]

The difference between inculturation and contextualization, though subtle, can now be identified: inculturation relates two cultures, and is thus a broader and more inclusive process than contextualization, which is the fruit of, and dialectical pair of, contextuality. A local church seeking to read its contextuality will, by necessity, need to take into account the nature of Christianity they received. Was it from American Presbyterians? Spanish

---

36. Shorter, *Inculturation*, 20.

37. Gittins, "Deep Structures," 47–72.

38. Schineller, *Handbook*, 60.

39. Shorter, *Inculturation*, 11.

40. Ibid., 12.

41. Schineller, *Handbook*, 11.

42. Stanley, "Inculturation," 22.

Jesuits? British Anglo-Catholics? Brazilian Pentecostals? Such an historical awareness is central to the reading of contextuality because it means to remember God's *missio dei* (the term Coe uses) in the past, with the goal of interpreting God's acts in and will for the world today. That is the contextuality of Coe—it includes an analysis of the evangelizing culture, but is a broader category, for contextuality includes the insight that the evangelizing culture needs to be critically analyzed and, like the culture being evangelized, challenged and formed and reformed by the Gospel.

Having reviewed three possible models which might assist in identifying a framework for theology-making, I believe that the most helpful model for this book is the ecumenical model of Coe, which I call organic contextualization. Directed contextualization is not helpful because it does not represent *theology by* but *theology for*. As for inculturation, it is a helpful theoretical model for analyzing the meeting a non-Christian culture with another Christian culture, but is not in itself a model of how theology-making might take place. Rather theology-making could be one process or facet of the larger process of inculturation.

While insights from scholars of inculturation will be used in this dissertation, and while inculturation and organic contextualization have much in common, the ecumenical model of contextualization is a more suitable theoretical framework and will be preferred throughout.

WHAT COUNTS AS GOD KNOWLEDGE? ROBERT SCHREITER ON TYPES OF THEOLOGICAL OUTPUT

If we think of theology only as systematized, certain knowledge about God, and understand the theology-maker as a professional devoted to that task, then CMBs are, with a very few exceptions, not theology-makers. But theological understanding can be done by believers who are not systematizing certain knowledge. This issue must be addressed because we seek to understand if ex-Muslim Christians are making their own theologies, and we therefore need to have a rough idea (at least) of what the theological artifact or output might look like.

Robert Schreiter begins chapter 4 of *Constructing Local Theologies* by noting that different societies envision, experience and understand what constitutes knowledge in different ways, because "How human knowledge is experienced, although communicable across cultural boundaries, is nonetheless largely shaped by local circumstances."[43] Drawing on the discipline of the sociology of knowledge, Schreiter proposes four broad categories of what constitutes theology or, in its most etymological meaning, God knowledge.[44]

The four varieties of God-knowledge he proposes are theology as variations on a sacred text, theology as wisdom, theology as sure knowledge, and theology as praxis. The first form of theology includes commentaries on Scripture, narrative, and anthology. The second form envisions theology as wisdom, and is "concerned with the meaning of experience" and "the interiority of human experience,"[45] in "being able to see the whole world, both the visible and the invisible, as a unified whole."[46] It is common to find in wisdom theology mention of mystical experiences and principals for "It is a pathway where learning, though indeed important and essential, is subordinated to devotion."[47] Schreiter mentions the *Interior Mansions* of St Teresa of Avila and the *Ascent of Mount Carmel* of St John of the Cross as two examples of such theology. I would argue that Eliot's *Four Quartets*, from which the epigraph of this book comes, is also such text.

The third form is theology as sure knowledge. This "is probably the most common form of theology in Roman Catholicism and mainline Protestantism in the West today": "Whereas wisdom theology tries to discern the unity of the world, theology as sure knowledge constructs a system to explain it."[48] This is the sort of theology which the Anglican priest in Egypt had in mind when he said that the CMBs there aren't concerned with theology. Schreiter, in a brief but fascinating historical synopsis, argues that the rediscovery of Roman Law in Western Europe in the eleventh century was instrumental in the rise of influence of this form of theology.[49] He also says that urbanization in Europe and the concomitant division of labor made the formation of professional teacher guilds and universities possible, and so "Theological reflection came to be understood as the work of full-time, trained professionals. They were teachers who engaged in theology, rather than persons who taught because they had reflected theologically (such as

43. Schreiter, *Local Theologies*, 75.

44. It is this differentiation between *types of contextual theology* and *sociology of theological knowledge* which makes Schreiter's book more useful, in my opinion, than Bevans's *Models of Contextual Theology*, which, while having much in common with Schreiter's book, does not sufficiently differentiate between the two.

45. Ibid., 85.

46. Ibid., 86.

47. Ibid.

48. Ibid., 87–89.

49. Ibid., 89–90.

bishops and novice masters)."[50] While not denigrating this form of theology, he rightly notes that " . . . often attempts have been made to impose the methods and results of theology as sure knowledge in cultural contexts where they do not fit . . ."[51]

The fourth form is theology as praxis, which is "the ensemble of social relationships that include and determine the structures of social consciousness."[52] Praxis begins with "pointing to false and oppressive relationships"[53] and attempts to "disentangle true consciousness from false consciousness."[54] Theology as praxis is closely related to liberation theology (one of his forms of local theology). This is not to say that other forms of theology do not lead to some practical application though. The word *praxis* here is used technically and specifically to refer to the claim that God-knowledge—by *its very nature*—leads to and is incomplete without the transformation of society and the subversion of unjust social structures.

With Coe's theory of the dialectical process of contextualization, and with Schreiter's refinements of Coe's theory in relation to theology-making, we are in a position to understand what the process of theology-making more or less looks like. With Schreiter's sociology of theology, we are also in a position where we can be perceptive to the diversity of forms of God-knowledge (theology) which ex-Muslim Christians may be producing.

POWER

Steven Lukes's Three Dimensions of Power

The very act of theology-making is closely tied to the topic of power, for it is an expression of agency, which involves the formation and reformation of overarching social and cultural orderings. Also, as will be clear in the next chapter, the issue of power over people, power to act, and power to control people, either directly or indirectly, is crucial to our understanding of both apostasy and conversion, which are fundamental to our understanding of the context in which ex-Muslim Christians act and live and might be making their own theology.

With this in mind, it is necessary to explore in greater detail the concept of power. In this section, the theory of Steven Lukes (1st edition 1974,

50. Ibid., 90.

51. Ibid., 91.

52. Ibid.

53. Ibid.

54. Ibid., 92.

2nd edition 2004) will be described. His theory of power will be useful to us in two related ways. Initially in chapter 2 it underlies our examination of the use of power by Islamic rulers to prevent the spread of the "pollu-tion" of apostasy. In subsequent chapters it informs the various efforts made by authorities to contain the "pollution" of apostasy and conversion to Christianity and by converts to survive persecution. Finally, it underlies both empowerment and disempowerment in the context of living out their Christian faith with attendant theology-making.

Lukes espouses what he calls a "radical view" that has "three dimen-sions." The first and most basic sort of power is that whereby an agent can cause another agent to decide to do something not in his interest (Lukes chapter 2). But there must be more to power than this, he argues, for causing certain issues not to be raised is itself an exercise in power, as the agent can *control the issues*. This second dimension is able to analyze " . . . the question of control over the agenda of politics and the ways in which potential issues are kept out of the political process."[55]

Lukes is aware as a social scientist that it is more difficult to observe such instances of the use of power because, unlike the first dimension, there is commonly an absence of action. Nonetheless, he insists that it is possible to observe such currents of power in society and gives some examples. The first dimension is a decision to *do* something, it is active, and it results in observable behavior. The second is a non-decision, but as such, is a decision that thwarts/suppresses an issue/interest before it can even be raised. That act of suppression is still an action (Lukes chapter 3).

But Lukes goes on to propose a third dimension (Lukes chapter 4), wherein one can identify a still more nuanced (if difficult to observe) use of power "in which *potential issues* are kept out of politics and other in-stitutions, whether through the operation of social forces and institutional practices or through individuals' decisions" whichever side of the power divide they are on.[56] That is to say, while the second dimension understood power as being able to keep *real* issues off the political agenda, this third dimension of power is understood as the ability to prevent *potential* issues from becoming *real* issues.

Much of the rest of Lukes's book is concerned with teasing out how his subtle third dimension can be empirically observed and tested (a req-uisite for a social science). He also argues that power may indeed be coer-cive or violent, though it need not be (Lukes chapter 5). He addresses the

---

55. Lukes, *Power*, 21.
56. Ibid. 24.

complication of interest when agents misunderstand what *really* is in their interest, and considers whether persuasion is also a use of power.

This three-dimensional theory of power has ample explanatory capacity. It can help us both understand the relation of the weak to the powerful, as when converts experience persecution. But it can also help us to understand the dynamics of empowerment, as when a convert stands up to persecution or distributes her experience of being in, say, an Egyptian jail. In so doing, she is converting her record of powerlessness into an instrument that shames the country of Egypt, revealing its unethical behavior. Finally, Coe's theory assumes that contextualization may well lead to social transformation, or at least an effort to transform society. The claim to be able to transform a society relates to all three dimensions of power in Lukes's theory, and also recalls Anthony Giddens's identification of power as *transformative capacity.*[57]

Power and the Word of God

Let us briefly look at one example of how power, identity, and *diin* are all linked in a web of mutual influence by examining the way in which these two communities, Muslims and Christians, interact with their holy books.

For reasons of economy I will limit myself to two communities, notably, an overwhelmingly Sunni Muslim community in the Arab world whom we meet again in chapter 4, and contemporary evangelical Christians. I have chosen the Sunni community because it is fairly typical of how Muslims in much of the Arab world interact with the Qur'an, and contemporary evangelicals because it is to these forms of Christianity—evangelical ones—that most CMBs are turning.[58]

Both evangelical Christianity and orthodox Islam tend to treat their books in specific ways: there is some overlap, but there is also significant divergence. It is sometimes difficult for non-Muslims to grasp how writing, reading, and comprehension relate very differently to the context of the Islamic world. Perhaps most centrally, the Qur'an is not often read to be understood: it is a form of divine speech, it is the pre-existent word of God present with him from all eternity, but instead of becoming incarnate in a man, it was made to descend to the Prophet of Islam who recited it. After

57. Giddens, *Social Theory.*

58. I am aware that there are many varieties of evangelical Christianity in the world. If emphasis is placed on American and British forms it is because they are influential an, on the whole, the sort of evangelicalism that these Muslims are encountering, rather than, say, Indian or Latin American streams of evangelical faith.

the battle of Yamama, "in which a number of those who knew the Qur'an by heart died,"[59] it became necessary to collect the recitations and record and codify them.

The content of the Qur'an is also more uniform than that of the Bible, consisting primarily of poetic summons to obedience and worship and warnings of punishment for those who resist, and then of laws and rules touching on everything from dividing the spoils of war to the treatment and procurement of slaves, inheritance laws, ritual and dietary laws, and so on. The person speaking is always (or almost always) God through the mediation of an angel, though often he is instructing the Prophet what to say. The book is to be recited in Arabic and is, ontologically speaking, incapable of being translated, for "in the context of religious activity, the recitation of the Qur'an can only be done in its original Arabic language, and such recitation tends to carry with it a sense of engagement in a religiously meritorious action."[60]

That is, the Qur'an cannot retain its identity upon translation. Only recently have translations of the meaning of the Qur'an been made widely available, though Christians had early on translated it into Latin, and Luther himself sponsored an early edition of the book in Germany.[61] A non-Arabic Qur'an will usually indicate that it does not claim to be the Qur'an but rather a "translation" or "translation of the meaning" of it. The consequences of this inability to be translated are manifold. On the level of interreligious dialogue it is often used to discard the opinion of anyone who does not know Arabic, because they cannot read the Qur'an. On the level of education one finds the *madrasas* of Pakistan, where children who do not know Arabic spend years memorizing the entire book in Arabic. To people used to a more Western style of education this may seem unproductive, but that misses the point. To memorize the entire revelation of God and be able to recite it is a supreme achievement, for the power of God flows in the very sounds and syllables whether or not they are connected to the cognition of the hearers. I have at times asked Arab Muslim friends about the meaning of a verse or phrase in the Qur'an (some of the grammar is infamously obscure). They would recite the verse from memory, but when asked about its meaning would say something like, *you know I've never thought about what it means.*

The Qur'an is also central to Islamic art. The iconoclastic tendencies of Islam mean the use of images is frowned upon, so the words of the Qur'an

59. Abdel Haleem, *Qur'an*, xvi.

60. Pratt, *Challenge of Islam*, 37.

61. Francisco, "Luther," 295.

are written in Arabic calligraphy, different places and times producing different styles of calligraphy.

> Reading calligraphy can be difficult, requiring preparation and application, and the consequent pleasure of the achievement is a reflection of our success in understanding God more profoundly, moving in his direction and developing a conception of the deity.[62]

The calligraphic use of Qur'anic verses, coupled with creative use of geometrical design and colors, is at the heart of much Islamic art.

The physical object—the book itself—is also something that is, one might say, sacramental, being a visible and tangible expression of God's invisible majesty and splendor. So the Qur'an is generally not placed on the floor or in one's pocket. On the other hand, one may find a miniature version of the Qur'an—which may not actually contain the entire book—hanging apotropaically from the rear-view mirror of a Muslim's vehicle. Some Muslims in the UK have requested that religious texts be placed on the highest shelves in public libraries;[63] this is an appropriate gesture in the Muslim mind, though some non-Muslims mentioned that this would be counter-productive because it would just make the books harder to access. It may seem a trivial matter, but it represents well two different approaches to the religious book: is this text one that somehow conveys and signifies the presence of God, or one to be read and understood and analyzed? Douglas Pratt, in his analysis of how Muslims interpret the Qur'an, explains what he views, correctly I think, as the hermeneutic that most Muslims employ in relation to the Qur'an, calling it a hermeneutic of *revelational positivism*:

> This denotes the view that the substantive message, as given in revelation and by virtue of its source, is fixed: it is not amenable to any change or modification whatsoever. The Absolute has spoken; what is given is, by implication, itself absolute and unchangeable, and so "transferable" as it stands to other times, places and contexts without any substantial modification of understanding or application. The divinely given datum of revelation is immutable.[64]

With this background in place a few conclusions can be drawn about power. First, in the sending down of the Qur'an which is itself *eternal* with Allah, the divine power is made manifest. The power of God is affirmed

62. Leaman, *Encyclopedia*, 73.
63. Cockroft, "Bible moved to library top shelf . . . "
64. Pratt, *Challenge of Islam,* 38.

in that it informs humans of the divinely ordained conduct which humans must follow, rules which are "absolute and unchangeable" and to be applied at all "times, places and contexts." Second, one can access or participate in this power by hearing, reciting or wearing it (as in an amulet) or looking at it (as with the artistic calligraphy), but this must be done in Arabic. Understanding the text or critically reflecting on its meaning is not required (nor is it necessarily encouraged) for otherwise the great majority of Muslims in the world would not be able to participate in this divine *baraka* or blessing. The concept of coming up with novel interpretations of the Qur'an is often viewed as highly suspicious, for the reasons Pratt mentions. Indeed, there is a specific form of heresy in Islamic jurisprudence called *bid3a* which translates as "innovation," to which individuals who propose novel interpretations or applications of the Qur'an may lay themselves open.

Evangelical Christianity prides itself on being "Biblical," and uses the word extensively: there are "Bible churches"; there are nominal Christians, and then there are "Bible-believing Christians" or just "believers." Arab evangelicals, when they need to differentiate between a true believer and a nominal Christian, will often use the words *mu'min* (believer) and *masiihi bi 'ism* (Christian by name) to make this distinction. It is hard to not see such language as being at least slightly derogatory towards other Christians, because the implication is that non-evangelical churches are not "Biblical" and that their Christians are deficient in their belief. Some evangelicals use such words with those beliefs in mind, but others do not, being simply a matter of convention. Evangelical piety is indeed centered on the Bible: a man should spend quiet time every day reading his Bible, it should be underlined and marked so he can go back to it for future reference—writing in the margin of the Qur'an being unthinkable for most Muslims. A woman brings her own Bible to the evangelical church and does not use the pew Bible, nor is she content merely with listening to the reading. The sermon, which is supposedly tied to the Biblical reading, can be quite lengthy, especially when compared to the ten minute homilies found in some Catholic and Orthodox churches. (Ironically, a Catholic mass or the Sacred Liturgy with all its readings—Psalm, Old Testament, Gospel, Epistle—usually has more actual reading from the Bible than does a service at an evangelical church.)[65] The most successful form of evangelical art has not been architecture or painting, but rather Contemporary Christian Music (CCM). In terms of musical dynamics it is almost identical to secular popular music. While not always explicit, Biblical themes are present throughout.

---

65. There is also an intersection of churches that are both liturgical *and* evangelical, as with some Anglican and Lutheran congregations.

Nor does evangelicalism have one, universal and coherent hermeneutic. All evangelicals agree that the Bible is the supreme authority over the Christian and the church, although it may be difficult to arrive at a consensus regarding what precisely the Bible teaches on a given point. Nor is there any way to discern an essential core of doctrines which must be agreed upon without making appeal to historical formulae (like the Nicene Creed or the Articles of Religion), which are, by their very definition, traditions of the church which communicate how it read the Bible at a given point in history. All of this has resulted in a community that to some degree resembles the *umma*: decentralized and pluriform, sometimes divisive, somewhat intimidated by modernity, but certain of its unique role in God's beneficent plan for the world.

Nevertheless, the evangelical Christian does seek, in her own way, to understand the Bible. The goal is not to simply understand the historical background and linguistic nuances of the book, but to know the Bible and live it in the context of a personal relationship with God. The young lady who has marked her Bible well shows her community by that physical object (the book) that she has been with God through thick and thin, and just as the pages of the book are tattered and worn, so her faith has, by God's grace, weathered the dangers, toils, and snares of life. Evangelicals are encouraged to engage with the Scripture critically, while remaining within an unspoken hermeneutical boundary. And here is one avenue whereby evangelical Christians encounter the power of God in their Scriptures, in that Scripture provides comfort and guidance for the difficulties and challenges of day-to-day life. As long as the individual does not step outside of certain parameters, like saying they have figured out when Jesus will return or discarding Trinitarian doctrine, they are free to identify verses and stories in the Bible which, according to the believer, the Holy Spirit has led them to in order to provide guidance and comfort. This in itself represents a form of power, but not the same sort of sacramental power found among (some) Sunni Muslims, which I described above.

Islam espouses the idea that Scripture "descended" (*nazala*) from God.[66] Christianity proposes something quite different—inspiration. If Muslims believe that the Qur'an is the verbatim word of God, eternal and increate with him, Christians generally believe that

> God speaks to us in this book. But God speaks through human writers who used the languages of an ancient Near Eastern people and of an ancient Western civilization. Moreover, the biblical writings reflect their writers" education or lack of it, their

66. Qur'an 3:3, 57:16, etc.

local environment and culture, their ancient views of geography, physics, and astronomy. As God in the infant Jesus came to us wrapped in swaddling clothes, so the word of God comes to us in the words of these human beings (Luther's analogy).[67]

This is the doctrine of inspiration. There are variations of this doctrine, and a proportion of evangelicals hold to the view that God did not permit any factual errors to be recorded in the Bible. Nonetheless, that the personality of the human author(s) of the inspired, biblical text—his story, his history, his life experiences—come through in and are an important key to understanding a text is widely acknowledged.

This means that, for Christians, the Bible is both a completely human book *and* completely a divine book. If this seems paradoxical or illogical then one should remember that Jesus Christ, in Chalcedonian Christianity (of which evangelicalism is but one tradition), is "at once complete in Godhead and complete in manhood . . ." (*Definition of Chalcedon*, 451 CE). In the doctrine of "God with us," which is called incarnation, and in the doctrine of the inspiration of the Bible, there is an intimation of the human and the divine (though they are not combined into a single new thing) that is to many Muslims illogical and incoherent and, what is worse, an affront to God and his power. For evangelicals, their God rejoices over the believer's well-worn, noted Bible for their reading it and interpreting it (within limitations) is of value to him. Intertwining their own biographies and theologies with his inspired book by making notes appears to evangelicals to be a sacramental (though evangelicals rarely use this word) way of making the invisible visible: they write their lives in the book of God, and conversely God writes their own lives into his own story. The power of God is thus encountered in intimacy as God shows his power in his vulnerability. God, in this theology, is taking a huge risk by partnering with human beings who are concupiscent by their very nature, by revealing to them his own word and will in the Bible. He is risking that readers will not clearly recognize the divine quality (and power) of the words in that he has shared them with fallible human authors.

Muslims and Christians agree that self-revelation is both a uniquely divine prerogative and a demonstration of divine power, but Christians state that the deity has associated himself with human beings in this activity. To many Muslims these doctrines are illogical, bizarre, and/or unacceptable. Technically, their vision of power and God will not allow for such a sharing of the divine prerogative. The power and authority of Allah are absolute and

---

67. Guthrie, *Christian Doctrine*, 58–9.

undiluted by the need of anything more than a "warner," as Muhammad is called in the Qur'an,[68] who can relay that message to humanity.[69]

Christians also approach the issue of translation very differently. Christianity is, one might say, incapable of *not* being translated. The doctrine of the incarnation itself can be read as a theology of translation, that the *kalimat allah* (word of God) is most authentically his word when it is being spoken to humans *in the flesh*. Andrew Walls has shown how essential translation was to the early spread of Christianity which co-opted the Septuagint, thus permitting the incorporation of large numbers of gentiles who otherwise would not have had access to the Hebrew Scriptures.[70] One might recall that the Cyrillic alphabet itself is the fruit of missionary work to the Slavs—it was developed by Saint Cyril who upon finding that they did not have an alphabet developed one, and this was a key step towards their conversion. Examples could be multiplied.[71]

This impetus towards translation coupled with the hunger for practicality/relevance—a key concern of evangelicals—has resulted in a bewildering assortment of translations of the Bible in some languages, often with notations regarding everything from grammatical and historical information, to quotes, to eschatological observations, to practical ways of applying a verse to one's life: one can purchase an English-language Bible with commentary/advice for mothers, high school students, college students, families, and so on. All of this is immensely confusing to many Muslims who can point to one Qur'an which is not translated and is the same over all the face of the earth. Between the commentaries and different translations, the awareness that these Bibles are all translations of the same texts in the original languages is sometimes lost on the Muslim. The deity of Islam, in his power and majesty, has no need to partner with humans to see that his Scripture be translated, for its very nature defies such attempts, but even in its foreignness and unintelligibility it is capable of mediating divine power

---

68. "But you are only a warner . . ." (11:12, but see also 7:188, 13:7, and 29:50, which have similar statements).

69. Muslim piety interferes here though. For many Muslims, Muhammad has become something close to an object of worship. The reasons for this are complex, but suffice to say that in the Qur'an the divine will and the will of the Prophet are very difficult to separate from each other. Thus the Prophet can say, "If you love Allah, then follow me, Allah will love you and forgive your sins . . ." (3:31).

70. Walls, *Christian Movement*, 30ff.

71. Calvin Shenk, in his "Church in North Africa," has gone so far as to suggest that Christianity in North Africa, which gave the church great figures like Tertullian and Cyprian, did not survive because it did not translate the Bible into the original, indigenous languages of the region (Punic and the Berber languages), but remained reliant on the recently imported, urban language of Latin.

and favor. From this point of view, translation (like inspiration) appears to imply that God is willing to lower himself to a demeaning level by allowing fallible humans to translate and (by necessity) perhaps mistranslate his divine message. From the point of view of the Christian though, being able to translate the Bible into a community's indigenous language is actually an empowering act. A missionary who had spent many years with a Berber tribe of North Africa related to me how surprised one group was when they were presented with the New Testament in their own language, asking how a divine book (the *injiil*) could be in any language but Arabic, which for many of them is associated with colonialism and racism. The missionary responded that the *injiil*, unlike the Qur'an, could and should be translated into every language without losing its meaning. This represented a form of empowerment to the Berber group and a validation of their identity *as Berbers*.

To conclude this section, there are similarities and differences in how evangelicals and Arabophone Sunni Muslims tend to interact with their holy books. Among both communities there is a strong tendency to believe that God would not allow for any factual error to be present in the book, and neither tradition has a centralized juridical power that can regulate the interpretation of said books. But there are some very significant differences as well. For evangelicals, the deity is happy to relate personally to the believers, as they read and mark their Bibles, and as they weave their own biographies into the divine narrative. For Muslims the power of God is revealed in its otherness, for the book, like God, is completely independent of any human activity whatsoever. In orthodox Islam, even without the Creation, the Qur'an would have existed as the eternal speech of God.

In spite of all of this, both communities end up with a similar confession: "For yours is the kingdom and the power and the glory forever. Amen" (Matt 6:13), and "To Allah doth belong the dominion of the heaven and the earth, and all that is therein, and it is He Who hath power over all things" (5:120, Yusuf Ali trans). But what it means for God to be powerful, to show power, and willing to share his power is precisely the issue of contention as has been shown in relation to two important doctrines: revelation and translatability.

An analysis of the two doctrines has been presented from the point of view of power to give an example, but as will be seen through this book, these two issues—revelation and translatability—will resurface a number of times. Theology-making, if it occurs, must occur by necessity within a given cultural, religious and political context, and an examination of contextuality is a necessary first step as we seek to discern if contextualization is taking place. Understanding the nature of power and how God's power can be mediated is an important step toward understanding that context. We will learn more about how revelation and translatability are integral aspects of the context wherein theology-making may be taking place in chapters 2 and 3. But first it is appropriate to present an overall map of the entire book.

STRUCTURE OF THE BOOK

Chapter 2 considers religious conversion, and, specifically, the type of conversion called apostasy and becoming Christian. Since the majority of current ex-Muslim Christians are evangelicals, special attention will be paid to how most evangelical Christians understand conversion and what is expected of the convert. Lewis Rambo's theory of conversion will be described and evaluated. Since some Muslims deal rather harshly with apostates, the realities faced by these apostates are an integral aspect of their context.

In chapter 3 the recent historical context will be explored. Since roughly the 1960s hundreds of thousands of Muslims have come to identify themselves as followers of Christ as portrayed in the Bible. Estimates of the numbers of converts will be provided. Based on a questionnaire distributed to Christian practitioners with experience in the Muslim world, those factors will be discussed which they feel have facilitated the increase in the number of Muslims who decide to follow Jesus. Then these factors will be related to the concept of power, and the increased inability of some Islamic groups or governments to limit the growth of Christianity among Muslims will be presented. Chapter 3, then, tries to address the question: what are the new realities that have facilitated the growth of Christianity among Muslims? Another way to put it is that we are trying to understand additional aspects of the globalizing *context* of CMBs.

Chapter 4 is a case-study of an evangelical, Arabic-speaking, largely Christian congregation in the Middle East. This community is unlike most other such communities in that it actively welcomes Muslims and converts from Islam for whom it forms a bridge. Some of the members of this community live and/or work in a context where they may suffer violence or imprisonment for their activities. Furthermore, this community started a Muslim-background congregation that almost entirely consists of converts from Islam. The context is one where Christians are a small percentage of the over-all population. The chapter will explore the linkages between conversion, power, and identity-formation in the context of a Muslim-background congregation (MBC).

Chapter 5 examines some texts written by CMBs and asks whether these are theological texts. I will argue they can and should be read as such, and that the predominant form of theology which ex-Muslim Christians produce is a liberation theology, one of its main goals being the transformation of Muslim societies. I will also argue that in these texts we find a wisdom theology, according to the model of Robert Schreiter's "local theologies," itself an expansion of Coe's model. Examples will be provided wherein CMBs are engaged in the process of discerning their own needs, selecting a medium of communication, and then proposing possible solutions for how those needs (or desires) might be met through this theology-making.

Chapter 6 is a case study of Iranian Diaspora Christians in the USA and the UK wherein I will argue that they are engaging in theology-making. ICs, who are mostly converts from Shi'a Islam, represent one of the largest movements from Islam to Christianity ever.[72] Specific characteristics pertaining to political and economic and religious realities in Iran will be discussed to suggest some reasons to explain this numerically significant conversion movement. Then, based on interviews and participating in Iranian worship and events, I will discuss how ICs utilize anti-syncretism, ritual and kerygma in contextual theology-making, and the special place of baptism. Some of the key challenges (facets of their contextuality) facing the communities I researched will be presented. As a diaspora study, these ICs are not under threat of state-sponsored persecution, although relatives in Iran may be so affected.

Chapter 7 is an analytical chapter that returns to the core issues of this thesis—contextuality, contextualization, conversion, power—and proposes some overarching themes and concerns that connect the varying ex-Muslim Christians studied in this book.

CONCLUSION

In this first chapter possible candidates for understanding theology-making were presented: directed contextualization, organic contextualization and inculturation. While not perfect, the most helpful model among them for this project is the framework of organic contextualization developed by Shoki Coe. Robert Schreiter's work clarified some varieties of theological knowledge. As to the question of *who* makes theology—it is the community that is the theology-maker, though it is common that a leader or representative of that community will act as a spokesperson.

---

72. It is likely the second largest single movement from Islam to Christianity, after the conversion of many Javanese "folk" Muslims to Christianity in the sixties and seventies, largely for political security. For more on the Indonesia movement, see Willis, *Indonesian Revival.*

It is impossible to understand the context of ex-Muslim Christians and religious conversion without an adequate theory of power, thus the topic of power was explored. After outlining Lukes's radical theory of power the example of how two different traditions within Islam and Christianity relate power to their Scriptures was provided.

Central to a reading of the contextuality of ex-Muslim Christians is an understanding of religious conversion. In the following chapter conversion will be approached from a number of different angles—why Muslims convert, what the repercussions are, what is expected of the convert, and how Muslims understand the act of apostasy, among others.

2

The Context of the Ex-Muslim Christian
Conversion and Apostasy

CONTEXT AND CONVERSION

Coe's model of organic contextualization proposes that prior to understanding any contextual theology-making which may be taking place, an understanding and evaluation of the *contextuality* of the theology-maker is necessary. A key facet of that contextuality for CMBs is their conversion, both away from Islam and to Christianity. Therefore, in this chapter some background on how Christians, and specifically evangelical Christians, understand conversion will be outlined. A summary of Lewis Rambo's theory of conversion will be presented and then applied to a specific CMB conversion narrative. Reference will be made to biblical material related to conversion that still inform evangelical piety and practice today, including baptism.

Ex-Muslims, whether they consider themselves Christians or members of some other religion or no religion at all, are apostates. So the specific form of conversion called "apostasy" will be described, with special reference to how the Islamic shari'a has often addressed it, and how the status of the apostate may be affected. It is not uncommon for the apostate or enquirer to face coercion or threat, which is an instance of direct power. Lukes's three dimensions of power will be used to help us understand the various uses of power to attempt to contain the "pollution of apostasy." Having explored these topics we will have become familiar with some important facets of the contextuality of the ex-Muslim Christian.

RELIGIOUS CONVERSION

Arthur Darby Nock's Definition

Conversion, on a very basic level, can be defined as a turning away from something, and turning to something else. As Nock wrote in his important study of conversion in early Christianity:

> By conversion we mean the reorientation of the soul of an individual, his deliberate turning from indifference or from an earlier form of piety to another, a turning which implies a consciousness that a great change is involved, that the old was wrong, and the new is right.[1]

That definition, while somewhat antique, is quite fitting for our study of conversion among ex-Muslims. Many early Christians were engaged in what other people saw as deviant behavior, as is true for Muslim converts today. Similarly, it was often the case that a person's Christian faith might well lead to marginalization or persecution, if not outright martyrdom. This is also the case in much of the Muslim world today, and may be true even for Muslims living in the West.

Lewis Rambo and contemporary conversion theory

Traditionally, religions often had monopolies on groups of people, and were largely able to convince (or compel) people to remain loyal to their brand, and sometimes measures were taken to limit people's awareness of other religions altogether. This does not mean that people "believed" in the religion, in the sense that evangelical piety desires, but it did mean that, regardless of their private opinions, they would engage in a minimal demanded public involvement. An example of this is during Elizabethan England when many individuals who were not convinced by the Protestant "reforms" nonetheless maintained a minimal, public conformity for the sake of not causing problems.[2]

But with the advent of modernity and globalization a panoply of options and ideas have become available to many religious enquirers. It is possible to acknowledge this while also recognizing that Islamic communities and families still possess multiple methods whereby they can exercise their power to circumscribe the options available to the religious consumer. This

1. Nock, *Conversion*, 7.
2. MacCulloch, *Tudor Church Militant.*

will be discussed later in the section on apostasy, and then in detail in chapter 3.

Lewis Rambo, in his influential 1993 volume *Understanding Religious Conversion,* is able to bring together results from a variety of disciplines, such as psychology, anthropology, sociology and history, and distill the collective research of decades in one book. Following is a summary of his "hypothesis," as he modestly calls it. Points relevant to conversion among ex-Muslims will be emphasized, while some material that is not relevant will be passed over. He starts by saying that his is a holistic model, one which takes account of the environment and the individual as well. He provides a helpful list of types of religious conversion: Apostasy; intensification (becoming more involved in the life of your religious community); affiliation (ie, movement from no affiliation to a new affiliation, not increased participation as with intensification); institutional transition (i.e., a Baptist becomes a Methodist); tradition transition (i.e., from Islam to Christianity).[3]

Drawing on the work of Lofland and Skonovd,[4] he suggests several conversion motifs as well: intellectual, mystical, experimental (trying something new and seeing if it works), affectional (belonging to a community, then believing with them), revivalism (emotional arousal, and then peer pressure), and finally coercive.[5] He then goes on to outline the central feature of his proposed model of the stages of conversion.

Context (Rambo chapter 2) is the first element, and refers to the entire, holistic environment around the person, included economic and social and gender status to political and religious surroundings. Context is not simply "one step," but is the first concept to be understood and interpreted, and it remains relevant through the entire process of conversion. After context comes crisis: "Some form of crisis usually precedes conversion; that is acknowledged by most scholars of conversion."[6] A crisis (Rambo chapter 3) is any event or series of events that calls into question the previously held beliefs of the person. It need not be sudden (like Paul on the Damascus Road) or dramatic, and may include a vision, healing, existential doubt or worry, or a moral dilemma.

The crisis then occasions a quest, the third stage in a conversion. The goal of the quest is to try to resolve the crisis, and the potential convert is actively engaged in resolving his problem. That is to say, the convert is not a passive observer who is merely an object of manipulation for some

---

3. Rambo, *Religious Conversion,* 12–16.

4. Lofland and Skonovd, "Conversion Motifs," 373–85.

5. Rambo, *Religious Conversion,* 14–16.

6. Ibid., 44.

preacher. The nature of the quest will be affected by several factors such as whether the person has the time, education or ability to travel or read, and whether they need to keep this quest secret from family.

Encounter is the fourth stage (Rambo chapters 5–7). Here the person comes into contact with an advocate for the new religious position. Lewis devotes ample energy to explaining the various aspects of encounter. Some examples of aspects of encounter he discusses are the strategy and goal of the advocate: it could be polemical, irenic or manipulative. The goal of the advocate is integral to understanding this phase of encounter, and some general evangelical goals will be explored later in this chapter. Rambo notes that sometimes encounter can come before crisis, and this is indeed the case in a number of conversion narratives among MBBs.

Interaction is the fifth stage (Rambo chapter 8). In this stage, the seeker interacts with the advocate and her community as well. Drawing on the work of Greil and Rudy,[7] he proposes that during this stage the nature of the interaction can be analyzed using four components: relationships, rituals, rhetoric, and roles. It is during this time that "Potential converts now learn more about the teachings, life-style, and expectations of the group, and are provided with opportunities, both formal and informal, to become more fully incorporated into it."[8] This may be a brief period of time or an extended one, depending on the community, and, for some Muslims seeking Christ, may lead to persecution.

Commitment (Rambo chapter 9) is "the fulcrum of the change process."[9] CMBs, following the broader evangelical tradition, tend to place this at the moment of making a confession of faith in Messiah, but baptism is also seen as important. This stage is often couched in terms of "surrender," after which the person will start to use a changed rhetoric in speaking about her past as she reorganizes and reinterprets it to fit her emerging religious identity. It is after this point that certain things may well become forbidden to the convert.[10]

The final stage in conversion is consequences (Rambo chapter 10). One can discuss the consequences of a conversion in several ways. For instance, one might investigate the psychological consequences by examining the converts' mental health, or in a large movement of conversion the historical consequences.

---

7. Greil and Rudy, "Social Cocoons," 260–78.

8. Rambo, *Religious Conversion*, 102.

9. Ibid., 124.

10. Though with CMBs things may be no longer forbidden, like pork or alcohol.

Consequences for CMBs are related to persecution, identity formation, finding a church, relations with Muslim family members, and questions related to marriage and children. All of these will surface in this book at different points. Theology-making may be part of this open-ended stage which itself is the context of theology-maker.

Applying Rambo's Model: The Conversion of Timothy Abraham

Unfortunately, Rambo's extensive bibliography does not have a single book on converts from Islam to Christ. This is the case even though years before its publication good-quality volumes on the topic were available, like Willis's 1977 Indonesia study and Syrjänen's 1984 Pakistan study. Nor does he use CMB conversion narratives, though there were by 1990 several such books.[11]

It is appropriate now to apply Rambo's hypothesis to an actual conversion narrative, and then evaluate it. Timothy Abraham was born into an Egyptian Muslim family and now lives in the USA. His conversion narrative has been available on the Internet for over a decade.[12] Moreover, I have been in personal contact with him for over four years, so I have been able to ask him for clarifications on several points. Also, given Rambo's emphasis on the advocate, I felt it important to choose a convert with whose advocate I could converse. I was able to interact with both Timothy and John via email and telephone interviews (2011).

Timothy describes his context: a bucolic village in the Nile Delta, and "There was not a single reason to doubt a religion which emphasized fearing God, doing good work and living a moral life." During his childhood he was seeking deeper knowledge of God. He became involved with the Muslim Brotherhood. This in itself is a type of conversion, according to Rambo's terminology. He started to fast more and "I diligently imitated every thing the Prophet Muhammad did, even the sitting posture of the Prophet as he was eating." He also started to engage in Islamic *da3wa*, which initially meant calling Muslims to a more devout imitation of the Prophet; he forced his sister to veil. Eventually he desired to expand this *da3wa* to calling non-Muslims to conversion. Via a magazine that offered to connect international pen-pals with each other, Timothy and John started to correspond: "I wrote

---

11. Sheikh, *Call Him Father*; Esther and Sangster, *The Torn Veil*; Masood, *Into the Light*.

12. Available online at http://www.answering-islam.org/authors/abraham/testimony.html and http://www.truthnet.org/islam/timabr.htm.

to John from Pennsylvania back and forth for two years, each trying to convert the other. I read every book I could get hold of to refute the Bible."

John described an initial "deluge of correspondence." Eventually John was working in Kenya and decided to travel to Egypt. He had come from a devout evangelical family, but he was not a professional missionary or minister. Nonetheless, he had grown up with "a lot of exposure to foreign missionaries" who visited his church. His goal was "to convert" Timothy, which in the context of American, non-denominational evangelical Christianity means to elicit a confession of faith in Jesus Christ as "Lord and Savior," eventually to be accompanied by baptism and attendance at a local church.

This is Rambo's stage of encounter, as John and Timothy are interacting, and in the case of Timothy it appears to have preceded the crisis. If Timothy had a quest at this point in time, it was that of furthering Islam. But John's visit, and their personal interactions, would occasion the crisis stage. John went to live with Timothy and his family for a few months. John was intentional about living the normal village life—eating their food and drinking the same tap water they did. That John was about the same age as Timothy and lived at the same socio-economic level is a significant aspect of the context of the advocate, for his self-communication was not of greater power or status relating to someone inferior. Indeed, by staying at Timothy's home he was putting himself at the mercy of Timothy who could have presumably told him to leave.

Timothy portrays this time in a positive light:

> That was the first time I saw a real Christian. His sincerity, frankness, genuineness, and openness impressed me. John stayed with me for two months. He had an amazing prayer life which served as a model for me in my latter life. I did not know that Christians prayed until I saw a "living epistle" right in the middle of my house, a man from a far off land who became one of us and genuinely incarnated the love of Christ . . . I became jealous of John's intimacy with God and increased my recitations of the Quran.[13]

John's memories are less rosy. He describes how Timothy would taunt him until he lost his temper and then Timothy would say, "now calm down!" John was in his 20s at the time, and his perspective today is that he should have been less polemical and more patient. Timothy's perspective is that God was doing something in him to call into question his previous commitments and open his eyes to a new reality. The two narratives do not disagree on any material facts, but they do illustrate how differently people interpret

---

13. From Abraham's Internet testimony, n.p.

the same narrative. John is still an evangelical Christian, but older and, from his point of view, more mature.

Timothy describes the moment of crisis:

> After John left, his influence stayed . . . His intercessory prayer moved the LORD to wake me up in the middle of the night as I had no sleep or rest. Inner conflict reached its zenith. Restless, I reached out to my Bible and opened it at random. I found, "Saul, Saul, why do you persecute me?" I remember one day in the heat of a debate between me and John, I made fun of the Bible and said, "John, your Bible is the most absurd thing! How can you believe the story of Saul who became Paul, the servant of the Gospel?" John said, "The story is true, and that is why I am patient with you. You will be another Paul one day!" I replied, "John, you must be out of your mind to think for a second that I could leave the religion of all religions, Islam!" Reflecting on "Saul, Saul. . ." I said "Lord! Me? Me persecute You? I did nothing to You in person . . . I remember I turned in a female medical student to the police . . . but I did nothing to You. Is it true that He who touched one of Your people touches the apple of Your eye?" (ibid.)

This crisis started Timothy's quest. Timothy started to question Islam. He started reading a great deal, including evangelistic literature from publishers like Call of Hope and Light of Life.[14] He was about 20 at this time and was, in his own words, "working as a tinkerer and fixing kerosene stoves." Eventually Timothy came to the conclusion that the Bible was the true "inerrant" word of God, and that Jesus was the Word of God as well. He describes himself as intellectually agreeing with Christianity, but, as he said, in need of a miracle so that he could fully "yield" to God. He was aware that apostates are to be executed, and that he would be ostracized by his family. Then he had a dream:

> One night Christ appeared to me in a dream and said with a tender sweet voice, "I love you!" I saw how obstinately I had resisted Him all these years and said to Him in tears, "I love You, too! I know You! You are eternal for ever and ever." I woke up with tears all over my face filled with abundant joy, believing that Christ Himself touched both my mind and my heart, and I yielded.[15]

14. Online: http://www.call-of-hope.com/new/site/index.php?lang=eng and http://www.light-of-life.com/.

15. Ibid., n.p.

This, and not the moment of *intellectual* assent, is his moment of surrender. The difficulty is that it is hard to account for stage five, interaction. I explored this in conversations with him, asking if he had been part of a church in his town while he was exploring the Bible and reading Christian literature. He responded that there was a Coptic family, and that they made an impression on him, but since he was being watched by state security his interaction with them was limited to avoid endangering them. Broadly speaking, reading the evangelistic material was a form of interaction with Christians, but there is no regular attendance to a church or fellowship during this period, which is central to Rambo's definition:

> For people who continue with a new religious option after the initial encounter, their interaction with their adopted religious group intensifies. Potential converts now learn more about the teachings, life-style, and expectations of the group, and are provided with opportunities, both formal and informal, to become more fully incorporated into it.[16]

This lack of an interaction phase, or having a very tenuous interaction phase, is common in the accounts of CMBs, mostly due to security reasons. The Muslim may endanger himself by attending a church, and a church may endanger itself by allowing a Muslim to attend. Moreover, these activities mentioned by Timothy more closely resemble the quest stage. Today, Timothy is and has long been a member of a church, but it appears that his interaction came *after* his conversion, a possibility that Rambo never entertains.

The final stage is consequences. Timothy recounts those in his narrative:

> Since my secret conversion was now made public and Muslims plotted to kill me, I had to flee. I was hunted by Muslims from my village in the Delta, to Ismailia until I arrived in Cairo where my Christian friends lived. Yet Christians were not willing to shelter me and I had to go back to the village, seeking refuge in His protective hands. I came back from Cairo and found an angry mob of Muslims filling up our house. My mother was wearing the garment of mourning, dressed in black as is the custom in Egypt. To them by deserting Islam, I was dead!!![17]

These consequences are not uncommon for a convert in Egypt, or most anywhere in the Muslim world. Eventually he was able to flee to the USA. He is married to an American woman and they have two children.

16. Rambo, *Religious Conversion*, 102.
17. Ibid., n.p.

He is a great lover of Arabic and French literature and is active in Christian apologetics to Muslims. I asked him if return to Egypt would be possible and he answered, "Of course I can't and won't ever go back to Egypt. I am on two lists of the Egyptian intelligence and the security department there."

All in all Rambo's model works satisfactorily, though with a few qualifications. In this case, the two most important ones are that interaction appears to come after conversion, and that encounter occasioned the crisis, rather than encounter resulting from the quest. A third issue is that Rambo doesn't seem to address the possibility that religious conversion need not come from "spiritual" motives at all. During my fieldwork with Iranians in the UK I was informed by more than one leader that sometimes an Iranian asylum-seeker would start to attend a Christian church and seek baptism because they had heard it would increase the strength of their claim for asylum before the government. According to the evangelical understanding of conversion this is not a valid conversion because it lacks repentance/surrender, which is seen as essential. But the leaders also informed me that sometimes those very people became "true believers." That is, after attending church and Bible study for the reason of assisting their asylum case, they actually came to that interior state of repentance/surrender. It is difficult to see how Rambo's framework could make sense of such a scenario. Sometimes religious conversion is not spiritual at all—a person wants to marry someone, or they need a job, or they need their debts forgiven. It is important to at least acknowledge the reality of such conversions.

Most CMBs have converted to some sort of evangelical Christianity, and evangelical Christians (the advocates, in Rambo's model) have identified in the Bible some key aspects of conversion that influence their practice and doctrine today. In order to understand "the new" that CMBs have turned to we will now explore some dominant themes in the New Testament that strongly influence how Christians, and evangelical Christians in particular, understand "the new."

Scripture and Conversion

First century Judaism had a detailed system for receiving converts. Gentiles attracted to their faith could have a limited involvement in the local synagogue without a full conversion. These were called "God-fearers" and several are mentioned in the Bible.[18] Full converts to Judaism had to be baptized with water, and, if male, circumcised. The practice of water baptism would

---

18. For example: Cornelius in Acts 10.

be retained by Christians as the church gradually became a community that was identified as something other than just another Jewish sect.

The initial and most primitive proclamation of the Gospel originates with John the Baptist, who preached, "Repent, for the Kingdom of God is at hand," and this prophetic message was endorsed by Jesus.[19] *Repentance*, then, would come to form a key aspect of how Christians were to understand conversion, and is often emphasized by evangelicals. A "genuine" repentance that leads to a changed life is one of the pillars of the evangelical perception of what constitutes a "valid" and "biblical" conversion.

The repentance-conversion preached by Jesus was *holistic* and touched every aspect of the convert's life: relation to family, Empire, Temple, ritual purity, Torah, money, the poor and hungry, prayer, persecution, ethnicity, the eschaton, and, very significantly for this work, to power.

In the New Testament, Jesus commissioned certain leaders to propagate his teaching and instructed them in how to initiate new members into the Kingdom of God. These believers came to understand themselves as belonging to the church, perceived of both discrete congregations but also a pan-ethnic, universal assembly. An unprecedented number of gentiles joined what was originally seen as a Jewish sect, and the question of what constitutes a valid conversion came to the fore. Baptism, reconfigured around the person of Jesus, was unanimously preserved as an important initiation rite.[20] But to what extent should this new *ekklesia* retain the old (Jewish) conversion theory? In Acts 15 the gathered leaders discern that the Spirit's will is that male converts need not be circumcised, and that only some rudimentary Jewish customs need to be observed. Thus much of the traditional theory of conversion was abandoned, which, in practice, threw open the gates to non-Jews.

Here it is necessary to examine with more care the significance of Paul and his conversion, because, "The Pauline conversion experience greatly influenced both theological conversion models and psychologists of religion."[21] Paul was a persecutor of the early disciples of Messiah, and on the Damascus road he encountered the risen Jesus who then commanded him to go see a man named Ananias. Paul was struck blind, but Ananias healed him, and then Paul "got up and was baptized."[22] While Paul continued to identify himself as a Jew, his transformation in relation to Jesus was unequivocal and took place in a short period of time. This led to the as-

19. Matt 11:12.

20. Green, "Apostasy in Pakistan," 152; Humphries, *Early Christianity*, 156.

21. Gooren, *Conversion and Disaffiliation*, 11.

22. Acts 9:18.

sumption that "proper" conversions should take place along the same lines. While sudden, dramatic conversions sometimes take place, they are not the norm, as was noted above.

These, then, are the fundamental ideal qualities of conversion as they generally relate to the context of evangelicals engaging in Muslim evangelism and thus also the CMB. First, conversion is related to repentance,[23] a turning[24] away from an old life and towards a new life[25] that has been made possible through the life and death and resurrection[26] of Jesus. Second, conversion is holistic in that it affects every area of the convert's life.[27] Third, conversion is communal, or ecclesial, in that the true convert is, by the very act of conversion, a member of the body of Christ, his church.[28] Fourth, it is baptismal, in that conversion is, sooner or later, symbolized and announced by the ritual of water baptism and a concurrent confession of faith.[29]

The baptismal quality of conversion should not be understood on a soteriological level though, as most evangelicals do not believe that water baptism is necessary for salvation. It is almost universally practiced by Christians. Among evangelical Christians the confession that Jesus is one's "Lord and Savior" is often used, recalling Jesus's authority (*lordship*) over the entirety of life (the holistic aspect mentioned earlier), and the person's inability to *save* their self by their own efforts. Furthermore, most evangelicals do not practice infant baptism, and prefer baptism by immersion. Baptism recurred as an important locus of reflection and discussion throughout my fieldwork. Therefore, greater detail on the actual function of baptism as a rite of initiation is appropriate.

Baptism as Initiation for Converts

Arnold Van Gennep, in his effort to analyze rites of passage, proposed a three-fold structure: 1) separation, 2) liminal period, and 3) reassimilation (also called reincorporation).[30] This concept was later made popular by British anthropologist Victor Turner in his 1967 book *The Forest of Sym-*

---

23. Matt 3:2.

24. 1 Thess 1:9.

25. Rom 6:4.

26. Rev 1:5.

27. Matt 5–7; 8:22, etc.

28. Matt 8:17; 1 Cor 5:12; Eph 3:10; 1 Tim 3:15; and also Abu Daoud, "Sacrament and Mission" [3 parts].

29. Matt 28:19; Acts 2:38; Eph 4:5; and also Green, *Evangelism in the Early Church*.

30. Van Gennep, *Les Rites de Passage*.

bols. Van Gennep's ritual cycle and specifically liminality / the liminal phase are useful for understanding conversion from Islam to Christ. The concept of liminality refers to the stage of belonging to neither world, of being "in between," and it comes from the Latin word *limina* meaning threshold. At the threshold of a house one is entering, but is neither outside nor inside of the house itself. The period of engagement to being married could be interpreted as liminal, as the couple is neither free to date others, nor do they yet have the new status of a married couple. Another example would be a Catholic seminarian—he is not merely a student who is gaining academic knowledge, but nor is he yet a priest with the obligations and prerogatives of that office. Crossing a threshold can be symbolically communicated in gestures that people do not even realize they are doing—taking off one's hat when saying grace, making the sign of the cross upon entering a church, removing one's sandals on entering the mosque.

Baptism is a *right of initiation* whereby one is separated from a previous community, enters a stage of liminality (preparation, in this case), and then is incorporated or assimilated again into a new community, having a different status than before. For Muslims converting to Christianity, this stage of liminality is best construed as the entire period of pre-baptismal training. Baptism is also a *rite of passage* in that it marks a shift from one station in life to a different one. As such it is closely related to conversion, even if it is not considered to be the "moment" of conversion, per se. Images of baptism in the Bible[31] are related to death and deliverance and are drawn on today by CMBs when they speak of baptism.

If baptism points to a rupture or transition point in the life of the CMB, we must also acknowledge that there are individuals who purport to follow Jesus not as Christians (as our CMBs) but within the context of Islam. To them we now turn our attention.

Forms of Conversion: ex-Muslim Christians and Muslim followers of Jesus

This book is primarily interested in those who understand themselves to have left Islam for Christianity. But there are also individuals who continue to identify themselves as Muslims, and understand themselves to be followers of Jesus as he is portrayed in the Bible.[32]

---

31. Matt 3:11, Rom 6, etc.

32. Sometimes called "insiders" or "Messianic Muslims." The topic will resurface in chapters 3 and 7.

Regarding CMBs and Muslim followers of Jesus, these are not discrete, immutable categories, for someone could move from one category to the other. Furthermore, there is a commonality between them, in that both a) originate in an Islamic society, and b) hold a commitment to Jesus Christ and his message as portrayed in the Gospels.

Regarding the Muslim followers of Jesus, they are a second and *apparently* less common form of Christ-follower. They appear to understand Islam more as a civilization or a culture rather a religion. Therefore, according to them, it is possible for a person to remain, in some cultural manner, within Islam, and thus remain, in a certain understanding of the word, Muslim, or at least Islamic. Mazhar Mallouhi, who was a Muslim, then became an evangelical Christian, and then became a "Muslim follower of Christ," explains such a view of Islam:

> I was born into a confessional home. Islam is the blanket with which my mother wrapped me up when she nursed me and sang to me and prayed over me. I imbibed aspects of Islam with my mother's milk. I inherited Islam from my parents and it was the cradle which held me until I found Christ. Islam is my mother.[33]

Individuals in this group would tend to use self-identifiers like Muslim follower of Christ, Jesus Muslim, or, in the case of one group I heard of, followers of the Straight Path. There is a tendency in such groups to retain as much Islamic and local custom or tradition as possible and to find creative ways of accommodating their new allegiance to Jesus and his message and their Islamic context, namely Muslim family members, dietary rules, dress codes, and so on.

It is difficult to know what to make of these believers utilizing Rambo's model. The closest approximation *appears* to be what Rambo calls institutional transition, which is to say going from one sort of Islam to another, like a Shia Muslim who becomes a Sunni Muslim. Another option is that they understand themselves to be forming a different religion altogether and this would again be influenced by the local context, and specifically how much exposure they have to Christians, and their opinion of those Christians. It is also significant that traditional, orthodox Muslims generally regard such groups as heterodox (at best) or heretical (at worse), or even as outright crypto-Christian liars. Ultimately it may not be possible at present to broadly classify such groups. Each one has its own context and most information

---

33. Mallouhi, "Insider Movement," 8.

available on such groups comes from hearsay or anecdote, making a careful analysis impossible.[34]

It is not necessarily easy to differentiate between a CMB and "Muslim follower of Jesus." For example, in the course of a conversation a believer from a Muslim background quotes from the Qur'an. It could mean that he is a "Muslim follower of Jesus." But it could also mean he is trying to keep his (Christian) faith to himself and not get into trouble. It could also be the case that he dislikes the Qur'an, but is willing to make use of it for the purpose of evangelism. Or that he simply views the Qur'an as part of the general public discourse, and does not intend any religious implication at all. This complexity may be diminished in countries with freedom of religion,[35] which excludes many countries with a version of the sharia. In countries with freedom of religion I have often found that ex-Muslims who have a negative opinion of the Prophet or the Qur'an have no qualms about sharing it.

There is also the complexity of self-identification in relation to the two forms of conversion outlined above. What does it mean *for them* to have turned from the old to the new, to use Nock's expression, and how do they talk about it? Using a self-identifier like "Muslim-background believer" for one's self does not necessarily reveal much. Muslims by and large understand Christianity to be something *other* than Islam, and that when a person says they are a Christian, that they are *ipso facto* no longer a Muslim. So even if a person is strongly committed to the Christian faith and has little appreciation for Islam, it does not mean they will necessarily be willing to use such a disruptive term ("Christian") in conversation for self-reference. In sum, due to a lack of freedom of religion or fear of punishment, it is sometimes difficult to determine which form of conversion a person has undergone or is undergoing.

All of these groups can be referred to as Muslim-background believers (MBBs). When that term is used in this book, it is with the intention of speaking about any or all of these kinds of believers. On the other hand, when the term "ex-Muslim" or Christian from a Muslim background (CMB) is used it intentionally excludes the "Muslim followers of Jesus."

In closing the section on conversion, I want to clarify that in this book there is no presupposition regarding the time-frame involved, understanding that conversion may take place over a relatively short period or many years. Furthermore, no assumptions are made regarding the motives for the conversion. In reading ex-Muslim conversion narratives there is always

---

34. Abu Daoud, "Victory of Apostolic Faith," 55.

35. Here the term is understood as freedom to criticize Islam, the Prophet or the Qur'an.

some spiritual or religious motive, but there are commonly some political, relational or economical factors that were very important.

> It may be best . . . to see conversion not as a unitary entity but as involving a diverse collection of social and psychological processes that manifest in unique arrays within each individual, though different aspects of these arrays may be highlighted in various traditions.[36]

While Zehner made the comment regarding Buddhist conversions to evangelical Christianity, it is equally applicable for the individuals and communities dealt with here.

Identity, which will be discussed in a coming section, is central to this entire issue. In sum, there are reportedly Muslims who understand themselves as having converted to Christ but still identify themselves as Muslims in some sense of the word. There are also Christians from a Muslim background who understand themselves as having converted from one religion to another, mutually exclusive religion. It is the latter converts who are the topic of this dissertation and are generally called Christians from a Muslim background (CMBs) or simply ex-Muslim Christians. The former do not understand themselves to be apostates, though they may be aware that others do; the latter understand that they are apostates, and now it is necessary to turn to a discussion of the meaning and consequences of apostasy.

APOSTASY (RIDDA OR IRTIDAAD)

It is not possible to understand the dynamics of conversion from Islam to Christianity without understanding how the dominant Islamic tradition deals with apostasy, which is both a form of conversion in itself as well as the "turning away from the old" in Nock's usage. Furthermore, since Coe's model of contextualization requires a critical and detailed understand of the theology-makers' context, it is imperative to understand the effects of apostasy.

Apostasy in the Dominant Islamic Tradition

In the previous section on conversion mention was made of how violence or fear of violence can affect a person's or community's discourse and behavior. Leaving Islam for any religion or no religion is a capital crime in all four

---

36. Zehner, "Unavoidably Hybrid," 75.

schools of the Islamic sharia as well as in Shi'a jurisprudence.[37] A diplomatic way of putting this comes from Cragg:

> It is assumed that Islam is a faith that no Muslim would conceivably wish to question. Consequently the option to do so is neither valid nor feasible. It is nonexistent. Looked at from this side Islam is a faith that no adherent is free to leave. And that which one is not free to leave becomes a prison, if one wishes to do so.[38]

Regarding the female apostate, An-Na'im writes:

> There is also disagreement on whether a female apostate is to be killed or merely imprisoned until she returns to the faith. Her offense is not regarded by any school or jurist to be of less magnitude, the disagreement merely relates to whether the appropriate punishment is death or life imprisonment.[39]

While the Qur'an itself does not explicitly command the execution of apostates, a hadith which is considered to be authentic (*sahiih*) reports the Prophet doing so in no uncertain terms: "Whosoever changes his religion, slay him" (*man baddala diinahu, faqtaluuhu*).[40] The other main hadith quoted in reference to the death penalty for the apostate is also from Al Bukhari, which one CMB quoted from memory:

> Allah's Messenger said, "The blood of a Muslim who confesses that none has the right to be worshipped but Allah and that I am His Messenger, cannot be shed except in three cases: in Qisas (equality in punishment) for murder, a married person who commits illegal sexual intercourse and the one who reverts from Islam (Apostate) and leaves the Muslims."[41]

The question of interest here is not why this is part of the authoritative, legal Islamic tradition. Nor is the question being asked, to what extent, if any, is it possible to amend or change the positions of these legal schools (*madhaahib*). While these are important questions for Muslim scholars to discuss, they lie outside the purview of this specific work.[42] Of significance

37. Fatah, *Chasing a Mirage*, 117; Lewis, "Heresy," 59.

38. Cragg, *Call of the Minaret*, 307.

39. An-Na-im, "Islamic Law of Apostasy," 211.

40. Al Bukhari, *Sahiih*, volume 4: number 260.

41. Ibid., volume 9, number 17.

42. For an opinion arguing in favor of revising the traditional "theology of intolerance" see Abou El Fadl, "Tolerance in Islam," 3–26. He states that the Qur'an "can readily support an ethic of diversity and tolerance" (15), though he does not address

here is that, while many contemporary Muslims today would feel uncomfortable advocating the execution of apostates, this is an authentic and, until recently, undisputed part of the Islamic legal tradition, and has been for many centuries. This reality has made a significant impact on the patterns of thought and behavior of both Muslims and non-Muslims in Islamic societies. One Christian minister in Jordan, when asked what would happen to a convert, answered, "That is simple: they kill him." CMBs are also familiar with this legal consensus, and often referenced it during interviews and discussions as evidence of how in their view Islam is incompatible with modernity and human rights.

In terms of Muslims and how some of them tend to view apostates, there is a strong tendency to dismiss any conversion from Islam to Christianity as the effect of bribery, the promise of a visa to the US, or a foreign bride. When Muslims asked me what I was researching I generally give them the short answer, "Muslims who become Christians." This has met with numerous reactions. One common response is to say that while there may be a few Muslims who become Christians, it is not due to some religious conviction, but to convenience (as in the examples just given). Another response is to point to the allegedly large numbers of Christians who convert to Islam in Europe every year, and which they have heard about through Islamic media. The quote from Cragg above is helpful here, when he describes this view of Islam as seeing it as "a faith that no Muslim would conceivably wish to question."

Making conversion from Islam to Christianity (or indeed to any other religion or no religion) a taboo topic has led to a situation wherein even asking questions about it is seen as a dangerous and possibly polluting activity. Apostasy can indeed be interpreted as a polluting action, and an incredibly grave one at that. "A polluting person is always in the wrong. He has . . . crossed some line which should not have been crossed . . ."[43] The gravity of the act of apostasy in the Islamic tradition, including in the legal tradition referenced above and the sayings of the Prophet, make the

---

apostasy. It is hard to envision how a consensus of great antiquity and supported by two *sahiih* hadiths can be amended. Islamic jurisprudence is, after all, the practice of understanding God's eternal laws based on the Qur'an and the Prophet's life, both of which are considered to be divine revelation. Some modern figures like Sayyid Ahmad Khan in India, Muhammad Abdu and Rashid Rida in Egypt, and Hasan Turabi in Sudan have argued that the death penalty is only specified for apostates who become traitors of the Umma, and not for all apostates (Ali and Leaman, *Key Concepts*, 10). Their views have not been well-received. As of 2008, "Muslim-majority countries frequently ban proselytizing and the majority of contemporary Muslim scholars uphold the premodern view that apostasy merits death" (Ibid).

43. Douglas, *Purity and Danger*, 140.

claims of the apostate *ab initio* unacceptable and unworthy of being heard. "Some pollutions are too grave for the offender to be allowed to survive."[44] In the Islamic legal tradition, and in many parts of the Muslim world today, that is often how apostasy is interpreted—a pollution whose spread must be halted and may lead to execution; the apostate is "a dead limb that must be ruthlessly excised,"[45] and the use of power in any of its forms is licit to accomplish this.

Apostasy in Contemporary Muslim Societies

Some Islamic countries have laws explicitly forbidding apostasy. For others it is not written into the legal code, but it is implicit insofar as the written constitutions must be in accordance with the sharia. Canadian Muslim Tarek Fatah explains the implications:

> the majority of the Arab constitutions declare the sharia as the basis of legislation, or at least consider it as a main source of legislation. This prevents most of the countries that pretend to be Islamic States from living up to the standards set by the 1948 United Nations Declaration of Universal Human Rights. It also legitimizes the notion of racial and religious superiority, and allows for multiple levels of citizenship and widespread and systemic discrimination against racial and religious minorities living within a state's borders. Invariably, the human rights of the weak and dispossessed, the minorities and women, the disabled and the heretics, are trampled upon without the slightest sense of guilt or wrongdoing. Men and women are imprisoned, routinely tortured and often killed, while numbed citizens, fearful of offending Islam, unsure about their own rights, insecure about their own identities, allow these violations to continue.[46]

This quote demonstrates that this is not *only* a matter of religious freedom, but that ethnic minorities, the poor, and women are also affected by this context.

---

44. Ibid., 168.

45. Lewis, "Heresy," 59. It appears that even questioning the apostasy rule is in some cases interpreted as pollution. For instance, Islamic scholar Ahmed Subhy Mansour (b. 1949) argued that the hadiths reported above, which have for centuries been regarded as sahiih or authentic, were in fact not authentic. See Mansour, "Penalty of Apostasy," and, "Killing the Apostate." For his views he lost his position teaching at Al Azhar in Cairo and had to flee Egypt.

46. Fateh, *Chasing the Wind*, 17.

When the Islamic Council in 1981 produced an alternative Universal Islamic Declaration of Human Rights, it referenced Qur'an 2:56—*there is no compulsion in religion*—to guarantee that non-Muslims would not be forcibly converted to Islam. Article XIII of the document[47] reads, "Every person has the right to freedom of conscience and worship in accordance with his religious beliefs." However, there is no freedom for Muslims to change or leave their religion.[48]

Patrick Sookhdeo, a CMB and advocate for persecuted Christians, makes this point: "While most Muslim states have signed the United Nations declarations on human rights, they usually add caveats stating these are accepted as long as they do not contradict Islamic law (sharia). Sharia is inherently discriminatory to non-Muslims. . . ." The result is that "In several Muslim states such as Saudi Arabia, Qatar, Iran, and Sudan, the law specifies the death sentence for a Muslim who converts to another religion."[49] To this list one *might* add Pakistan, where defaming the Prophet is a capital crime, and apostasy, which is departing from the Prophet's religion, can possibly be made to fit that offense.[50]

These countries form the first category regarding reaction to apostasy. In such countries the state itself may well be the primary agent of persecution and perhaps even execution. The process is not necessarily expedited and attempts are often made to persuade the person to return to Islam or perhaps expel them from the country, but in such states the apostate can realistically anticipate in some circumstances *de jure* capital punishment. To what extent such executions are effective today can be debated, but certainly there is, at least, an attempt to control the polluting presence of the apostate by silencing his voice.

Other Islamic countries form a second category, wherein the state itself will not carry out the sentence of execution but will allow or even encourage other agents to do so.[51] This allows the government to maintain a positive image on the international stage while at the same time not allowing the legal conversion of a Muslim to any other religion. This is a very important reality and will be discussed at greater length later on, but for the moment it is enough to say that religious status in Islamic countries has many ramifications on everything from family law to education to being

47. Available online at http://www.alhewar.com/ISLAMDECL.html.

48. See also Meral, *No Place to Call Home*.

49. Sookhdeo, "Persecution."

50. Tim Green's 1998 study, "Apostasy in Pakistan," of 70 apostates from Islam in Pakistan found that while they almost all faced some persecution or opposition, a mere 6 percent of them were actually killed.

51. See chapter 6 for an alleged instance of this in Iran.

able to get a certain job or flat to where one is buried, what names one may give their children, and so on. These are Rambo's "consequences" of conversion. An indigenous Christian in the Middle East gave an example of this to me: the government of a neighboring country (which he visited often) was heavily dependent on a certain Western country for a large portion of its yearly budget, which made it necessary for them to silence their apostates discretely. If an apostate were willing to keep her faith to herself, and not seek to have her conversion recognized by the government, then all would be well.[52] But if the apostate engaged in evangelism, openly questioned Islam or the Prophet, asked the government to change her religion on her national ID card from "Muslim" to "Christian," then it would become necessary to compel silence. Informing the person's family of the situation was a first step, with the hope that they would enforce silence. If the apostate was unwilling to quiet down, then finding a way to expel her from the country (and thus remove her polluting presence) might be sought. If the person desired to stay in her country, and was furthermore unwilling to conceal her conversion, then the family would be encouraged to "preserve their honor" in the only way left to them. The government would look the other way, or at worst the person carrying out the sentence would be given a symbolic slap on the hand—a few months in jail, perhaps.

Gabriel Said Reynolds provides assorted examples:

> But if converts rarely are brought to court, they often are threatened or killed by Muslims acting outside the courts. In 2006, Bashir Tantray was shot and killed in Kashmir after his conversion to Christianity was noted in the local media. In 2007, two Turkish Christians of Muslim origin who attracted attention with their missionary work were brutally tortured and stabbed to death. In January 2010 a Christian church leader of Muslim background was killed by members of the Shabaab movement in Somalia. In 2003, Jamil al-Rifai, a Jordanian Christian convert and a former classmate of mine, was killed by a bomb planted in a missionary's house in Tripoli, Lebanon. Such vigilante attacks are sometimes justified by Muslim religious leaders with the Islamic principle of "forbidding evil" (see Qur'an 3:104), which they take to mean that individual Muslims should play a role in enforcing Islamic law. In this way the Saudi author Salih Ibn Abdallah insists that shedding an apostate's blood is still licit even if the state does not impose the death penalty.[53]

52. See Meral, *No Place to Call Home*, 62 for another similar example.

53. Reynolds, "Evangelizing Islam," n.p.

This represents a second category of governments: ones that will use various measures, often indirect, to silence the voice of the apostate. If the apostate is willing to accept status as an inferior citizen and relegate herself to quietism, her continued existence within her own country may be possible. If not, then the polluting presence of such a person must somehow be eliminated, whether it be through incarceration, exile, or extra-legal execution. Many countries in the Middle East fit into this category: for instance Morocco, Algeria, Tunisia, Libya, Egypt, the Palestinian Authority, and Jordan.

There is also a third category in which there is relative freedom, including the possibility of legally changing one's religion from Islam to Christianity if the government keeps such information in its records. This does not mean that the process is easy, but it is real and with persistence can be carried out. Nor does this mean that the family of the apostate will welcome their conversion, or that they will not, of their own initiative, try to silence the voice of the apostate somehow. It does mean that the government will not directly or indirectly encourage the persecution of the apostate. Examples of such states are Turkey, Israel and parts of India. It is difficult to discern where to assign Lebanon. Anecdotal evidence seems to affirm that it is still possible to legally convert from Islam to Christianity there, but I know of no recent cases to confirm or deny this. Pakistan is another country where it is technically possible to legally convert, whereas in reality the government may belong to category two, or where the apostate may be charged with defamation of Islam / the Prophet. Countries in the Americas, Europe, and those that do not have a large Muslim population, will often belong to this category, though sometimes the police will not ensure the safety of the convert against Islamic vigilante justice.[54] In certain areas in the UK, USA and France, families may arrange for the apostate to return to the ancestral homeland for a "vacation," where they can be forced to marry or interned in an insane asylum or killed. The extent to which this occurs is unknown, but what is important here is that apostates believe it happens.[55]

---

54. As was the case with a converted couple in Bradford. As news of their conversion spread among the Pakistani community people started to insult them, throw stones at them, and eventually their car was set on fire. When the man complained to the local police the officer told him to "stop being a crusader and move to another place" (Meral, *No Place to Call Home*, 63).

55. In reference to the UK, for instance, an article in *The Telegraph* by Graham Wilson, dated 29 January 2007, reports that " . . . 36 percent of the young [Muslim] people questioned said they believed that a Muslim who converts to another religion should be 'punished by death'" (Cited 25 July 2012. Online: www.telegraph.co.uk/news/uknews/1540895/Young-British-Muslims-getting-more-radical.html#). See also Rusin, "Fear Stalks Muslim Apostates in the West."

Finally, there are states where, due to the lack of sovereignty, the actual law or practice of the state matters little because the central government simply does not have a monopoly on violence in all areas that, *de jure*, are part of that state. Examples are Somalia, and large swathes of Yemen, Iraq and Pakistan, where the official position of the government will be of little or no import. Rather, these areas operate by *lex loci* and the will of the tribal leader will dictate how the apostate is treated.

The Status of the Apostate

In addition to the general practice of the state, there are other factors that will influence how apostates are treated in Islamic societies. As mentioned above, one of the key factors is how vocal she is. A vocal apostate is a constant reminder to the Islamic society that someone not only has violated a taboo, but wants others to consider taking the same step. It is also an instance of agency—an awareness that one has power, and is willing to use it for the sake of furthering their interests, which here means spreading their "pollution."

If one individual is polluted, it may be permissible to allow for her continuing presence as long as the discourse of the person is silenced, thus assuring that her "pollution" will not spread to other people. In other words, it has been contained, but without going to the distance of imprisonment, exile or execution.

The question of social status is also significant, though at times ambiguous, and may depend largely on the specific location of the apostate. In some contexts a poor person converting is suffered, precisely because of his poverty and lack of education. Such a powerless source of "pollution" is considered unlikely to spread to "the people that matter" in most societies. On the other hand, if the government or some other group desires to carry out the punishment for apostasy designated by the Prophet, it is all the easier because of the apostate's lack of power. Sometimes if an old person converts (which is not common), they will be left alone, as their conversion can readily be dismissed as an aspect of senility. Similarly, in the case of an older woman who no longer has children in her care it is unlikely that her "pollution" will spread, so for this reason she may not face persecution.

The person of high social status is in an ambiguous position, with the advantage and disadvantage of being visible and having influence, or at least belonging to an influential family. A key factor determining the person's fate will be the disposition of his family. If the family is particularly strong in their adherence to orthodox Islam, the visibility of the apostate may well work against him. It becomes all the more urgent for the family to preserve its dignity by eliminating the source of "pollution." If the family of the apostate is more secular or liberal in their practice of Islam then they may try to save the person by encouraging them to emigrate or may even, in rare cases, support the religious freedom of the apostate, even if they do not agree with the outcome. These complexities mean that each case must be evaluated on its own. It is most often the case that within an extended family there will be representatives of various points of view.

In concluding this section on apostasy and its consequences, three broad categories or *tendencies* have been identified. These are not static categories, and a country (or region) can shift from one to the other. These are, 1) countries wherein the state will be a direct agent of punishing the apostate, including the possibility of execution. 2) Countries that may be involved in punishing the apostate indirectly, and will not directly take part in her execution. This does not exclude the possibility that such a state will permit or even encourage the apostate's execution or exile by means of a non-governmental agent. 3) There are states wherein conversion is legal and feasible, though this does not mean that the elements within the state will not hinder the process, or that the state will protect the apostate from non-state actors. Nor does it mean that family members or religious authorities will not intervene. Some regions are beyond these categories because they operate according to tribal custom and *lex loci*.

Apostasy, Persecution, and Power

Now I will apply the three dimensions of power to the topic of conversion to Christianity from Islam by providing models of past practice. Then I will provide examples of how the power of Muslim societies has eroded (in all three dimensions) to the point where conversion from Islam to Christianity is a real possibility that people are increasingly aware of. The following three examples are all hypothetical but realistic.

The first dimension is explained as the ability of one agent to cause another agent to do something that the second agent would not normally do. History provides us many examples of such acts of power. Churches would normally not desire to remove crosses from the exterior of their buildings under Islamic rule, but in some cases, they did. Churches did not desire to stop ringing their bells, although under some cases of Islamic rule, they did. Christians did not desire to have their children taken by the Ottomans, forcibly converted to Islam, and then have them trained as Muslim soldiers and officials, but under the system of *devshirme*, they allowed it.[56] Christians did not desire to convert the Hagia Sophia in Constantinople or the Cathedral Church of St John the Baptist in Damascus into mosques, but under Islamic rule, it occurred.

The second dimension of power is not difficult to illustrate: Ahmad has been going to a local church secretly for some time, he has been reading a Bible, and he expresses interest in being baptized. This becomes known to the secret police and they pay him a visit and inform him that quietly attending church is one thing, but the act of baptism is too much, and that, while the secret police would never do anything to hurt him, they will not be able to ensure the safety of his home, place of business, family, or person. The veiled threat succeeds. Ahmad wants to be baptized, and that is his interest. After the visit from the secret police he decides that it is too dangerous to act on his interest and therefore abandons his plan. The salient feature here is action—Ahmad was doing something, actively following a path, and the secret police actively countered his action. By means of "suggestion" they cause him to change his plan to act on his interest. Here power is shown by its ability to enforce non-decision. The topic of baptism is simply abandoned, even if he continues going to church, though Ahmad will likely be changed by this experience.

The third dimension of power involves foreclosing the recognition of an interest, and is particularly relevant to our topic. From the point of view of ex-Muslim Christians, this has been carried out in several ways. Historically, this can be seen in the treatment of the non-Muslim *dhimmis*, who were sometimes segregated from the Muslim population. Often they had their own neighborhoods in towns, and, importantly, their safety was contingent on their use of an ethnically restricted language like Syriac or Armenian in their liturgy and worship. There was no problem with them knowing and using the local lingua franca for commerce and trade, but the polluting force of Christianity had to be quarantined and isolated linguistically. Thus a rather daring Turk could perhaps attend the local Christian church, but would have no ability to understand what was being said in Armenian or Greek. The curious ethnic Iranian could attend the local Assyrian church (again, in itself a daring move) but would not understand what was being said. Neither could these enquirers easily or safely procure a Bible in their mother tongue until relatively recently.

Here, the prohibition of translation, for instance, meant that potential interests could not materialize into real interests. That is, Muslims were

---

56. In effect roughly from the fourteenth through the eighteenth centuries and was levied against Christians in the Balkans.

prevented from being exposed to the Christian message, even though some Muslims may have had a potential interest in hearing it. Moreover, indigenous Christian communities were forbidden from evangelizing Muslims, and if it was attempted coercive power in its first or second dimension could be deployed, and the decision to evangelize reverted to a decision to not evangelize, or if the evangelist was imprisoned or killed, then an inability to evangelize.

From the point of view of some Muslim rulers, these acts of power, including coercive and violent power, are not only ethically permissible, but mandatory. In relation to the first dimension examples, power is understood to flow from God, and is a sign of God's favor. The career of Muhammad is validated in that he went from being powerless to being powerful. So in this reading the ability to coerce and to use that coercion to force people to comply with God's will is the very reason that power is given in the first place. Since having power is an indication of God's will, it is appropriate to deprive certain people and groups of people of power. Specifically, this is the case when such groups (like Christians and Jews) are recalcitrant in accepting the full truth of God revealed in the person of Muhammad and the Qur'an. Insofar as Jews and Christians do not completely reject God by resorting to atheism or outright polytheism, they need not be deprived of *all* power by expulsion from *dar al islam* or execution. Christians and Jews have some things right, such as prophets, a belief in the resurrection and final judgment, but other things wrong, notably a refusal to accept the prophethood of Muhammad. So power is, in this reading, a measure of orthodoxy. And it is the will of God to demonstrate the orthodoxy of one community versus another by allowing for the orthodox to exercise power over the heterodox.

Because of this, the use of the mosque and the state to prevent Islamic society from being polluted by the Christian message is, in their view, a virtuous act. It is an act whereby they "command that which is just and forbid that which is evil."[57] In this reading, the real interest of every Muslim is to stay a Muslim. If some Muslims hear the Christian message then they may depart from this real interest and a perceived interest (to leave Islam) may arise in them. But that perceived interest, no matter how sincerely held, is impossible to reconcile with their real interest, which must inhere with the revealed interest of Allah, and indeed the interest of the Muslim rulers, whose power would decrease if apostasy became widespread. Moreover, following the example of the Prophet who used violence and coercion on multiple occasions, and sometimes with great success, it is permissible to wield power in such a manner to preserve the interest of God (and the rulers).

---

57. Qur'an 3:104.

The use of such coercion and violence, however, do not mean that the use of power is oppressive, but rather a just and responsible use of force to ensure the maintenance of the will of God and of the ruling earthly order.

Persecution and having to possibly face violence and coercion as a consequence of religious conversion are realities for many ex-Muslim Christians as they live out the consequences of their conversion. Given that changing from Islam to Christianity is often accompanied by so much stress and danger, it is helpful to review the reasons that converts give when asked why they have converted.

REASONS WHY MUSLIMS CONVERT TO CHRIST

The main focus of this book is not why Muslims convert, but rather on their subsequent theology-making. Nonetheless, understanding the contextualization that CMBs may be doing requires an understanding of their contextuality. And the motives for and consequences of their conversions are recurring themes and integral facets of how they read their own contextuality. Multiple studies have been done on why Muslims convert to Christianity, and this section summarize and critique them.[58] Many of these themes will recur throughout this book, especially when I relate conversion narratives, like those of John and Ayya in chapter 4.

Probably the most well-known study is that directed by Dudley Woodberry. In the 2001 article "Muslims tell . . . 'Why I Chose Jesus,'" co-authored with Russell Shubin,[59] the results of their research were presented. Woodberry and Shubin received around 600 responses to questionnaires. The conclusions are based on a sample of 120 of the 600. We do not know anything about the gender or nationality or self-identification of the respondents, other than that they come from over 50 ethnic groups and 39 countries. Six key factors are presented which the researchers have identified as why these converts chose Jesus. It should be noted that this would, presumably, include both streams of conversion—ex-Muslim Christians as well as Muslim followers of Jesus (accommodationists). The results do not appear to be given in any specific order.

One, "A sure salvation," which refers to the Christian belief that through Jesus Christ's death and resurrection one's sins can be forgiven.

58. Portions of this section appeared previously in Miller, "Christ's Converts from Islam," 15–27, and are used with permission.

59. Similar findings are in Woodberry, Shubin and Marks, "Why Muslims Follow Jesus." I have opted to use the older article because it is more widely available and I saw it referenced more often.

That humanity's sins are forgiven means that humans have not merited forgiveness of their sins, rather, it was Jesus who merited it. And he merited forgiveness *for us*, as an act done by one person for the benefit of another. Since Jesus has merited forgiveness *for us*, it is no longer our responsibility or burden to earn God's mercy/forgiveness. Thus the believer need not rely on her own righteousness to merit salvation, and this "sure salvation" attracted a number of Muslims to faith in Christ.[60]

Two, "Jesus": The person of Jesus as he is portrayed in the Bible is attractive. For instance, he did not retaliate when he was offended. Others are attracted to his humility, his teaching in the Gospels, and his willingness to die for the sake of humanity.[61]

Three, "A holy book: the power of the Bible": Muslims are aware of previous revelations through the Qur'an—the Torah given to Moses, the Psalms (*zabuur* in Islamic Arabic) given to David, the Gospel given to Jesus. In the Bible they find these sources and are affected by them. The Sermon on the Mount (Matt 5–7) is specifically pointed out as recurring often in survey responses. This point overlaps with the previous one about Jesus, for it is in the Bible that Muslims can learn more about Jesus than the relatively few narratives found in the Qur'an about him.

Four, "Christianity answers questions": Some Muslims find truth in the Bible, particularly in its message about God. Others find the Christian account of life, ethics and religion to be satisfying. They feel that Islam was not able to successfully answer questions, but that Christianity does.

Five, "I have had a dream": Muslims have had dreams (or visions) of Jesus or another figure. This may be Rambo's crisis, or it may confirm someone to continue on their quest.

Six, "Love": This was the most important factor, according to Woodberry and Shubin:

> By far, the reason found most compelling for the greatest number of Muslims who have turned to Christ is the power of love. Like Paul, many a believer from a Muslim background has found that "the greatest of these is love." Nearly half of all Muslims who have made a shift of faith allegiance have affirmed that the love of God was a critical key in their decision.[62]

---

60. The CMBs I interviewed felt the Qur'an was equivocal on the matter of forgiveness. That is, one could never know for sure whether one would be forgiven or not.

61. It does not appear in Woodberry et al., but a number of converts I met both male and female, noted that they were attracted to how Jesus interacted with women, which they found to be superior to Muhammad's interaction with women.

62. Woodberry and Shubin, "Why I Chose Jesus," n.p.

This includes both love demonstrated by Christians, and also a sense of the love of God.

My reservations about this study are related to the lack of knowledge that we have about the method of the research. Were all of these converts to evangelicalism? What would a study of converts to Catholic or Orthodox Christianity look like? Are the factors different based on where the converts live in relation to the status of apostasy and how it is treated by those with power? We know too little about the methodology of the research to be able to answer such questions, which is a weakness of the study. The strength of this study is that it drew on a large pool of data and had a skilled team of scholars working together.

A second study, *Called from Islam to Christ* (1999), was composed by a Catholic priest, Jean-Marie Gaudeul, of the White Fathers, and is based on his reading of around 170 publicly available conversion narratives. The majority of the converts he studied were Africans, with 70 alone coming from Sudan, which at the time of his writing included South Sudan.[63] Based on reading these texts Gaudeul proposes five key factors that attract Muslims to Christ.

One, "Jesus is so attractive" (Gaudeul chapter 2). Gaudeul lists several reasons why Muslims find Jesus attractive: he is present in the Qur'an[64] where he is portrayed as working miracles (unlike Muhammad), which can pique the curiosity of Muslims. Prayers offered in his name or prayed to him are answered. There is also a recurring theme of the power of Jesus's name to deliver people from addiction and oppression.

Two, some Muslims find in Christ satisfaction for their "Thirst for Truth" (Gaudeul chapter 3). Many Muslims understand the claims of Islam but did not feel it provided viable or satisfying answers. These questions, whether related to ritual, politics or ethics, are like Rambo's crisis phase, and the "thirst for truth" that Gadeul refers to is Rambo's quest phase, as the converting individual is active in trying to find satisfying answers to their questions. Gaudeul lists some of the topics that provoke a crisis in the converting individuals. For instance, Muslims are taught about the unity of the Islamic *Umma* but in reality "Islam has been divided into a number of sects from the outset: Sunnites, Shi'a, Kharidjites, each of which in turn is subdivided into a number of factions . . . ."[65] The differences between Muslim

63. Gaudeul, *Called from Islam*, 25–26.

64. 2:87: "And we gave unto Jesus, son of Mary, clear miracles." Among other things he summons a table of food from heaven (5:112–114), he speaks while still in the cradle (3:46), he forms a clay bird and breathes on it and it comes alive, he heals and raises the dead, and he has access to secret knowledge (3:49).

65. Gaudeul, *Called from Islam*, 59.

groups have led to outright violence on some occasions. There is also the question of whether Islam can peacefully flourish in the modern world.[66] Some Muslims leave Islam because they come to the conclusion that Islam's teaching on the treatment of women or non-Muslims are simply incompatible with modernity. Others refer to perceived scientific discrepancies between Islam and modernity, relating to the theory of evolution or some of the purported miracles of the Prophet (which are not in the Qur'an), such as he split the moon in two pieces.[67] There is also the question of evil. Islam proposes that humans are born good, in the state of original innocence, but when one looks at the evil around us, and the inability of humans to obey God's rules even when they know them well, this can lead to doubt in Islam. Other questions that occasion a quest are related to ethics, piety, or the Bible. In sum, some converts claimed to have found the explanatory power of Christianity superior to that of Islam.

Three, some Muslims feel like they are "without family" (Gaudeul chapter 4) and then they find a new family in "God's community" (Gaudeul chapters 5 and 6). "Islam proposes an ideal of fraternity and equality," but in reality, "the actual organization of Muslim societies creates institutionalized inequalities . . ."[68] Because of the experience of violence, corruption, divorce, unfair treatment of women, lack of compassion for orphans and the disabled, and of Muslim oppressing Muslim, some Muslims become disappointed with Islam and start to look for another community. Here we are talking about something that is turning Muslims away from the old and the incorrect (to use Nock's image), not something turning them *to* the new and correct. Gaudeul notes that disenchantment with Islam alone is not enough warrant for accepting a convert into the church, but that "a positive experience of Christ and his church" are also requisite.

If the realities of the *Umma* today have driven some Muslims away from their *diin*, the life of the church—whether Catholic or otherwise—can draw them to conversion. Sometimes faith in Christ comes before involvement in a community of believers (as seems to have been the case with Timothy Abraham), sometimes it is the life of the church at worship or in education or as charity that provokes the "crisis" and begins the converting person upon their quest. Sometimes contact with a single Christian calls into question stereotypes the Muslim had been taught since childhood. As one convert asked, "How was it possible for an unbeliever to be so virtuous a

---

66. Ibid., 61.

67. Ibid., 62.

68. Ibid., 87.

man?" a question which became part of his crisis.[69] That Gaudeul explicitly brings a communal dimension to his analysis of conversion is a strength of his analysis.

Four, "the need for forgiveness" (Gaudeul chapter 7). This category is closely related to that of Woodberry and Shubin above under the category "a sure salvation." A brief quote from Gaudeul will suffice to identify where his scholarship has identified a bifurcation between Islam and Christianity. In Islam, "Divine forgiveness can only be given when divine justice has been satisfied and sins have been expiated." While in Christianity "God offers an unmerited forgiveness which heals and transforms the sinner, pouring into his weakness the strength of the Holy Spirit."[70]

Five, there is "a thirst for God" (chapter 8), and specifically, a personal relationship with God. Gaudeul describes Islam as tending towards "overwhelming transcendence,"[71] and as holding "mysticism under suspicion."[72] This is related to the debate about power in relation to Scripture seen in chapter 1 of this book. The Christian deity is transcendent, but imminent as well, willing to lower himself to our level in the Incarnation, the Cross, the Church, the indwelling of the Holy Spirit, and in the inspiration and translatability of the Bible. To many Christians these doctrines are cherished and show the compassion and love of God for humanity. Muslims, with their tendency towards overwhelming transcendence, may be highly suspicious of these doctrines and their implications for what constitutes divine power/ authority. But according to Gaudeul some Muslims experience a "thirst for God" which cannot be sated within the Islamic metanarrative. Christianity does, however, allow for a relationship with a God at once transcendent *and* immanent. Speaking of the converts, he says, "They have met the living God, they feel themselves loved by the Father, they live in continual intimacy with the living Christ, they pray and act with a new strength—that of the Spirit of God."[73] Gaudeul says that converts have experienced this intimacy in something as simple as calling God "Father" or being able to pray informally, using their own words, either alone or in a group.[74] Being able to pray or read Scripture in one's own language (rather than Arabic) is

---

69. Ibid., 130.

70. Ibid., 154.

71. Ibid., 184.

72. Ibid., 185.

73. Ibid., 191.

74. Ibid., 208.

also a sign of a personal relationship with God for people for whom Arabic is not their primary language.[75]

The studies of Woodberry & Shubin and Gaudeul are the most widely-quoted and referenced studies on why Muslims convert to Christ (and most of those to Christianity, as a religion). There are also scattered studies of conversion motives by region or country. Patrick Cate (1980) researched some 52 converts from Islam in Iran. For decades it was sitting in a filing cabinet, but with Cate's permission I have made a scanned version of it available online.[76] This document contains a section on reasons for conversion. The first category of reasons are related to the person of Christ and the Bible: the main reasons listed are reading or studying Scripture or Christian tracts, the "superiority of Christ's teachings and the encounter through his perfect Character," the love of Christ as seen in his Cross and his working of miracles, doing Bible studies at church or with clergy, especially of the book of Matthew. The second category of reasons are related to the lives of Christians and the church, "A Christ-like lifestyle and testimony," and this includes participation in Christian worship, including songs sung in Farsi, still others heard the testimonies of Christians who were converts. The third category is related to "discontent with Islam."[77]

Seppo Syrjänen (1984), a Lutheran missionary and scholar in Pakistan, studied a group of Pakistani converts. While he is most concerned with questions related to identity, his research includes his findings on why they converted. A more recent study of Palestinian converts in the West Bank was carried out by South African missiologist Ant Greenham.[78] A study was done on why Muslims leave Islam, whether for Christianity or no religion at all,[79] but apostasy alone (without become a Christian) is significantly different from what we are studying here.

The findings of Syrjänen, Cate and Greenham[80] do not differ substantially from the conclusions of Wooderry and Gaudeul. While Gaudeul and Woodberry classify their findings using different titles, it is easy to see how much they overlap. For instance, Woodberrry and Shubin have the category

---

75. Ibid., 213ff.

76. Links are online at http://www.duanemiller.wordpress.com/2012/06/19/a-survey-of-muslim-converts-in-iran-for-patrick-cate-by-dwight-singer-1980/.

77. Cate and Singer, *Converts in Iran,* 5–6.

78. Greenham, "Palestinian Muslim Conversions," 116–75.

79. Khalil and Bilici, "Conversion out of Islam," 111–24.

80. Greenham, "Palestinian Muslim Conversions," 72 identifies the top four reasons for conversion among his 22-person sample (equally divided between men and women). These factors are 1) the Person of Jesus, 2) God's miraculous involvement, 3) Truth of Jesus's Message, and 4) Role of believers.

of "love," and this includes both the love of God as seen in the Bible and the person of Jesus, as well as the love of God as mediated by Christians or the church. Gaudeul has room for both of these, but the experience of God's love would probably come under the heading of Jesus, or forgiveness, while the love of Christians would likely come under the heading "God's community." The categories "a sure salvation" and "forgiveness of sins" overlap nicely, and both have the category "Jesus." Woodberry does have a category of dreams and visions which is lacking in Gaudeul's findings, but again a dream of Jesus would fit in the category "Jesus" or correspond to the immanence of God reaching out personally to the individual.

While I find Gaudeul and Woodberry overlap substantially, there are some advantages to Gaudeul's categories. Specifically, they allow for a better understanding of the reality that CMBs are often driven away from Islam as much as they are drawn to Christ or Christianity. Gaudeul does not think that disappointment with Islam is sufficient warrant for baptism, but he does acknowledge that sometimes disillusion with Islam is the crisis that provokes the quest—a quest which may lead to Christianity. Acknowledging this reality also enables us to take into account political and economic factors in religious conversion. Islam is, in many places in the world, understood as being inextricable from the political (and hence economic) order, and "Political and moral considerations influence conversion not simply as extrinsic constraints, . . . but as intrinsic aspects of the conversion experience."[81] Some of the converts I interviewed held up the perceived failures in the Muslim world in areas like education, human rights, and government corruption as being, necessarily, failures of Islam. This is never the entire story, as they also relate their positive encounter with Christ. But Gaudeul's framework allows us to note and research these perceived failures: Woodberry and Shubin's does not.[82]

I also appreciate that Gaudeul's explicit use of communal language—"God's community'—resists the tendency of American evangelical scholars towards individualism, as if religious conversion could ever be a totally private affair. During an interview with an Iranian convert named "Frances" she listed as important to her conversion the poetry of Gerard Manley Hopkins, a Jesuit poet, the Narnia novels by C.S. Lewis, and the architecture and aesthetics of the Catholic church she used to walk by as a child.[83] It is difficult to see how any of this could fit easily into Woodberry's structure.

81. Hefner, "Conversion in Muslim Java," 119.

82. The later 2007 article by Woodberry, Shubin and Marks does acknowledge the importance of disappointment with Islam.

83. Miller, "Secret World of God," 1–14.

But they do fit into Gaudeul's quite well—because we are speaking of novels and poems and buildings of God's community as expressions of that community's life.

In conclusion, the question of why Muslims convert to Christ (and again, most of these converts have explicitly become Christians), has been researched in some detail. The findings of the two main studies overlap substantially. Studies of smaller samples confined to one region or country, like those of Cate (Iran), Greenham (Israel-Palestine), and Syrjänen (Pakistan), do not contradict the overarching findings of the two primary and international studies. All in all Gaudeul's categories are slightly more suitable, though they should be supplemented by one of Woodberry's categories for the sake of clarity and precision, which we might call "visions, dreams and miracles."

IDENTITY

Religious Conversion and Identity

Religious conversion and identity are closely related to each other. Religious conversion entails the reinterpretation of one's past precisely because it involves a turning away from the old and assumedly wrong, to the new and hopefully right. Thus one must reinterpret one's life pre-conversion, when one was still living in old and incorrect ways.

Another reason why identity is important to this study is that our modern, globalized context has given rise to a number of new forms of identity that previously had been seen as impossible. For instance, in some places one can find openly gay, non-celibate Christian clergy, or a female imam. It appears that some of the identities being formed by CMBs may also be novel, and an understanding of identity theory would be helpful in exploring this issue. Furthermore, two major studies of CMBs that have been published (Kraft and Syrjänen) have both identified identity-formation as key areas of concern, activity and stress for these converts.

Finally, identity formation is all the more important because the consequences of conversion in antagonistic contexts often entail the use of coercive violence against the convert, who is seen as a polluting presence.

Tim Green, who has researched converts from Islam to Christianity in the context of a Muslim-majority region in South Asia, proposes a helpful model of identity in his 2012 study relating the topics of identity, religious conversion, and marriage. Adapting the model of Benjamin Beit-Hallahmi,[84]

---

84. Beit-Hallahmi, *Prolegomena*.

he identifies the deepest and most profound level of identity as *core identity*,[85] though it has also been called "ego-identity," and this refers to "who I am in my inner self." Social identity relates to "who I am in relation to my group or groups,"[86] or in the words of Syrjänen, "*Social identity* is the part of an individual's self-concept which derives from his knowledge of his member-ship of a social group together with the emotional significance attached to that membership."[87] As different people belong to different social groups (a political party, a tribe, a village, a guild, a particular mosque, etc.) so social identity is multifaceted and the claims of the different societies one belongs to may oppose each other.

Finally, there is collective identity, which "concerns the way a whole symbolic group is labeled and distinguished from other groups by its iden-tity markers."[88] Traditionally in many Muslim societies being "Muslim" was considered essential to one's membership in the community. Moreover, there is no ritual whereby one confirms one's membership in the com-munity (such as Confirmation or adult baptism for some Christians), "In the case of Muslim children[,] being Muslim is automatic, unless apostasy is deliberately chosen."[89] The identity of a person develops and changes as their core identity and social identity interact with and influence each other. Folk wisdom has long understood this reality, and it can be seen in say-ings like "birds of a feather flock together" or "bad company corrupts good character."[90]

One of the key difficulties faced by ex-Muslim Christians is in relation to forming a new identity, or resolving conflicts between the different layers of identity. For instance, can one be a Turk and a Christian? The answer is, legally speaking, yes. But will society accept this change of identity, or see converts as having defected from the community altogether with subsequent change in communal identity? A further question is whether it is possible to experience conversion at the level of core identity (which is important in evangelical Christianity) without also experiencing a different social iden-tity in the context of meeting with other Christians. Kathryn Kraft, after studying MBBs in Egypt and Lebanon, came to the following conclusion: ". . . because their Muslim communities are so cohesive, Islam continues to

85. Green, "Identity Issues for ex-Muslim Christians," 439.

86. Ibid., 440.

87. Syrjänen, *In Search of Meaning*, 57.

88. Green, "Identity Issues for ex-Muslim Christians," 440.

89. Syrjänen, *In Search of Meaning*, 60.

90. Which appears in the Bible, in 1 Cor 15:33, but it appears even then that Paul is quoting a proverb already in circulation.

be the ethnic identity of many converts, while Christianity becomes their religious identity."[91] The statement illustrates well the complexity of the topic. Green's model is detailed enough to be of assistance in this project. As he concludes: " . . . all three identity levels have a religious element. Since Islam lays claim to all these areas in a holistic way, those who leave it face a daunting task of renegotiating each aspect of their identity."[92]

Examples of Syncretism and Double Religious Belonging

Given the difficulty of converting from Islam to Christianity, it is reasonable to ask if there is the option of simultaneously belonging to both communities at the same time. Double-belonging is the status of belonging to more than one group at one time and is, in modern society at least, nearly unavoidable. Double *religious* belonging (or multiple belonging) is particularly of interest in the context of this study though. Double religious belonging is not the same as syncretism. Whereas syncretism brings elements of one religion into another, or combines elements of two religions to produce something that is not considered to be the same as either of its progenitors, double religious belonging is concerned with "people who do seem to feel at home in two different religious traditions."[93] Christianity and Islam have historically purported to represent two mutually exclusive communities, the church universal and the Umma. However, there are and have been people who claim, in some form, to belong to both groups simultaneously.

This book is primarily concerned with people who understand themselves as having converted *from* Islam, *to* Christianity. But this is not the only dynamic which has been tried in relating an Islamic identity to a Christian identity. In this section I will present a number of such examples. The great variety in approaches should remind us that Rambo's "tradition transition" *from* Islam *to* Christianity is one of many approaches to how to address questions of religious identity.

One example of double religious belonging were the so-called White Maronites of Lebanon. Under the Ottoman empire of the seventeenth century they wore the white turbans of Muslims and enjoyed the commercial and legal prerogatives of Muslims (which were superior to those of the Christian *dhimmis*). At the same time many of them were known to be, in terms of spiritual conviction at least, still Christian. When a number of them publicly reverted to Christianity in 1608, the Muslim governor allowed them to do

91. Kraft, "Community and Identity," 112.
92. Green, "Identity Issues for ex-Muslim Christians," 444.
93. Amaladoss, "Belonging and Liminality," 1.

so without fear of persecution.[94] Legally speaking, this was not a violation of the sharia which, as mentioned above, demands capital punishment, because it was possible to claim that these white Maronites or "Maronites of cotton and linen,"[95] as they were sometimes also called, had never in fact become Muslims. It was more like an annulment than a divorce. Nor is this is an isolated instance, as Jenkins writes about a Macedonian congregation "complete with its bishop"[96] that publicly converted to Islam, while continuing to worship in a Christian manner by night. Such conversion would allow families to keep their sons from being taken by the Ottoman authorities for use according to the system of devshirme. These appear to be examples of double religious belonging, insofar as the people mentioned claimed to belong to two religious communities simultaneously. On the other hand, one might interpret these examples in terms of double belonging, but not double *religious* belonging, in that the people belonged to the Umma on a political and economic basis, while on a religious basis they continued to belong to the church.

Just as there are examples of crypto-Christianity, there are examples of crypto-Islam, most notably in the example of the Moriscos of Spain, also called "new Christians" in the literature of the period. After the conclusion of the Iberian *reconquista* in 1492 Muslims were given the choice of departing to North Africa, or converting to Catholic Christianity. Many of those who decided to stay and "convert" did so out of convenience for the sake of staying in Spain. According to church law these people had been baptized and were indeed Christians, but from a subjective point of view they remained Muslims. The Christian response was one of anti-syncretism whereby the church authorities (notably the Inquisition) searched meticulously for evidence or a confession which indicated that the person's conversion was not sincere. This included observing whether the "new Christians" would drink wine, eat pork, curse Muhammad, eat during Ramadan, and even eat couscous![97]

In addition to double religious belonging, one can identify several instances of syncretism, both of Christianity mixing in Islamic elements, and vice versa. Jenkins (2008) mentions several instances of Christian syncretizations in Islam, such as the architecture of the Dome on the Rock which was designed and built by Orthodox Christians, and that the design is that of an Orthodox martyrion. He notes that the full prostration so common in

94. Makdisi, *Artillery of Heaven*, 35.

95. Naaman, "Maronite Society."

96. Jenkins, *Lost History*, 177.

97. Cardeillac, *Moriscos y Cristianos*, 23–27.

Islam may have been learned from Syriac Christians who did (and do) the same. On the level of doctrinal syncretism we find the suggestion that the SHOULD THIS BE 'EIGHTH CENTURY'? Adoptionist heresy of Spain was such an instance. The Adoptionist Christology proposed that the divine Sonship of Christ was eternal, but that in terms of his human nature Christ was the Son of God by adoption through grace. The occasion of syncretism here would be that the Adoptionist Christology would be more amenable to the Muslim rulers in Spain who objected to the persistent Christian use of the title "Son of God" to refer to Jesus, on the basis that this was the sin of *shirk* (association) and a violation of Qur'anic teaching that God neither is begotten, nor does he beget.[98] The Adoptionist could, to some extent, then agree with the Muslim, identifying that Jesus, in his humanity, was not the begotten Son of God, but an adopted one. Pope Hadrian condemned the heresy in two letters, one to the bishops of Spain, dated 785, and another to Charlemagne, dated 794.[99]

Even today, some Muslims in Egypt present their children for (incomplete) baptism at Coptic churches. Essam Fadle tells of the Virgin Mary Monastery in Assuit, and how Muslims bring their children for baptism during the yearly monastery celebration (Aug 7–21). The monks are careful not to apply the holy oil, which would seal the ritual and thus make the child Christian, according to their sacramentology. The ritual is administered, but not completed.[100]

The above examples include both successful and failed syncretism—non-coerced religious mixing. But in all cases the religious communities retain their identity as Christian or Muslim. There are, however, examples of communities that have so syncretized elements of Islam and Christianity to the point where the result is not considered to be either Islam by Muslims, nor Christianity by Christians. Two such examples, both going by the general name of Chrislam, have emerged in Nigeria. Since both movements go by the name Chrislam, it is preferable to use the Yoruba names of each to differentiate the two: *Oke Tude* and *Ifeoluwa*. Both movements appear to incorporate explicitly Christian and Islamic elements, like using the Bible *and* Qur'an, but unlike the examples above, the result is something that appears to be recognizably different than either Islam or Christianity as they are practiced in Nigeria.[101] In relation to identity, this represents a *claim* to

98. Qur'an 112:3.

99. Sollier, "Adoptionism," Cavadini, *The Last Christology*, Crisp, *Divinity and Humanity*, 38 fn.

100. Fadle, "Baptism."

101. For more on these two movements see De Sam Lazaro, "Chrislam," McLaughlin, "In Africa," and Janson, "Chrislam."

be both Muslim *and* Christian—to have both identities at the same time—but this claim is rejected by the larger Muslim and Christian communities.

In this section multiple examples have been provided that indicate that the interaction between Islam and Christianity has been complex, varied, and nuanced. Both have influenced and syncretized elements from one another. While the majority of the believers studied in this book identify themselves as ex-Muslim Christians, and understand the religion of Islam and the religion of Christianity to be mutually exclusive, it is important to be aware that this is not the only way to interpret the relation between the two faiths.

CONCLUSION

The first chapter set out the concepts of contextualization and power. This chapter has concerned itself with a discussion of several important terms that will surface again and again throughout this entire work such as conversion, apostasy (itself a type of conversion), persecution (the use of power to contain the "pollution" of apostasy), and identity. Examples of each of these were then provided from communities both past and present. Organic contextualization is a model of theology-making, it is the continuation of indigenization, whereby indigenous believers both ask their own questions and work out their own possible answers, while in conversation with fellow disciples of Christ throughout history and their contemporaneous setting.

In this chapter we have focused on religious conversion, which has many forms. Here we are concerned mostly with conversion as a transfer from one tradition to another one (Islam to Christianity, understood as mutually exclusive forms of relating to God and humanity), though there is also a group that understands conversion as allegedly happening within Islam, from being some form of Muslim to being another form of Muslim.[102] The former will be called ex-Muslim Christians or CMBs, insofar as they leave/reject Islam (the "old" in Nock's definition) and embrace Christianity (the "new" in Nock's definition); the latter will be called accommodationists, insofar as they attempt to accommodate elements of Islam and Christianity. Apostasy is a form of conversion, and consists in leaving one tradition (or religion) for a different religion or no religion at all. In orthodox Islam apostasy is punishable by death or, for females in some traditions, by permanent imprisonment. The use of power to contain or prevent the polluting

---

102. Other Muslims may not interpret it the same way. That is, they may see this as apostasy, regardless of how the Muslim follower of Jesus tries to accommodate Islam and the Christian message.

presence of apostasy in Islamic societies is a key challenge faced by converts as they live out the consequences of their religious conversion.

Chapter 2 has been about the *context* wherein converts might engage in the theology-making process described by organic contextualization. But there is another important question related to context which has not been answered: what is it about the modern (and late modern) world that has allowed for an environment wherein relatively large numbers of Muslims have confessed faith in the Christ of the Bible? That is the topic to be addressed in the next chapter.

3

The Twentieth Century

Changes in Context, Numbers, and Locations of Converts

The central research question in this book is about ex-Muslim Christians. In Chapter 2 we examined aspects of the contexts in which CMBs function, such as why they have converted, what it means to leave Islam (apostasy), and what it means to become an evangelical Christian. A careful understanding of context is essential if we are to answer the main research questions concerning theology-making.

Context leads to further questions of current numbers and distribution and also what has made it possible for a significant number of Muslims, two million at least, to make a commitment to follow Jesus Christ as portrayed in the Gospels. The point is particularly interesting given the relative failure of early modern attempts to bring Muslims to Christ.

A BRIEF HISTORICAL BACKGROUND: THE GREAT EXPERIMENT

During the nineteenth and twentieth centuries Protestants became interested in missionary work among Muslims, but prior to the 1960s it seems that few Muslims converted. Given the massive investments made in terms of time, money and personnel, why were there not more converts? A detailed study of this question would be beyond the brief of this book, but a sketch is in order.[1]

One reason, perhaps the most important one, for the early failure is that Islamic communities were able to use violence efficiently to stop the spread of "pollution"—a capacity currently being challenged. Missionaries

---

1. Livingstone, "34 Theses," 28–33, proposes 34 theses about the paucity of conversions.

were not allowed to enter many areas if it was suspected that they would engage in Muslim evangelism, which was difficult and dangerous, both for the missionary and the potential convert. Where there were indigenous ancient churches such as the Greek Orthodox, Maronite, Assyrian, Armenian and Coptic, most Protestants determined to "reform" these ancient churches with their "pure" Gospel. This gave rise to what Bob Blincoe labeled "the Great Experiment,"[2] namely that the ancient churches, revived and reformed by missionaries, would then evangelize the Muslims.[3] None of the ancient churches became evangelical and Reformed, but some from those churches did convert, and in some places indigenous evangelicalism took root (chapter 4 considers one such community). The Great Experiment was not the only missionary strategy, but it was the most popular one and consumed extensive missionary resources, both in terms of funds and personnel.

There are other figures who had looked favorably on the direct evangelization of Muslims—Ramon Llull (the father of mission to Muslims), Thomas Aquinas, Martin Luther, and Temple Gairdner, and there were indeed efforts at direct mission to Muslims.[4] One reason that few were successful is that very few were well-staffed *and* lasting. The American Lutheran mission to the Kurds of what is today Iran was intent on direct evangelism, for instance, but was interrupted by World War I, with all the missionaries leaving. The Free Church of Scotland medical mission near Aden, Yemen, suffered greatly when its brilliant leader Ion Keith-Falconer died in 1887, after only a couple of years there.[5] Such examples could be multiplied.

And then when there were converts the use of violence was usually effective in stopping the spread of the Christian message. Thus one Egyptian convert, Ahmed Fahmy, was forced to flee to Edinburgh, where he studied medicine, and went on to become a medical missionary to China.[6] We find a well-funded, well-staffed, joint missionary effort in Constantinople

---

2. Blincoe, in his *Lessons from Kurdistan* coined the term. But he is not the first to note its existence. Lyle Vander Werff, in his magisterial book *The Record*, uses the accurate if unwieldy label "via the Eastern Churches" for this missionary strategy for Muslim evangelism.

3. Those words are from one of the most important texts that advocated this strategy, Smith and Dwight, *Missionary Researches in Armenia*, ix.

4. For more on Gairdner see Cragg, "Gairdner's Legacy," 164–67.

5. Grafton, "Pax Americana"; Vander Werff, *The Record*.

6. Vander Werff, *The Record*, 151. A fascinating story which remains to be researched and written. Other than the few lines in Vander Werff I have found no other information on Dr. Fahmy.

(1858–1877) where multiple societies were cooperating in Muslim evangelism and distributing books, pamphlets and portions of Scripture. The Ottoman Porte had issued in 1856 the Hatt-i Humayun, guaranteeing equal rights to all his subjects. Between 1857 and 1877 over 50 Turks were baptized, and "Prospects of a convert church seemed hopeful."[7] However, in 1864 the government seized all the missionary literature, locked up the meetings halls, expelled the missionaries, and imprisoned Turkish believers: others simply disappeared with the "pollution" contained. One rare exception where a church containing a number of CMBs was formed was in Iran, under the leadership of Anglicans and Presbyterians.[8]

The prominence of the Great Experiment as a strategy meant that many missions did not even try to evangelize Muslims. When they did, the missionaries had to confront the effectiveness of Islamic coercion and frequent lack of resources, stability or manpower. All of this together meant that known converts were, in most places, few and far between. Later in this chapter we will see how the context and strategy of mission have both shifted dramatically. But first it is appropriate to try to discern where the converts are.

DIFFICULTIES RELATED TO ESTIMATING NUMBERS OF CONVERTS

The number of known converts from Islam to Christianity has increased significantly since the 1960s. Calculating the number of converts is very difficult, and in this section I will explain why. I will then present what appear to be the most credible or reasonable estimates for some countries.[9]

The first problem is collecting reasonably accurate numbers. There are multiple motives for people to both over and under-report the numbers. On the side of over-reporting, or at least using overly-optimistic figures, one reason is related to fundraising. When Christian missions are raising funds for their endeavors, or when indigenous Christian ministers (including CMBs) are doing so, the bigger the number of converts, the better. Thus if one reads something like, "In country X 50,000 Muslims have already decided to follow Christ!" it is worth scrutinizing the number and asking how it was calculated. If the context is related to fund-raising, such caution is all the more vital. Edward Ayub, a CMB pastor in Bangladesh, writes of his frustration regarding this issue:

7. Ibid., 162.

8. Ibid.

9. Figures for other countries are in Miller and Johnstone, "Global Census."

> . . . because numbers are held to be the most important evidence
> of God's blessing, they produce exaggerated reports. Someone
> abroad asked me whether 10,000 mosques have been converted
> into Christian Churches in Dhaka. I had to answer that I know
> of none.[10]

This is not, however, to say that none of such material can be used,
but when it is, there is a tendency to use the most generous possible way of
counting converts.

Over-calculation is also used by Muslims at times. Sheikh Ahmad al
Katani stated on Al Jazeera the rather surprising conclusion that in Africa
six million Muslims convert to Christianity ever year.[11] This was presented
in the context of encouraging Muslims to support his efforts at *da3wa* in
Africa. His message was clear: Muslims are losing ground to Christians in
Africa, so the Umma must support him.

Regarding terminology, it is important to examine carefully what exactly is being claimed in different kinds of literature. For example, if one
reads that 50,000 somewhere have made a "decision for Christ," this does
not mean that they are necessarily attending a church, reading the Bible,
praying, or much less that they have been baptized. It generally means that
during some sort of encounter with a Christian person (or website) they,
in some form, usually a short extemporary prayer, accepted Jesus as their
"Lord and Savior," and asked God to forgive them their sins. This does not
mean that the person really understood what was happening, or that what
he actually felt he was doing was what the Christian had in mind. I recall
how one Muslim lady related that she had said this prayer as a matter of
courtesy to her Christian friend with the understanding that since Muslims
already accept the Prophet Jesus, there was nothing un-Islamic about it. All
of these realities are implicit in the phrase "decision for Christ."

A slightly more helpful measure is baptisms. Because baptism normally requires commitment to a local church and a period of pre-baptismal
training, it is more likely that the person being baptized is serious in making
a commitment to the new religion. But even with baptism we find a specific
problem in relation to MBBs, which Stricker and Ripken, who interviewed
hundreds of MBBs, explain:

> The interviews also reveal that most MBBs, within five years
> of their declaration of faith in Christ, (regardless of whatever

10. Ayub, "Observations and reactions," 25.

11. "Because of the Christian missionaries every hour Islam loses 667 Muslims
[who] convert to Christianity, every day 16,000, [and] every year six million." From
Abdallah, "Six million Muslims."

process they have been a part of), have been baptized and re-baptized three to five times. In countries where missionaries representing different agencies are beginning to partner and share statistics, it is clear that the number of annual baptisms of MBBs is significantly inflated as MBBs are baptized time and time again within different mission bodies.[12]

I have also seen a variation of this with the Iranian churches in the UK for legal reasons. Even if someone was baptized in Iran at a home church, they often cannot get a baptismal certificate from the pastor there, as the church exists illegally and cannot create such documents. Thus they must be re-baptized in the UK, where a church can issue them a baptismal certificate, which can then serve as physical proof to the Home Office that they have in fact been baptized, and are thus no longer Muslims but Christians. Such documentation is often important for the government in determining whether or not to grant the person refugee or asylum status. This should not be interpreted as an effort at bolstering numbers of claimed converts, but simply addressing a difficult situation in a pragmatic manner. Baptism may also be re-administered due to differences in practice (namely immersion v. sprinkling). In spite of all these limitations, "baptism is in fact a rather rough index of who is and isn't a Christian."[13] So baptism, while still problematic, appears to be somewhat more reliable than "decisions for Christ."

There is, however, also the real possibility of under-reporting. This commonly occurs in public forums likely to be read by local Muslims. Using the lowest possible estimation, or indeed below that, is considered to be a way of maintaining safety, especially in countries where the government actively punishes apostates, or turns a blind eye while the family is permitted or encouraged to do so. Under-reporting is also used by political and religious leaders in such formats. "[C]onversion ranks among the most destabilizing activities in modern society, altering not only demographic patterns but also the characterization of belief as communally sanctioned assent to religious ideology."[14] While Viswanathan was not speaking specifically of the Muslim world, her point is germane to our topic. So even when conversion is taking place in significant numbers, it is often considered to be in the best interest of society to ignore it, conceal it,[15] or when that is not pos-

12. Ripken and Stricker, "Believers and Baptism," 6.

13. Cooper, *Muslim Sahel*, 389.

14. Viswanathan, *Outside the Fold*, xvi.

15. An example of this is cited in Madany, "New Christians of North Africa," 51 where the Algerian government allegedly claims that the number of converts to Christianity is "a state secret." According to "Conversion rate," in *The Economist* the Catholic Church in Kosovo, where substantial numbers of Muslims are converting, would not

sible, to dismiss the number of converts as negligible or insignificant. This is not meant to imply, again, that *no* such sources (newspapers, specifically) should be used, but rather that they require a good deal of scrutiny.

Perhaps the most reliable sources of information available are research articles largely internal to the missionary community and missionaries themselves. Firstly, some research articles are published in journals like the *International Journal of Frontier Missiology* (IJFM) or *St Francis Magazine* (*SFM*) or the *International Bulletin of Missionary Research* (IBMR). These publications are available to the non-specialist, but their readership mostly consists of scholars of mission and missionaries. There are also documents that are never published, but are shared via email, exchanged at conferences, or downloaded from secure websites. These are even less publicly available than the articles published in the journals just mentioned. Examples of such documents are *Mapping People groups in [Country Name] for Informed Church Planting*[16] and the *Camel Training Manual* (ND). It is in these documents that missionaries and mission strategists may evaluate their progress or lack of progress in certain regions and try to share their findings. Therefore, these documents tend to value accuracy, and where there is not a specific number, they will often provide a range of numbers that represents the best estimate, including the high and the low.

Secondly, the other source of information is the missionaries themselves and databanks collated from their reports. Speaking with someone who is doing academic research, knowing their name will not be published, and knowing that what they say will have no financial or professional repercussions for them—all these factors are conducive to an environment where the urge to minimize or maximize numbers is not present, or at least not in so pronounced a manner. At times it is possible to speak with individual missionaries, but in addition to this, most missionary agencies collect detailed data from their missionaries. And groups like the Joshua Project at the US Center for World Mission (USCWM) or the Center for the Study of Global Christianity at Gordon-Conwell Seminary have as a main purpose keeping detailed, up-to-date records on information such as what people-groups live in a given country, to what extent are they Christian, whether they have the Bible in their own language, and so on. Thus, in distilling information from hundreds or thousands of missionaries and indigenous ministers, such databanks can be very helpful.

---

release specific numbers of baptisms to a journalist.

16. Farah, *Mapping People Groups.*

COUNTRIES AND REGIONS

Patrick Johnstone is one of the world's foremost experts on mission and Christian demographics. In 1964 he published the first edition[17] of *Operation World*, a series of books which would, over the decades, deeply affect the evangelical world and its interaction with prayer, missions, and World Christianity. The original 32-page book communicated basic information on 30 countries and how Christians could pray for the needs of the churches in those countries. Since 1964 *Operation World* has been greatly expanded and now contains information and statistics on every country in the world.

If a person has recently met a foreign student from Kazakhstan, for instance, and they are curious to learn more about the country and the church there, they will find in the most recent edition of *Operation World* that Kazakhstan is 2,717,300 sq. km, that in 2010 the population was about 15,753,460, and that the population density is 6/sq. km.[18] Since 1991 there has been "massive emigration of Europeans," who made up 35.9 percent (mostly Russians) of the population, while 63 percent of the population was Turkic (mostly Kazakh). They will also learn that evangelical churches are not recognized by the government, and thus may be limited in their activities, that the largest church is Russian Orthodox with 206 congregations and 825,175 members, with Evangelicals and Baptists having 315 congregations and 11,000 members. Evangelical Christianity is growing at about 3.5 percent per year, and Pentecostalism is growing yearly at about 6.6 percent. Then follow two answers to prayer, and nine challenges for prayer, all of which indicate a detailed knowledge of the context of the local (evangelical) Christians in country.

The book is almost 1,000 pages and contains data on every country in the world. It is evident that a great deal of research has been carried out for the sake of this project, which has as a main goal to assist Christians in praying for the specific needs of churches in every nation. From the first through the 6th edition (2001), Patrick Johnstone was the editor of the volume.

In trying to discern numbers of MBBs by country I contacted Johnstone, and I am grateful to him for sharing the results of his research with me. The figures below are based on the data that he gathered from missionary agencies and missionaries. Note that the numbers here are not for baptized believers, but for "believers," which may well include un-baptized people who have made a confession of faith. Where I have found additional information or question his numbers I have added footnotes. This book is

17. Published by Dorothea Mission, South Africa.
18. Mandryk, *Operation World*, 497.

interested especially in CMBs in/from the larger Middle East, the USA and the UK, so those are the countries I have included here. When the Arab World number of MBBs is calculated, Johnstone comes up with 485,123.

- North Africa

    - Algeria   50,000[19]

    - Egypt   10,000

    - Libya   300

    - Morocco   2,000

    - Sudan[20]   25,000

    - Tunisia   300[21]

- Europe

    - United Kingdom   20,000

- The Americas

    - Canada   40,000

    - USA   300,000[22]

- Asia

    - Afghanistan   3,000

    - Bahrain   1,500

    - Iran   50,000[23]

    - Iraq   1,000

    - Israel   300

    - Jordan   5,000

    - Kuwait   250[24]

19. This figure seems realistic. Guera, "Berbers of Algeria," provided an estimate of 20,000 to 100,000.

20. Information was gathered prior to the independence of South Sudan in 2011.

21. Madany, "Christians of North Africa, 51, has an estimate of 500.

22. Many ex-Muslims move to the United States if they are able to. The same thing can be said of Canada, Australia, Germany, and the UK, among others. These numbers include such individuals.

23. This figure is almost certainly too low. Knowledgeable contacts of mine place this figure in the hundreds of thousands *within* Iran.

24. Some of the Gulf States are mostly populated by non-citizens. Per my 2012

☐	Lebanon	2,000
☐	Oman	50
☐	Palestine	200
☐	Qatar	200
☐	Saudi Arabia	50,000
☐	Syria	1,000
☐	Turkey	3,000
☐	UAE	200
☐	Yemen	100[25]

The next question to be addressed is about the factors which have enabled the increase in conversions. It is true that there is information on why individual Muslims decide to follow Jesus, but such research focuses on individual motives, and was reviewed in a previous chapter. Here I am trying to look at the global level, and ask "what are the characteristics of the world in the second half of the twentieth century that have made possible (though not necessarily caused) a significant number of conversions to Christ?" The question is not as ambitious as it might seem, for I am not trying to establish a direct relationship of causality, but rather a general description of the global context that has made such a shift a possibility.

METHODOLOGY

Given the dearth of material, it was necessary to devise a way of collecting information touching on the issue. I determined that asking ministers, both local and foreign, with experience in an Islamic context would give a useful foundation if critically appraised. The validity of this approach rests on the premise that such individuals are privy to knowledge that is not readily available from other sources. Therefore, a two-part questionnaire was circulated by secure email to selected missionaries and ministers, the basis for selection being more knowledge of their existence as long-term workers than assumptions about individual competence. The responses ranged from a few lines to two pages. Five of the respondents are originally from the Muslim world or their parents were. One was a CMB. Almost everyone

---

correspondence with Johnstone, the figures here include the large migrant populations, and not just citizens.

25. Knowledgeable sources of mine place this figure somewhere between 300 and 500.

contacted answered, and a total of 30 responses were received. Of the respondents 27 were men and three were women. One was Catholic, two non-evangelical Anglicans, and the rest were evangelicals from different traditions. All had at least five years of experience ministering in an Islamic setting. I was assisted in establishing contact with and obtaining information from a few of the missionaries and ministers by two colleagues who wish to remain anonymous.

The sample is not representative in any way. It is not weighted according to where missionaries are sent in the Muslim world, where most Muslims live, or where most Muslims are converting. Rather, the contacts available were dictated by pragmatic circumstances in which sending sensitive material could affect respondents' security. Thus I was limited to people my colleagues and I had met personally over the years. The benefit of such an approach was a high response rate.

Of the 30, 24 had experience in a region where the government might realistically use coercion to silence, imprison or expel apostates. The other seven were in "secular" countries where the convert might well face pressure from their family but probably not the state.

There were only two questions. They were:

> Were there any books/articles/speakers that personally influenced your understanding of Christian witness in the Muslim world?

And:

> Over the last decades there has been a significant increase in Muslims making some sort of commitment to Jesus and his message as they are portrayed in the Gospels. What are some of the factors in your opinion that have led to this?

The language in the last question intentionally allows for the full spectrum of identities of Muslim-background followers of Jesus, as discussed in chapter 2.

QUESTION ON INFLUENTIAL FIGURES

The purpose of this question was to discern who/what were the main figures/texts that influenced how these ministers engaged in witness to Muslims. Given the relative decline of the Great Experiment as a strategy for Muslim evangelization, what figures influenced and helped to bring about new approaches to Christian witness to Muslims?

One scholar mentioned by six different respondents was the Anglican Kenneth Cragg, formerly an assistant bishop of the Anglican Diocese of Jerusalem. After him is a Baptist from the USA, Phil Parshall, mentioned by four respondents. Three sources were mentioned by each of three respondents: Fouad Accad, Rolland Muller, and the book *Answering Islam* by Geisler and Saleeb. A brief summary of the approaches of Cragg and Parshall will help to show that this is a diverse and multi-polar conversation, and that the respondents are drawing on varied resources that are far from univocal in how they approach the topic of Christian witness to Muslims.

Kenneth Cragg (1913–2012) worked both in the Anglican Church and academia, and was consecrated assistant bishop in Jerusalem in 1970. He authored many books such as *The Call of the Minaret* (which was mentioned by name by one respondent, originally published in 1956 and since republished numerous times),[26] *Sandals at the Mosque: Christian Presence amid Islam* (1959), *Jesus and the Muslim: An Exploration* (1985), and *The Arab Christian* (1991). In seeking to ensure that Christians properly understood Islam, he also translated a book by a Muslim author into English, Kamil Husayn's *City of Wrong: a Friday in Jerusalem* (1959), which is a dramatization of Good Friday. Cragg emphasized inter-religious dialogue, and his approach was irenic. That said, he never subscribed to religious relativism. Behind his measured, scholarly works for Muslims and Christians there was always an insistence that Muslims who desire to follow Messiah should be free to do so, and that when Muslims persecuted converts they were compromising the integrity of their own *diin*.[27]

Phil Parshall,[28] American and Baptist, was a missionary in Bangladesh for over 20 years. His main book has already been mentioned in connection with the topic of contextualization, *New Paths in Muslim Evangelism*. In that book Parshall explores then-uncharted territory in terms of witness to Muslims. As an indication of how far he is willing to go in questioning traditional missionary methods, he asks if, given how baptism is so scandalous to Muslims, there is not a dynamic equivalent for that ritual.[29] In other words, Parshall is willing to discuss jettisoning the traditional Christian rite of initiation involving water and the Triune formula in favor of some

26. And incidentally, was the first book I ever read on Islam.

27. For a helpful summary of Cragg's overall approach to dialogue and witness see Bridger, "Take up and Read," 37.

28. See his autobiography: Parshall, *Divine Threads*.

29. See page 209 of the 2003 re-release of the book, under the name *Muslim Evangelism: Contemporary Approaches to Contextualization*: "In view of the fact that baptism is so misunderstood in Muslim lands, would it be feasible to construct a functional substitute for baptism, one that would retain the biblical meaning but change the form?"

other ritual which will be less provocative. On the other hand, in an oft-quoted 1998 article he stated that MBBs should *not* continue to attend the mosque on a regular basis. He also expressed dismay that some Christians had legally converted to Islam so they could "become Muslims to Muslims" for the sake of evangelism. In other words, he felt some missionaries had taken his suggestions too far. Parshall's importance lies less in his formula for how to carry out mission to Muslims, but rather in his willingness to explore "new paths." He helped to start a conversation (or controversy) that continues today, and is still active in mission scholarship and publishing. All in all, Parshall was a trail-blazer in advocating greater creativity in directed contextualization.

There are multiple voices in this conversation. Cragg's irenics and the polemics of a figure like the Orthodox Coptic priest Zakaria Botros (mentioned by two people) are similar in that they are both built on a foundation of erudite scholarship. While irenics and polemics might appear to be mutually exclusive, more than one respondent mentioned representatives of both of these approaches as being influential. The Lebanese Fouad Accad, whose book *Building Bridges: Christianity and Islam* (1997) was referenced by name by more than one respondent, takes Cragg's irenics even further and represents yet another approach. Roland Muller in *Honor and Shame* asked if it is possible to explain the gospel on those terms, rather than innocence and guilt. These voices do not represent a single approach to the topic of Christian mission to Muslims, but include almost every possible approach to Muslim evangelism, and some voices, which might seem mutually exclusive, were listed by the same person. This seems to be evidence that at least a portion of the respondents are actively engaged in continually forming and re-forming their opinions and practices in relation to this topic, and are not unwilling to hold what appear to be opposing opinions in tension while evaluating them. In sum, the list of influences is *eclectic*.

The large majority of books and articles published that relate explicitly to the topic of Muslim evangelism are written by evangelicals because they are, of all Christians, the group that is most involved in that endeavor. However, a number of influences are surprisingly *ecumenical*. For instance, Kenneth Cragg does not easily fit into the evangelical mold; nor do other influences mentioned like Zakaria Botros (Coptic Orthodox) or Mazhar Mallouhi (Muslim turned evangelical Christian turned Muslim follower of Jesus) or Samir Khalil Samir (Egyptian Jesuit). Perhaps what accounts for the influence of such figures is that they are all firmly committed to sharing the Christian message with Muslims, a common concern which bridges or supersedes other disagreements. If that hypothesis is correct, then it might be the case that the concept of who exactly is an evangelical within the context of Christian mission to Muslims has, to some extent, been redefined. That is, the *ethos* of evangelism supersedes the *doctrinal* characteristics which had historically been used to delineate who is or is not an evangelical.

Third, this is an *international* conversation, though not a global one, for the voices from Latin America and East Asia are largely absent. That is probably due to the fact that missionary efforts to Muslims from those areas are relatively new, and the publishing and translation of scholarship is a demanding task. As missionary efforts from such countries mature it seems likely that the influence of their scholars and practitioners of mission will increase. Now, the authors mentioned are from North America, Europe or somewhere in the Muslim world, with the Arabophone countries being predominant.

As a final note, it is not only people who write and publish books who are influencing how this missionary work is conceived and undertaken. Numerous respondents mentioned fellow ministers, many of them who served for decades in obscure corners of countries like Pakistan or Lebanon, but whose influence was largely limited to their immediate sphere of activity.

The influences listed by the respondents point to a conversation that is evangelical in tone while also being eclectic, international, and ecumenical. Moreover it appears that the strategy of the Great Experiment is no more, because while some evangelical missionaries continue to partner with the ancient churches, it is not with the goal of reforming them in an evangelical mold to evangelize Muslims. Not one respondent referred to the influence of one of the architects of that strategy as having informed her outlook on mission and Islam. On the contrary, many of the cited authors advocated Muslim evangelism in some form or other. The next section will help us to evaluate this hypothesis: how far do the respondents still subscribe to the Great Experiment or have new strategies taken its place?

QUESTION ON FACTORS FACILITATING CONVERSION

The information presented here does not pretend to be comprehensive, and once again the biases and personal backgrounds of the respondents have influenced their answers. With those caveats, it is appropriate to discuss some of the answers given by the respondents.

Broadly speaking, there are three categories that emerge as the respondents try to explain some of the "factors" which they think have led to, or at least allowed for, this increase in the number of known conversions. In the following sections, each of these categories will be examined with quotes from respondents. Some of their claims will be tested with available data. In the conclusion to the chapter I will argue that frequently the factors facilitating conversion (FFCs) augment each other, and will provide some examples. Nevertheless, what follows is not in itself a history of specific conversion movements, but a description of factors that, according to my respondents, *allowed for* or *facilitated* the increasing number of known conversions from Islam to Christ in the latter half of the twentieth century.

Transcendental Factors: Prayer, God's Timing, Dreams, Visions, Miracles

Like many Christians, the respondents believe that God is, in some sense, sovereign over the course of human history, and that prayer is an effective way of changing the direction of that history. It is therefore not surprising that eight respondents explicitly mentioned one or more of the following. One, more people are praying for Muslims to convert. Two, there is a movement of God's Spirit drawing people to convert. And three, that in God's plan for human history it is simply the right time for more Muslims to convert. No clear explanation was given by the respondents regarding causality, leaving it open whether God's Spirit was moving because of increased prayer, or more people were praying because God's Spirit was so moving them. The respondents seemed comfortable acknowledging the power of prayer to influence God, but also his absolute rule over human history, without seeking to reconcile the implicit tension. As one Western minister in the Arab world said, "some of the increase [in conversions] is not explainable—it's the Lord's . . . timing, and His movement of the Holy Spirit, and we just get to enjoy it . . . Also there has been more concerted prayer for the Muslim world than probably ever before." The increase in prayer for the region was also mentioned by another person[30] who has noticed "more prayer focused on our region[31]—evident in several region-wide prayer networks, more prayer trips into the area and more access via internet and technology to see and pray with insight for things on the ground."

One person[32] noted that churches in the West are praying specifically for the Muslim world more than ever before: "the most important [factor] I feel is the focus that many groups and organizations have placed on prayer for breaking down the walls of Islam in general and focus on the [Muslim] people groups in particular. There would not be the response if it were not

30. A Western man in the Arab World.

31. The Middle East and North Africa, in this case.

32. A Western woman minister in the Arab world.

for the prayers." The implication here is that increased prayers have brought about "God's timing" for Muslims to convert. Interviews with missionaries, including ones who did not complete this questionnaire, indicate that events like 9/11 and the July 7 Tube Bombings in London have forced Christians to think about Islam. While some have reacted with xenophobia, fear or even conversion *to* Islam, others have turned to prayer and sending out missionaries.[33]

Is it true that there has been more concerted prayer for the Muslim world, the conversion of Muslims, and missionary work focused on Muslims? The evidence indicates this is indeed the case. One concrete example, though not explicitly mentioned by name by any respondents, is a widely-distributed and attractively-produced prayer guide to be used by Christians praying for Muslims during Ramadan. Each day of Ramadan a different people group from the Muslim world is described, some facts are given about it, and then some specific pointers are given for how to pray for that people. It is used not only by individuals, but also by entire churches, one website[34] giving tips on how to get the whole congregation praying for Muslims during Ramadan. One influential missionary agency[35] is in the process of composing a book with the profiles of 50 unreached/unengaged people groups—that is, ethnic groups with a common language and identity that have little or no indigenous Christian presence. Previously this kind of detailed information was only the province of anthropologists, missionaries, or aristocratic travelers, and was not available in an easy-to-understand, attractive format with pictures, maps and interesting facts about groups from the Sanani Arabs of Northern Yemen (est. population 10.5 million)[36] to the Circassian Muslims of Jordan (est. population of 97,000).[37] The multiple editions of *Operation World* mentioned above are also a good example of this development.

The first quote above connects the increased prayer to speedier communications. The implication is that missionaries and ministers can both

33. That there are more missionaries in the Muslim world was a factor mentioned by four of the 30 respondents. A review of various editions of the *Mission Handbook*, which is published twice a decade or so, and collects information about the number of missionaries sent from the USA serving in different parts of the world, supports this claim in reference to the Arab world. See also Miller, "Woven in the Weakness," 21–22, and Dawn BSA, "Preaching the Gospel."

34. Online: http://www.ramadan.everypeople.net/. The prayer guide is produced in connection with the US Center for World Mission.

35. Online: http://www.frontiers.org/home; the book is titled *Called to Pray: Frontiers' Guide to Praying for the Unengaged.*

36. Online: http://www.joshuaproject.net/peopctry.php?rop3=108627&rog3=YM.

37. Online: http://www.joshuaproject.net/peopctry.php?rog3=JO&rop3=100079.

ask for and receive prayer more quickly, and that these prayers will be more efficacious because they are more specific. The same person mentions "prayer trips into the area." This refers to the increase in the number of people who travel to the mission field for a week or two, perhaps a little longer, as "missionaries" and, among other things, pray for the people around them. However, these so-called short-term missions have come under bruising criticism from some within the evangelical community, including missionaries, as being "holy tourism" which expends huge amounts of financial resources with relatively little in the way of results.[38] In fact some missionaries have reported to me negative results as individuals with little or no knowledge of the culture or language are apt to do more harm than good to the local church, local Christians and long-term missionaries being left to repair the damage after the visitors leave.

Also within this transcendent category, multiple mentions were made of dreams, visions or miracles. As one Western minister in the Arab World said, "it is a known fact that God is revealing himself to Muslims through dreams and visions. However, they [the Muslims] think this would draw ridicule, so they don't tell anyone. Yet when we ask them [if they have had such a dream], they can't believe we know that they had dreams. This opens doors." Another Westerner in the Arab World connected the reported increase in dreams and visions to the increase in prayers just mentioned: "The Holy Spirit is answering the prayers of God's people by sending dreams and visions and evangelists."

An increase in dreams and visions was noted by seven respondents, but one missionary[39] felt that the change was not *more* dreams and visions, but rather that in the past they had gone unreported: "I believe that Jesus has been revealing himself to Muslims for thousands of years via dreams and visions and appearances but those folks have had limited ways of communicating with the outside world to tell their story . . ."

In studying conversion narratives of Muslims, dreams and visions are fairly common although not always present. Among the Muslim converts whom I have met, it is not uncommon for someone to mention a dream or vision or miracle as one factor that contributed to their conversion. Woodberry and Shubin[40] mentioned dreams and visions as one of the key reasons that MBBs give when asked why they have decided to follow Jesus, similar

38. See, for instance, Jaffarian, "North American Missions," 35–38.

39. A Western missionary with experience in the Arab World and with Internet evangelism.

40. Woodberry and Shubin 2001, "Why I Chose Jesus."

to Timothy Abraham whose conversion narrative outlined in chapter 2 included a dream of Jesus.

The matter of dreams and visions has been much publicized in the Christian press. Some of the reports may well be exaggerated and sensational, but the statement that these are being reported more than in the past withstands scrutiny. Moreover, when one reads a number of the reports it is hard to think of them as "evangelical inventions" because so many of the elements in them are not evangelical at all. One missionary complained to me that so many women were having dreams of Mary, too Catholic for her liking. Another man had a dream of a priest holding a chalice and host, which is rather un-evangelical imagery and not what one would expect from a fabrication.

These conversion narratives that include dreams/visions have been parlayed into an evangelistic tool, to date five of them having been made into short movies of surprisingly good quality. These were produced by a ministry named *More than Dreams*. They are about characters from Nigeria, Egypt, Turkey, Iran, and Indonesia who came to the Christian faith and attributed that conversion—in part or in whole—to a dream or dreams.[41] An article by *More than Dreams* in a popular missions publication gives some background information:

> For decades, a well-documented phenomenon has been occurring in the Muslim world—men and women who, without knowledge of the gospel, or contact among Christians in their community, have experienced dreams and visions of Jesus Christ. The reports of these supernatural occurrences often come from "closed countries" where there is no preaching of the good news and where converting to Christianity can invoke the death sentence.[42]

There is no appeal for funds either in the movies, the website, or in the article. The overall tone of the movies as well as the sinner's prayer at the end indicate quite clearly that they are the work of evangelical Christians, but any specific denominational connection could not be determined.

Pentecostal minister and TV personality Christine Darg has also written on the topic. Her book, *The Jesus Visions*, is available online for free in both English and Arabic.[43] Darg's treatment of the topic is from a

---

41. They can all be seen in multiple languages at www.morethandreams.org.

42. *Lausanne World Pulse*, January 2007. The article is attributed to the ministry More than Dreams. Online: http://www.lausanneworldpulse.com/worldreports/595.

43. Online: http://www.jesusvisions.org/content.shtml.

confessional point of view, and does not claim to be a scholarly work. None-theless, her general description of what her research yielded is helpful:

> A typical "Jesus dream or vision" with innumerable variations is usually described by Muslims as a peaceful face that they some-how recognize as Jesus. Often they encounter a compassionate figure in a white robe, calling them to come to Him. Sometimes His hands and arms are extended wide, or Jesus reaches toward them in love and invitation. Many dreams are preparatory expe-riences to encourage Muslims with the possibility of following Jesus. Other visions or dreams are "epic" experiences of such magnitude that the person knows unquestioningly that he or she is destined to walk the lonely path of faith, even martyrdom, with Jesus.[44]

A few respondents, after listing several political and cultural changes, ended their answers by admitting that, in their view, notwithstanding secu-lar changes, it is ultimately a question of God's sovereignty. This appeals to the concept that God has a specific plan for history (Acts 14:26, 27). Thus a missionary with experience in Turkey, the Arab World, and East Asia said, "When pressed for a theological explanation I fall back to my Reformed heritage: God will do what it takes to draw His own to himself."

None of the responses were limited *only* to the transcendent category, and some of the responses did not mention it all. But prayer / God's timing were mentioned explicitly by ten respondents, dreams, visions and miracles by eight. The indication is that in the view of the respondents there is a strong supernatural and transcendent element, without which it is difficult to explain the growth of conversions in the last decades. Over the last de-cades the topic of mission to Muslims has gone from being a rather eso-teric specialty to being an area of concern, and thus a focus of prayer, for Christians both inside and outside of Muslim lands. Improvements in com-munications and transportation have made more detailed prayer possible, which is interpreted by many Christians as being more effective in eliciting God's intervention. In sum, increased informed prayer for Muslims and an increase in reported dreams, visions, and miracles by converts are, accord-ing to my respondents, novel factors that have contributed to the increase in known conversions over recent decades.

From the point of view of the social sciences, it is not possible to ob-serve directly what God may or may not be doing. But, from the point of view of the respondents, God's active role in mission both undermines the powers that array themselves against the Christian message, and confers

---

44. Darg, *Jesus Visions*, n.p.

power on the convert. When MBBs are persecuted for their faith (the first or second dimensions of power) God is able to fill them with hope, boldness and joy and even deliver them from persecution. By sending dreams and visions, God is interpreted as undermining the third dimension of power by over-ruling Muslim censorship and allowing (or compelling) people to consider directions which they had perhaps not been aware of before. Furthermore, the claim to have had a mystical experience from God may confer upon the convert a subjective source of power in that as long as she continues to believe that she had a vision or dream, it is not subject to falsification—it cannot be disproved.

Factors Related to Missionary Strategies and Methods

Respondents to the questionnaire mentioned a plethora of missionary strategies, insights and methods which they had apparently seen being used effectively among Muslims. One person[45] wrote: "Not extracting them [Muslims who want to follow Jesus], but letting them remain as they were when they were called by God (1 Cor 7:17–24). Building bridges of relationship and truth from where they are (Koran) to Jesus. Not preaching Christianity but Jesus." A Westerner with experience in the Arab World made a similar point: "NOT to expect conversion [to Christianity], but simply to ask for faith (just as one would anywhere else) has given such discussions [about Jesus Christ] a very different character."

In these quotes we find a reconfiguration of the purpose of mission and evangelism. The respondents are envisioning people who in some way remain Muslim, while following Jesus. The approach presupposes that following Jesus Christ can be done independently of the historical Christian churches. Such followers of Jesus are sometimes called Messianic Muslims"[46] or "insiders." Mazhar Mallouhi, who grew up Muslim, became an evangelical Christian, and now identifies himself as a Muslim disciple of Jesus, explains the concept with these words: "An 'insider' believer is someone, like me, who comes from a family and country that is Muslim and chooses to maintain their culture after being irretrievably changed by the transforming power of our Lord."[47] Some of the interviewees found this concept highly problematic, seeing it as a violation of the precepts of the Bible, while others

---

45. A Western minister with experience in the Arab World.
46. Such as Travis, "Messianic Muslims."
47. Mallouhi, "Insider Movement," 3.

saw in this (apparently) new configuration of identity—both as Muslim (somehow) and as a follower of Jesus—a positive development.[48]

Another development in mission strategy is a different style of teaching often called "Bible Storying." This specific strategy was mentioned by more than one respondent. One Western minister simply listed the factor "Oral Bible Storying" while another went into more detail: "Presentation of the Gospel in more culturally sensitive ways . . . in a chronological fashion, from creation to Christ, which preserves the underlying biblical meta-narrative of creation-fall-redemption-consummation." Both the "insider" approach and oral Bible storying claim to communicate with Muslims within their cultural and social context better than previous forms of Christian witness.

As evangelical missionaries made use of information derived from fields like anthropology and biblical studies, it became apparent to some that the *manner* in which the Christian message is communicated is very important. In the two quotations above, reference is made to two such insights. The second quotation emphasizes the practice of being able to summarize the entire Christian meta-narrative and communicate it in oral, narrative form. This represents a shift to narrative rather than didactic communication, previously the case in Karl Pfander's famous *Mizan ul Haqq* or *Balance of Truth* (ca. 1830 [1910]). A well-known example of the didactic form of communication is the Roman Road, which consists of verses from Paul's epistle to the Romans which build on each other, attempting to persuade the hearers that they are sinners, their sin separates them from God, that the breach between God and man cannot be overcome by any human initiative, and that God in his love has provided a way to reconcile humanity to himself through the sacrifice of Jesus Christ on the cross.[49] The presentation of the Christian message moves step by step, logically building its argument.

In comparison to this didactic method of communicating the Christian message, Bible storying appeals to a metanarrative that most Muslims will already be familiar with, like Creation *ex nihilo*, and characters known to them like Adam, Eve, Abraham, John the Baptist, and so on. By the time the most scandalous element—the crucifixion—is mentioned, it is within the narrative context of a heroic, divine drama that is more likely to resonate

48. As this thesis is concerned with ex-Muslim Christians, the controversial topic of "insiders" and "insider movements" will not be explored at great length. For advocates of IM see, among others, Brown, "Biblical Muslims"; "Brother Jacob"; Ibn-Mohammad, "Tribal Chief"; and Rebecca Lewis, "God-given Identity"; "Integrity of the Gospel"; and "Natural Communities." For arguments against see, among others, Abu Daoud, "Victory of Apostolic Faith"; Nikides, "Emergence"; "Messianic Muslims"; Span and Span, "Report"; and Madany, "The New Christians." J. Henry Wolfe's 2011 doctoral dissertation on the topic is a valuable work.

49. The verses commonly used are Rom 3:10, 23; 5:12; 6:23; and 10:9–10.

with some Muslims than something like the Roman Road. This may lead to further communication or Bible study with the Christian, and consequently a higher rate of conversion to Christianity. Two authors report that Bible storying has been so effective that it led to several new churches being founded. The same report also tells how memorizing a story (like one of Jesus's parables) is something that children can do, with surprising results.[50] According to some of my respondents, such developments in the manner whereby the Christian message is communicated have played a part in the increase of known conversions to Jesus Christ throughout the world over the last decades. This shift in communication could have wide-spread ramifications.

I recall once chatting with a Muslim who asked me about the doctrine of the Trinity and why Christians believed this. I told him the story of the early church, how Arius from Libya was teaching in Alexandria that there was a time when God's Word/*kalima* was not, how his bishop Alexander resisted him in this, how the debate about monotheism and the relation of God to his *kalima* spread throughout the Empire, how Constantine became worried about this source of instability and summoned all the bishops to Asia Minor to settle the matter, and so on. He seemed very interested in the story because it is a great story, even if the hearer continues to believe that the Nicene Council did not reach the correct conclusion (as my Muslim friend presumably did). That was in the context of an unscheduled conversation and happened well before I started my doctoral research, but in retrospect I see the same principal at work, how a narrative kept him interested: pointing to verses from the Bible would either have confounded him or led instantly to the claim that the Biblical text was corrupted (*tahriif*).

The practice of formulating the Christian message for Muslims in the context of a story goes all the way back to Ramon Llull's *Book of the Gentile and the Three Wise Men,* wherein three companions are traveling together, a Jew, a Christian, and a Muslim, and they stop to rest in a meadow. During their sojourn they meet a gentile (pagan) who asks them about their monotheistic ideas, and they agree that each will present to him a summary of his views in the order of their religions' key figures: Moses, then Jesus, then Muhammad. Llull used this interesting setting to engage in a comparison of the different religions. A shift to narrative communication is not in itself radically new, but rather a return to a practice that had apparently fallen into disuse.

Translation has always been part of the missionary activity of the Christian church, and some have gone so far as to see in the doctrine of the

---

50. Bender and Sims, "Short-term Trips," 10–13.

incarnation a sort of theological analogue for this activity: In the incarnation the Logos of God is communicated to humans by becoming human, the Word of God *qua* Scripture being communicated to people by being translated into their language.[51] One respondent[52] listed as a factor the "Availability of Bible in local languages in [both] written and spoken form." Note how the emphasis on spoken form echoes the practice of Bible storying mentioned above.

While new translations into languages spoken by Muslim people groups are increasing, there has also, according to my respondents, been a great leap forward in making such translated material available, one respondent[53] mentioning "TV and radio programming in peoples' heart language, and distribution projects getting the Word in (including the Jesus film in various heart languages), and more Scripture translated and being made available in heart language . . ." Here there is an overlap of translation activities with advances in oral communications. Another respondent, indigenous to the Middle East, pointed out that physical distribution of the Bible has also increased: "Availability of Scriptures and distribution. Bible translation made this possible as well as a greater distribution effort by many organizations."

There is ample evidence to support the claim that the pace and scope of Bible translation has increased significantly during the modern period. In this section, multiple instances of translation will be provided and some of the factors that have made the increase in this translation movement possible will be listed. Lamin Sanneh, himself a CMB, said that, "as a translated religion, Christianity through history became a force for translation," and, "The overwhelming majority of the world's languages have a dictionary and a grammar at all because of the modern missionary movement."[54] Be that as it may, the translatability of the Christian faith makes it a very different sort of *diin* than Islam, which insists that its book is incapable of translation. The most widely-used Bible in Arabic today is the Van Dyke translation,[55] the fruit of the Presbyterian mission to Ottoman Syria and related to the Great Experiment. The Presbyterians, aided by the indigenous scholar Boutros al Bustani, not only did the work of translating, but also produced

---

51. Sanneh, "Muhammad," and *Whose Religion is Christianity?*

52. A Western minister with experience in the Arab world.

53. A Western woman minister with experience in the Arab world.

54. Bonk 2003, "Defender of the Good News," n.p.

55. This was not the first translation of the Bible into Arabic, the first one dating back to around 680, and the Vatican published an Arabic Bible in 1583, according to Goddard, *Christian-Muslim Relations*, 117.

the first-ever Arabic type with vocalizations.[56] This monumental translation effort is related to the Great Experiment, but it is mentioned here to emphasize the centrality of translation to the Protestant missionary effort which continues today.

More recently, though,

> The revolution [in Bible translation] started around the mid-1980s, when more and more translation projects began making use of the personal computer. Thanks to the PC, a text had to be typed only once. After that, only the corrections needed to be entered and upon completion of the project, the text could be sent to the printer in digital format.[57]

Harnessing advances in technology has resulted in improved productivity, quality, and cost-effectiveness. One instance of this "revolution" is the growth of Christianity among the Kabyle Berbers of Algeria after the New Testament was translated into their own language from 1990 to 1995.[58] Similarly, many Iranian and Pakistani converts identify the ability to pray and read the Bible in their language as an important factor that drew them to Christianity.

The drive to use local languages and dialects, or what one of the respondents called "heart language," comes through both in print and other forms of media and has been one reason for the increase in conversions. Ibn Warraq, an ex-Muslim who composed a voluminous study of contemporary apostasy from Islam, notes that, "The media have played a great part in the conversion of Kabylie. The majority of the radio stations have a strong following in this region, [many listening] to Radio Monte Carlo and particularly the popular broadcasts in Amazigh" (Amazigh is the Kabyle Berber dialect).[59] Daisy Marsh, a pioneer in radio ministry to the Kabyle, was instrumental in the conversion of many of the first converts in Algeria by their own admission.[60] The total number of Christian Kabyles is difficult to determine, but is probably somewhere between 20,000 and 100,000, mostly in Algeria with some in France.[61] In 1990 the number was negligible by all accounts.

---

56. *Centennial of the American Press*, 43.

57. De Blois, "Bible Translation," 5.

58. Guera, "Kabyle Berbers."

59. Ibn Warraq, *Leaving Islam*, 92.

60. Abu Banaat, "Daisy Marsh," 3.

61. For a global census of BMBs by country see Miller and Johnstone, "Global Census," 1–19.

Because of this impetus towards translation in modern evangelical missions—not unique in the history of Christianity—we should not be surprised to learn that, "In terms of population, at least a portion of the Bible exists in languages spoken by ninety-five percent of the world's population."[62] Much of that translation was done since the middle of the twentieth century, "In that time there has been an explosion of Bible translation. From 1950 to 2005 new translations have been made available in 1,196 languages."[63] It is the confluence of multiple factors that has resulted in this increase, such as developments in technology, communications, translation sciences, social sciences, and biblical studies.[64] Those are in addition to those missionary societies explicitly dedicated to translation like Wycliffe, founded in 1942 by William Cameron Townsend (d. 1982), a missionary to the Cakchiquel Indians of Guatemala.

One of the respondents explicitly mentions availability of the Bible in "spoken form." This appears to be a reference to the use of technology to present the Bible to non-literate populations. This is perhaps not, strictly speaking, translation, but it has been included because it was mentioned by the persons who answered the survey, and also because it seems that we find a similar motive and dynamic at play—the desire to assure that the message of the Bible is accessible and available to all. An example of this impetus to go to great lengths to ensure that people have access to the message of Scripture in an accessible format can be found in Starling 2009, where he describes his own ministry with Global Recording Network (GRN). He states that "as much as two-thirds of the world's population, perhaps four billion people" are oral communicators (OCs), as opposed to text-based communicators, which is more common in the West.[65] Starling goes on to describe that OCs have a different communication style, which requires that Christian missionaries "adapt our communication style," provide a dynamic equivalence translation based on Scripture with "messages largely dictated by natural linguistic forms and local cultural dynamics."[66] This culturally-sensitive approach to translation and teaching become all the more effective because of the continual improvement of technology. "Over the years, GRN technology has changed from phonograph records to audio cassettes to CDs, DVDs, VCDs, MP3s, etc. GRN has freely downloadable recordings

62. Mitchell, "Bible Translation," 4.

63. Ibid.

64. "Into the New Millennium: The Changing Face of Bible Translation," 17–18.

65. He does not, however, give his source for this information.

66. Starling, "Oral Communications," 14.

on their website in over four thousand speech varieties."[67] The point is not that GRN is unique among missionary organizations in their creative use of technology and teaching, but that such work is being done across a broad spectrum of missionary agencies, of which GRN is a good example. This is also a case of creative strategy combined with the translation impetus inherent in the Christian missionary movement and the availability of new, affordable technologies and even the internet.

A final example that supports the claims of the respondents that increased translation has indeed taken place is the most translated movie in the world, the *Jesus Film*.[68] This is part of the missionary work of Campus Crusade for Christ and based on the Gospel of Luke.[69] Teams travel around and give out DVDs of the film in the local language(s), or in some places show the movie in a public place and invite local people to see it. As of 16 December 2009 the movie has been translated into 1068 languages.[70] Special versions of the film exist for children and one edition highlights the story of Mary Magdalene, designed to speak to the issues and difficulties faced by women.

Again we find that in terms of the increase in the number of conversions, the whole is greater than the sum of the parts—the use of technology, linguistics, advances in translation methods, increasing reliance on native-language speakers, and the Internet all augment each other's effectiveness. This in turn means that, over the last decades, a type of Christian witness to Muslims is possible and, in some places, a reality. This historically was not possible on a large scale.

This second category of factors relating to strategy is, like the list of influences, eclectic and broad. Insider Movements, Bible storying, and developments in translation and communications have all been discussed in some detail, but several other changes in strategies were mentioned by respondents, such as BAM (business as mission)[71] or CPMs (Church Planting Movements, Garrison 1999), and non-residential missionaries.[72] Translation as a missionary activity is not new, but in terms of range, speed, scope, and distribution there have been significant advances in the second half of

67. Ibid., 15.

68. Schmidt, *The Jesus Film*.

69. For an interesting description of how the *Jesus Film* is being used to evangelize Muslims in present-day rural Niger see Cooper, *Muslim Sahel*, 402ff.

70. According to the *Jesus Film* Project website, which updates the list on a regular basis: Online: http://www.jesusfilm.org/ film-and-media/statistics/languages-completed/.

71. Most of the February 2012 issue of *St Francis Magazine* (Volume 8:1) was devoted to BAM.

72. Garrison, *Nonresidential Missionary*.

the twentieth century. New missionary organizations and sodalities were formed, some with a view to engage in direct evangelism of Muslims. Evangelical mission to Muslims has become creative, diverse, entrepreneurial, and technology-focused.

In relation to power, we find that these shifts in strategy touch on all three dimensions of power, both in relation to empowering MBBs and those presenting Muslims with the Christian message, as well as compromising the power of those who seek to prevent this from happening. Advances in translation and non-written communication alert those who may previously not have been aware of another tradition or the possibility of converting to it. On the other hand, power is used in some Muslim states to keep foreign Christians who might be intent on evangelizing out of the country. This may be done by regulating entry visas, and it represents power in that the missionary is prevented from acting in his perceived interest in discussing Muslims' potential interest in following Christ. Business as mission (BAM) and non-residential mission (NRM) both represent ways of undermining this power hindering the Christian message.

Factors Related to Communications and Globalization

The factor most mentioned by respondents (fifteen of them) was media. One respondent indigenous to the Middle East wrote, "Modern technology became a facilitator of knowledge . . . media, satellites, and Christian programs targeting Moslem listeners are playing an important role in this increment of Moslems accepting the Good News as Light and Life granted by Christ the Lord." Another respondent mentioned the Internet:

> In a closed society, there is a limited amount of information that Muslims could get access to about Christ and rumors and pseudo facts about Christianity were (and still are) widely held (Bible has been changed, Christians worship 3 Gods). However, from the privacy of one's home or from the ease of a local internet café Muslims can search and try to find out for themselves whether it is true or not. Also, they can ask Google and not have to face the shame of asking a friend about their quest for truth.

The possibility of anonymity is worth noting. Muslims are aware of the very real dangers they might face in exploring the Christian religion, and being able to do so in relative privacy by watching a program on TV or reading the Bible online, rather than owning the physical book, disarms the power structures that traditionally made this taboo activity so dangerous.

Evidence supports the claim that outreach via media, especially satellite TV and the Internet, has dramatically increased throughout the Muslim world. For example, SAT 7, a well-respected Christian broadcaster, started broadcasting in Arabic in 1996, a children's channel in Arabic in 2007, Farsi in 2002 and Turkish in 2006.

One key development here is satellite television. At the time of the First Gulf War (August 1990 through February 1991) many households throughout the Middle East found that the only way they could get unbiased news was from international sources available via satellite TV and satellite dishes started to become more and more common:

> The era of satellite TV has changed (and continues to change) the politics, expectations and life styles of millions of people in the Arab world. The era began with the success of CNN during the first Gulf War in 1991, and sky-rocketed with the launch of another Arabic satellite channel in the same year as the launch of SAT-7, viz. the Qatar-based news channel Al Jazeera. Half of the population of the [Middle East] now has satellite TV at home (in some countries the figure is almost 100 percent). Satellite television is in most countries the only truly uncensored form of information or entertainment, and today more than 300 different Arabic-language satellite TV channels are broadcasting.[73]

Today throughout MENA they are ubiquitous. Jos Strengholt, an authority on Christian media in the Muslim world, commented on the developments after the First Gulf War:

> People began to realize the beauty of the dish on the roof that gave them direct access to world news without censorship. Now: 80% of homes have a dish, [there is] a massive TV industry for satellite now, including ten Arabic Christian stations broadcasting 24/7—Catholic, Coptic, Protestant . . . , TBN[74] . . . , etc. Since 1995 Miracle Channel and Sat7 [have been] broadcasting in Arabic. That was really the beginning of Christian TV in the Arab world.[75]

This proliferation of satellite channels is not isolated to the Arabic language alone, as Christian broadcasting in Turkish and Farsi also exists. Zakaria Boutros is an example of how successful such a ministry can be in terms of spreading the Christian message to a large number of people.

73. Schmidt, "Ecumenical Miracle," 290.

74. Trinity Broadcasting Network, a Pentecostal broadcaster based in California.

75. Interview, October 2008.

Most evangelistic channels have contacts within the Muslim countries that can then meet with the enquirers or new believers and perhaps incorporate them into an existing fellowship. One missionary told me that sometimes Muslims would start watching normal programming, like about how to discipline children or treat one's spouse, and find the material so interesting they would become regular viewers of a given channel. In other words, programming that was not intended to be evangelistic and was designed for a Christian audience on occasion resulted in or contributed to religious conversion.

According to my respondents, the growth in the variety and accessibility of media, especially Internet and satellite, has been the single most important FFC. These developments in media imply that a freer flow of ideas has made the Christian message available to individuals who previously would not have heard it. Previously, the Muslim in a large or cosmopolitan city might have access to Christians and perhaps even Christian literature, assuming they could read. But access to the Christian message was often restricted by the segregation of Christians from the Muslim population, punishments for apostasy, and the ability of authorities to destroy Christian material, prevent its dissemination or criminalize possession. The development of media that cannot be easily controlled or limited has compromised those coercive and successful manifestations of power. Lukes's third dimension of power—that of not even allowing a group to be aware of an option that could be in its interest—has also been severely eroded. Any illiterate Muslim in a small village can watch a program about Jesus on the television and evaluate for herself whether it is in her interest to follow this man Jesus.

According to the respondents, while developments in media mean that the Christian message is available to people who previously did not have access to it, there has also been a significant increase in migration of Muslims to non-Muslim countries, who then have access to the message. Nine of the respondents listed living abroad / migration as a factor facilitating conversion. "Muslims are experiencing first-hand life in societies in which Christian thought is widespread," wrote one Western minister with experience in the Middle East and East Africa. One minister indigenous to the Middle East listed various sorts of migrants, explicitly tying migration to globalization: "Globalization and the interaction of cultures due to travel, immigration [to non-Muslim countries], refugees, and international students." Another minister indigenous to the Middle East emphasized the role of economic factors in emigration, pointing to the increasing "number of Moslems who departed the region, looking for better conditions of life in the West, where they become, through their daily experience, exposed to Christian values and Christian education."

The respondents have the conviction that once out of the Muslim world Muslim migrants can "experience first-hand life" there, as one wrote, and evaluate it for themselves. Whereas before they had probably heard of the evils of the West and the sexual immorality prevalent there, either from local imams or Hollywood, after migrating they are in a position to come to their own conclusion regarding the value or lack of value of various metanarratives other than that of Islam, one of those metanarratives being that of the Christian faith. One of the respondents emphasized the role of friendship rather than coordinated evangelistic events, listing as a factor facilitating conversion "Christian friends." While having Christian friends may indeed be possible in some parts of the Muslim world, it is much more likely to occur outside of the Muslim world.

It is difficult to find precise figures for how many Muslims migrate to Christian countries every year because most countries, especially Western states, do not keep a record of the religion of people immigrating to their countries. Furthermore, nationality is not always an indicator of religion, as it may well be the case that religious minorities are emigrating in larger number proportionate to their percentage of the indigenous population of a country. Examples of this are Christians emigrating from Egypt, Palestine, Lebanon, Syria and Iraq.[76] Numbers of Muslim migrants are also politically sensitive, like the numbers of converts from Islam to Christianity. Some groups overstate the immigration numbers to stir up fear among non-Muslims, or even among Muslims of a different ethnicity. Figures could be overstated also to accrue greater political power to one or another Islamic society or organization: "Based on these large numbers of Muslim immigrants, it is clear our funding should be increased . . . " Similarly the figures might be minimized by some groups in an effort to stymie the tightening of immigration laws. A non-Muslim political group might want to do the same thing for similar reasons, to show the non-Muslim population that there is really nothing to worry about and there is no need for migration reform, thus courting the votes of groups who support such a stance. In any case, even after contacting the Migration Policy Institute in Washington DC, I was not able to find reliable, precise figures on how many Muslims immigrated to the countries of the West and other countries with greater religious freedom each year over the last half of the century.

According to the *World Factbook*,[77] many Muslim-majority countries have net out-migration, including that of their non-Muslims minorities.

76. Belt, "Forgotten Faithful."

77. Online: https://www.cia.gov/library/publications/the-world-factbook/. According to 2011–2012 figures, the ten most populous Muslim countries (85 percent Muslim or more) in the world are, in order, Indonesia, Pakistan, Bangladesh, Egypt,

According to my respondents, Muslim emigration of all kinds—from students to entrepreneurs to refugees—has increased significantly in the last half of the twentieth century. There are also figures like this, from the well-respected Pew Forum: "The number of Muslims in Europe has grown from 29.6 million in 1990 to 44.1 million in 2010. Europe's Muslim population is expected to exceed 58 million by 2030."[78] The source for this figure is considered by most to be reliable and apolitical, but the figure does not tell us how many of these are Muslims immigrants, or even children of immigrants. Some communities in Albania and Bosnia, for instance, have been both European and Muslim for at least two centuries. From this same source we do have helpful estimates about the number of Muslims immigrating to various European countries, but only for 2010. Without several other years of data for comparison it is not possible to identify with certainty a trend of increasing Muslim immigration.

Regarding Europe and North America it is clear that the Muslim population is growing both as a percentage of the population in most countries, and also in sheer numbers. The precise relationship of this to immigration is not possible to identify at the moment. Nonetheless, it seems impossible to account for these two measurements of growth without it being to some extent due to immigration. Here are some figures for major European countries, from the same Pew Forum report cited above, including projections out to 2030:

Country	1990	2000	2010	2020	2030
France	568,000 (1% of population)	1,401,000 (2.4%)	3,574,000 (5.7%)	4,613,000 (7.1%)	5,620,000 (8.5%)
UK	1,172,000 (2.1%)	1,590,000 (2.7%)	2,869,000 (4.6%)	4,231,000 (6.5%)	5,567,000 (8.2%)
Germany	2,506,000 (3.2%)	3,648,000 (4.5%)	4,119,000 (5.0%)	4,878,000 (6.1%)	5,545,000 (7.1%)
Spain	271,000 (.7%)	419,000 (1.0%)	1,021,000 (2.3%)	1,585,000 (3.3%)	1,859,000 (3.7%)
Sweden	147,000 (1.7%)	226,000 (2.6%)	451,000 (4.9%)	730,000 (7.5%)	993,000 (9.9%)
Italy	858,000 (1.5%)	1,267,000 (2.2%)	1,583,000 (2.6%)	2,425,000 (4.0%)	3,199,000 (5.4%)

Iran, Turkey, Algeria, Morocco, Iraq, Sudan, and Afghanistan. Turkey is the only one receiving more migrants than sending. Iraq is at 0. All other countries have a net out-migration, from 11 persons per thousand (Iran) to 4.52 per thousand (Sudan).

78. Pew Forum, "The Future of the Global Muslim Population."

Insofar as the Pew figures are reliable,[79] this means that from 1990 through 2030 the Muslim population of France will have increased by 989 percent, the UK by 475 percent, Germany by 221 percent, Spain by 686 percent, Sweden by 675 percent, and Italy by 373 percent. Without substantial continued immigration it is impossible to account for such figures.

The same Pew report gave the following figures for the USA and Canada:

Country	1990	2000	2010	2020	2030
Canada	313,000 (1.1%)	600,000 (2.0%)	940,000 (2.8%)	1,854,000 (5.0%)	2,661,000 (6.6%)
USA	1,529,000 (.6%)	1,727,000 (.6%)	2,595,000 (.8%)	4,150,000 (1.2%)	6,216,000 (1.7%)

According to the Pew figures, this means that from 1990 to 2030 the Muslim population of the USA will have increased by 406 percent, and that of Canada by 850 percent.

It is not possible to account for such a growth in the Muslim population of these countries merely through natural growth and conversion to Islam. Moreover, the factors listed by my respondents—education, economic hardship, political persecution—show no signs of changing at the moment. While the so-called Arab Spring held out the hope for greater human rights those promises have, to date, not yet been realized, and in some countries the human rights situation has actually become worse, especially for women[80] and Christians.[81] All indicators point to continued migration from Muslim countries to countries with a Christian heritage and some greater degree of freedom of religion.

The Pew information indirectly supports the claim of my respondents that migration from Muslim countries to non-Muslim countries (and specifically countries with a Christian heritage and freedom of conversion) has

79. One could argue that the Pew figures are in fact overly conservative. That is, they do not take into account new factors leading to emigration like the reality or likelihood of civil wars in countries like Afghanistan, Egypt, Libya, Pakistan, Somalia, Syria and Yemen, and the inability for countries to provide food and water for their populations in countries like Afghanistan, Egypt, Iraq, Pakistan, Somalia and Yemen. While birth rates are fairly low in some Muslim-majority countries (Iran, Tunisia), in many populous countries the birth rates are only declining slowly (Yemen, Egypt), while infant mortality is also declining. If dire climate change predictions come to pass, then increasing violence over already-scarce resources (especially water) will likely ensue. The result will be a number of asylum seekers and refugees, potentially much higher than anything produced by the wars in Iraq or Afghanistan.

80. Eltahawy, "War on Women."

81. Traub, "Exodus."

increased. Muslims in these new contexts are much more likely to enter into what Lewis Rambo calls "encounter," recalling his model as summarized in chapter 2. The respondents to my questionnaire did not use this technical word, but they did describe encounters that "are exposing Muslims to ideas and facts that challenge Islamic assumptions and the tribal systems that perpetuate them." In other words, such a setting also makes the quest and consequences phases of conversion less dangerous.

This increased likelihood of encounter is also possible due to the revolution in communications. The religious and cultural traditions that segregated Christians, Christian ideas, and Christian liturgy from Muslims have in many cases declined in terms of their efficacy. The "flattening" of the world, to use the phrase of Thomas Friedman,[82] in terms of travel/migration and communications are both integral aspects of globalization. Khalil and Bilici, in their 2007 study of why Muslims leave Islam, either for Christianity or no religion at all, confirm that globalization is a set of factors that enable apostasy:

> The process of globalization and digitization of the media seems to have created unprecedented spaces for both conversion and the mass communication of narratives of conversion . . . Testimonies of conversion to and from Islam continue to proliferate in the new public sphere of the Internet, where both anonymity and publicity can be easily found. New spaces like websites and the larger process of globalization have also undermined the conventional hold of religions on their adherents. In this new environment, religions seek to expand their discursive reach.[83]

In conclusion, globalization constitutes a third category of factors facilitating conversion. Within the larger scope of globalization I have specifically discussed two factors raised by my respondents—communications and migration. In their experiences these factors have made a number of conversions possible. Other available sources of information, like the conversion narratives of CMBs and the study by Khalil and Bilici, appear to corroborate the statements of my respondents. Those seeking to deliver the Christian message, and those who wish to explore it, are empowered by these developments, just as those seeking to limit its dissemination have seen their power to do so reduced.

82. Friedman, *The World is Flat.*
83. Khalil and Bilici, "Conversion out of Islam," 121.

CONCLUSION

This chapter started with an explanation of why gathering numerical information about MBBs is so difficult. With that caveat I supplied a list of what appear to be the most reliable approximations available. Then, the two central research questions of this chapter were presented, and the methodology for answering those questions explained. The first question sought to understand the shifts in how missionaries and ministers in Muslim contexts were being influenced in their understanding of Christian witness to Muslims. Based on the answers of my respondents several implications were presented, among them that the conversation is multi-faceted and not dominated by any one evangelistic strategy, but that it appears clear that the Great Experiment had largely vanished from the conversation.[84] The second question sought to identify factors in the changing context of the second half of the twentieth century that helped to create an environment wherein increasing numbers of Muslims could make a commitment to follow Jesus as he is described in the Gospels. Based on the information provided by the respondents, three broad categories of factors facilitating conversion were presented. Some specific examples within those categories were described: Factors related to prayer, God's timing, miracles, dreams, and visions; churches and Christians are praying more for the conversion of Muslims; churches and Christians having more knowledge about how to pray; an increase in short-term prayer missions; an increase in (known) dreams and visions; God's sovereign/ineffable will; better strategies and methods of Christian witness; Insider Movements; Bible-storying; an increase in non-textual communication; advances in translation; tent-making strategies, or Business as Mission (BAM); non-residential missionaries (sometimes called Strategy Coordinators); factors related to globalization; Internet; satellite TV; and migration.

Any of these factors might facilitate conversion on its own, but there appears to be a real synergy between them such that the whole is greater than the sum of its parts. The *More than Dreams* videos mentioned above, for example, actually related to all three categories. They are movies about dreams and thus related the transcendental category, but they are available for free on the Internet, linking them to communications in terms of distribution. Finally, they are part of a specific evangelistic strategy—to use well-produced, engaging films in local dialects to show how one conversion happened, and then to invite the Muslim viewer to consider religious

---

84. Which is not to say that Protestant and evangelical missionaries do not ever work with the ancient churches, but rather that when they do, the specific goal is not to "reform" them so that they will then evangelize Muslims.

conversion. Similar parallels could be drawn regarding the Bible itself, now translated into local dialects or audio media, and distributed much more affordably by the Internet or email, though probably still available in printed form. Or regarding prayer: communication advances mean that urgent, specific prayer needs can be distributed quickly to a large number of people, and developments in transportation have made it possible for groups of people to travel to a Muslim city or country to pray there. The production of specific, detailed, up-to-date prayer resources is also part of a larger research project which seeks to communicate the Christian message more accurately to the peoples of the world. So again here we have the intersection of strategy, transcendence, and globalization—with one factor augmenting the impact of another.

The research question of this work is about ex-Muslim Christians. Above I argued that prior to the twentieth century coordinated, well-staffed, sustained evangelistic missions *to* Muslims were rare. And where they existed, the use of power was often successful in stopping them. This chapter proposes that the Great Experiment has been replaced by an eclectic array of methods and strategies, many of them which emphasize the agency of local Christians, where they exist. Estimates of where MBBs live were provided. Then, based on a questionnaire, I provided a summary of the voices that have influenced the concept of Christian witness to Muslims, and the changing factors in the world that have helped to create an environment wherein known conversions from Islam to Christ have increased.

The reality of people from a Muslim background who have decided to follow Christ as he is portrayed in the Bible (MBBs) has been established, many of whom understand themselves to have left Islam and embraced Christianity (CMBs). With this background in place, and with the goal of better understanding the context within these people might go about making theologies—that is, the process of organic contextualization—let us now turn from the global to the local with a case-study from the Arabophone world of how a community of CMBs came into being.

4

Context and the Birth of a Muslim-Background Congregation in the Arab World

INTRODUCTION

The previous chapter presented a large-scale picture of some factors that have contributed to significant numbers of people opting for faith in Christ as he is portrayed in the Gospels. This chapter is a case study from the Middle East of Arabophone evangelicals who, working with a few non-indigenous Christians, founded a church consisting almost entirely of ex-Muslim Christians. Due to security reasons the names of places and people have been changed. Beyond the fact that Juduur and Kitma formerly came under the aegis of the Ottoman Empire, nothing else will be said.

In this chapter I will provide background regarding the people and places that were studied, examine the context regarding persecution and then summarize how the church in Kitma was founded. Issues related to power, empowerment and identity-formation will then be explored. At the end of the chapter we will return to reflect on the central research question of this book—theology-making.

THE CONTEXT AND BIRTH OF A CHURCH

In this lengthy section I will present the context within which these events have taken place, describe the main people in the narrative, and then give an account of how the congregations in Kitma came into being. The purpose of this section is principally descriptive.

The Setting: Juduur and Kitma

As discussed in chapter 1, during this research I conducted interviews in English and Arabic and met with lay people, lay leaders, and ordained leaders, both local and foreign. I also was able to observe first-hand the life of the community in contexts like prayer meetings, the weekly worship service, and evangelistic activities. Juduur is a fairly large city with a good number of non-locals and a small indigenous Christian community which had, in the past, been much larger. Through various factors, especially emigration and a relatively small family size, the Christian community has become a small minority while the non-Christian population has increased significantly. Nonetheless, the city has churches from many different traditions, including evangelical, although the number of indigenous Christians continues to dwindle. More than one evangelical leader told me that, "If we don't reach out to the Muslims then Christianity here is over." On the other hand, very few of the churches, including evangelical ones, are actually actively engaged in Muslim evangelism.[1]

Originally I had hoped to research the Muslim-background congregation (MBC) in Kitma, but it soon became clear to me that while I could meet with people at the Juduur Church, accompany that church's full-time evangelist in his activities, attend their church meetings, and do interviews with any of the church members or leaders I pleased, the church in Kitma was closed to me, though I did interviews with all of the lay pastors of that congregation. Because of these limitations, due in large part to the security of the MBC in Kitma, I had to decide whether I should abandon research on the believers at Kitma or redirect my research. In keeping with the research question of this dissertation I wanted to discern if these new believers were engaged in the activity of theology-making, and if so, what questions were they asking, how were they engaging in Coe's "double-wrestle," and what sort of answers they were proposing and then testing out in daily life. As it became clear that spending ample time with the MBBs in Kitma was not viable, but that the life, history and praxis of the Juduur congregation, which had given birth to the Kitma church, was wide open to me, I resolved to focus on a different question, but one that is nonetheless related to the central research question of this work. In the Juduur church I had a rare example of an indigenous community that had planted a MBC. I was able to interview people who had taken part in that process, and compare their experience with the factors just mentioned in chapter 3. This chapter will utilize Lukes's

---

1. For an example of a church in the Middle East which is faced with emigration of Christians and a policy of not evangelizing Muslims and also of not proselytizing other Christians, see Miller, "Episcopal Church in Jordan," 134–53.

theory of power to examine that process of starting and ministering to an MBC and ask if it is possible to discern if theology-making is taking place in that context.

The Agents

The history outlined here is by necessity piecemeal and based on the many interviews I conducted over my multiple visits to Juduur. The main sources of information were:

Andraus: When I started my research Andraus was the pastor of the church in Juduur, and on a board of leaders that coordinates ministry of the small denomination for the entire region. He is a seminary-trained, ordained pastor. He is still involved in the life of the church in Juduur and the denominational leadership, but is now more focused on ministry within the context of higher education, church-planting, and training leaders. He served as the pastor of the church in Juduur for about ten years. He and his family are first-generation evangelical Christians; he was born into one of the traditional churches. Andraus was the first person I met and, along with Matthias, acted as a gatekeeper—introducing me to many of the other people associated with this community. He is deeply familiar with the activities in Juduur, Aunf and Kitma.

Matthias: Matthias is a veteran missionary from North America who has served in the Middle East for several decades. He was serving as a missionary in Juduur at the time when Andraus and other people mentioned here experienced the religious conversion that is so central to much of evangelical Christianity. While he never served as the pastor of the church in Juduur, he has been involved in its life for decades, and is also on the same regional leadership board as Andraus. Married to Lara, he is nearing retirement.

Iskander is a lay leader in the Juduur church. At the time when this research started the Kitma church was led by a board of three lay pastors, one of them being Iskander. He is a first generation evangelical like most of the indigenous leaders. He owns his own business where he works full time. In the context of the ministry in Kitma, Iskander devotes himself mostly to preaching and teaching.

Atallah: Like Iskander, he is a lay pastor for the Kitma church. He also has his own business and is a first-generation evangelical Christian, his family belonging to one of the traditional churches. Atallah is gifted in forming relationships and personal evangelism. He is also married with children.

Ayya: The third of the lay pastors of the church in Kitma, and the only one of the leaders who is a convert from Islam. Unlike Iskander and Atallah, Ayya works full time for an evangelical ministry that raises funds from abroad to support indigenous evangelists. She came to faith over a decade ago. In her early 20s she started to investigate the status of women in Islam and mentioned explicitly the Qur'anic sanction to hit women,[2] mut3a marriage,[3] and polygamy (Rambo's crisis and quest). This caused her to cease wishing to be a Muslim or worship God as she knew him in Islam. After college she was working and one of her colleagues was an evangelical Christian (Rambo's encounter/advocate) who spoke to her of God's love and Jesus, and was able to answer her Islamic objections to Christianity (such as the Bible is corrupted). The idea of a loving God did not make sense to her, but it piqued her curiosity. She procured a Bible (part of her quest phase) from him and describes a turning point when she read the Sermon on the Mount (Mt 5–7), and wondered how the teaching of Muhammad, which came later on, could be inferior to this teaching of Jesus which deeply impressed her (a second crisis—the first causing her to move *away* from Islam,[4] and this one being *towards* Christianity). As she continued to read the Bible (interaction) she came to the conclusion that she must make a choice between Jesus and Muhammad, the Bible and the Qur'an, and that their messages and personalities were mutually exclusive. Upon her conversion (Rambo's commitment) her family turned her out and a local charismatic church accepted her (Rambo's consequences), but they didn't have any experience dealing with ex-Muslim converts, and thus were ill-prepared to assist during this difficult time of her life. Eventually she moved to Juduur and felt a vocation to full-time ministry. She is married to an ex-Muslim Christian from another Arab country. Her parents, who are secular Muslims, attended her wedding.

2. "Men have authority over women because God has made the one superior to the other, and because they spend their wealth to maintain them. Good women are obedient. They guard their unseen parts because God has guarded them. As for those from whom you fear disobedience, admonish them and send them to beds apart and beat them. Then if they obey you, take no further action against them. Surely God is high, supreme" (Qur'an 4:34, Dawood translation). Dawood translates *udrubuuhunna* as "beat them," as do Arberry and Shakir; Rodwell and Pickthall have "scourge them."

3. A contractual marriage lasting only a limited time, even an hour or two, during which sexual activity is permitted and the woman receives a dowry: proponents base their claims on Qur'an 4:24. Critics claim that it easily leads to sanctified prostitution with the "dowry" taking the place of payment.

4. Recall from chapter 2 that Gaudeul, *Called from Islam*, explicitly mentioned disappointment with Islam as a recurring theme in the conversion process from Islam to Christ. Woodberry, Shubin and Marks, "Why Muslims follow Jesus," and Abu Daoud, "Apostates," mention this factor as well.

Khalil: Another lay person from the church in Juduur, he is a full-time evangelist and focuses on Muslim evangelism both in Juduur and surrounding cities. He is also a first-generation evangelical. His ministry is supported by Christians, both local and foreign, and accountability is provided by some people from local churches.

The church in Kitma: Kitma is not one town, but a geographical region. Originally this was a Muslim-background congregation led by three lay elders (Atallah, Iskander, and Ayya). In late 2011 the decision was made to stop meeting together as one church and rather meet as small cell churches. Rather than the larger, unified congregation, the cell church model refers to "a small group of Christians in any given locality who meet, usually in private homes, for prayer, Bible study, and fellowship . . . ."[5] Both baptism and the Lord's Supper are part of the life of the church in Kitma (now the cell churches in Kitma).

I met many other people involved in the life and leadership of the churches in the area, and interviewed some of them, including people not directly involved with leadership. This was not easy since, as Matthias pointed out repeatedly, they try to emphasize the role of the laity in the life of the church, so almost every time I met a person they seemed to have some role or other in the ministry of the church. Having outlined some basic aspects of the people involved, it is now appropriate to present a historical synopsis of how the Kitma church(es) came into being.

The Danger: Persecution, Power, and John, a New Believer

In the previous chapters we have seen that there is a strong tradition in Islam endorsing the use of power to reverse apostasy or to eliminate the apostate, either by killing them or causing them to leave their homeland. Based on the conclusions in the previous chapter, however, it appears that the use of this coercive power has become less effective in some cases. In order to understand the context of the MBC in Kitma, it is necessary to examine the interplay of power and conversion there.

The Christians who come from Christian families who are ministering to Muslims in this chapter understand that their safety may be at risk. It is possible, if not likely, that ex-Muslim Christians who have formed the MBC will sooner or later face persecution from the government, and it is likely, if not certain, that they will face pressure, ostracism, and even violence from their families and neighbors. One time while staying at a guesthouse which was, unbeknownst to me, next to a safe house for converts from Islam, I

---

5. "Cell," in Douglas, *International Dictionary*, 206.

got to meet one of the local CMBs. Though he did not attend (or know about) the MBC discussed here, his story serves as a good example for the sort of difficulties and dangers faced by converts in the region. Following is a summary of my lengthy interview with "John" the night I met him at the safe-house, along with information from follow-up phone conversations and meetings:

> John was from an influential Muslim family known for its ties to Islamism. He enjoyed reading and first became curious about Jesus after reading an Arabic-language translation of Dan Brown's *The Da Vinci Code*. He also read *Holy Blood, Holy Grail* in Arabic during this time.[6] At this time (Rambo's stage of "crisis") he was either in his late teens or early twenties. Living in a heavily Muslim city with only a few hundred Christians, he spoke with one of the only Christians he knew, a Latin (Roman Catholic) dentist, who made a positive impact on him. He asked his dentist neighbor many questions about the Knights Templar, the Masons, and so on. (This seems to be the commencement of his "quest" in Rambo's model.) He also directed these questions to an evangelical European friend (Rambo's "advocate"?) who gave him a Bible, a book which he had been looking for "for a long time." This friend said, "I don't know about your questions, but I know about what is in here." John read the Bible cover to cover many times after that. He said at first he viewed the material as enjoyable and interesting fables, but eventually his viewpoint changed and he decided he wanted to be a Christian and get baptized. He started going to the Latin church where the dentist went. The first time he entered with a large pile of books and the priest told him to leave because they were praying: he felt deflated but was then informed that the priest thought he was a book-seller.
>
> Eventually, John informed the priest that he wanted to be baptized (an expression of his desire for Rambo's phase of commitment, though rebuffed), and the priest told him he needed training first and gave him some books to read, which John did. Then the priest informed him that only his bishop (who lived in Juduur) could do the baptism.[7] The priest eventually told

6. The original is by Baigent, Leigh, and Lincoln (Dell, 1983).

7. It should be noted here that the priest was quite right to be concerned about security issues. If he had baptized John and the word got out, it is not unlikely that Christian homes, churches or shops would be vandalized (Ajaj, "Baptism," 596–611). Recall the comment by Catholic bishop Paul Hinder from chapter 2: "we would not dare accept a Muslim's conversion to Christianity. It would just be too dangerous . . ." (quoted in Caffulli, "Catacomb Church," 1).

him that it was God's will for him to stay a Muslim, and that he would call the police if John ever came to the church again. He did however give him the phone number for a Byzantine-rite priest in town. That priest told him he could come to the liturgy and gave him a key to the church so he could pray alone, but said that he could not baptize him (more interaction, but again commitment is denied). One evening John was on the phone with the Latin priest and, unbeknownst to him, his mother was listening on the other line. Until this point his Christian faith was unknown to his parents. An explosive argument with them followed, including a physical scuffle, and he decided that he must leave the city and go to Juduur to demand baptism of the Latin bishop himself. He collected his pay from his work and met with his European friend who gave him the phone number of a Pentecostal pastor in a town on the way to Juduur. He got on the bus and left for Aunf, where the pastor lived. He met with the pastor, and as it was late he rented a room at a local hotel for John. This pastor (whom I later interviewed) had experience ministering to Muslim enquirers, and rather than sending him to the Latin bishop (who almost certainly would have also re-fused to baptize him), sent him to the safe-house where I met him.

Eventually John moved to Aunf and was taken care of by the Pentecostal pastor and was baptized (the ritual embodying and finalizing Rambo's commitment phase), but he lost his job at a grocery store when the owner learned he was a convert from Islam, rather than a Christian from a Christian family (Rambo's consequences). During this time, I called him during a trip to Juduur, and he told me he was having the first meeting with his mother since he had left, and asked me if I would come to this meeting, which after making sure it was safe, I did. During this meeting John's mother kept on inventing ways to refuse the reality of his conversion—he was psychologically unbalanced, for instance, or that he was a young, impetuous man just going through a temporary phase. It seemed incomprehensible to her that a right-thinking human being would ever leave Islam for Christianity.

John was later arrested and put in jail and given a blank sheet of paper to sign as a "confession," which he did. According to him, while in jail he was able to evangelize a number of the pris-oners, though there is no way to confirm this. He was released to his father's house and told he had to stay near his father's home. Eventually some relatives told him that other relatives were planning to kill him, so he fled to another country in the

Middle East, and then to North America where he studied at a charismatic Bible college and is applying for asylum while serving at a local church. He is now in his mid-20s and talks with his family by phone from time to time.

John was largely on his own, though his relationship with the European evangelical seems to have been important, in that he got him a Bible and referred him to the pastor in Aunf. The CMBs in the region of Kitma have mature and experienced pastoral care and direction, but John's experience is nonetheless informative, and the persecution he experienced is not uncommon in Kitma.

The church in Juduur is not very large in terms of membership, but it has been there for decades. It is the product of American evangelical missionary activity and most of its members came from traditional Orthodox or Catholic Churches. Arabic is the main language of the churches and homes, with English used with some missionaries and for some business purposes.

The Church in Juduur

The denominational presence in the Juduur region goes back over a century. Matthias and Lara arrived in the Middle East in the late seventies, and in Juduur in the mid-eighties. He has served as a missionary the entire time. When asked to describe the situation when he arrived he explained that there was no vision among the local Christians for Muslim outreach, and that he had been explicitly forbidden by his pastor to have anything to do with Muslims. Part of the motive for this was fear that the government would stop granting visas to clergy from this church if they engaged in Muslim evangelism, which is not an unfounded concern. According to him, during this time the idea of gathering young adults and church youth together for fellowship, worship and learning was very new for the local churches, and he considers this as a breakthrough for the evangelical churches in the country. He also describes the situation faced by young men who seemed to have a vocation to Christian ministry. The indigenous pastor had told them, "we have no more churches, there is nothing for you to do." Matthias then fasted for three weeks "for the church, revival, renewal," and he sees this as the occasion for another breakthrough, because the indigenous pastor then decided to train these young men to be leaders.

In the mid-eighties he and his family were reassigned to Juduur. He had hoped it would be a temporary assignment as he wanted to minister in a specific city in the Middle East in a different region, but told God, "If you do something within two years, we'll stay." Most of the 30 years prior to Matthias's arrival the church had been without an ordained pastor, being led by lay elders. Attendance was down to single digits and some people thought it would simply die out, as most attending were elderly. A refugee from a neighboring country was a zealous evangelist who lived in the church, bringing in new believers and making the church available for people at any time. A well-known Christian apologist was invited to speak, and "the church was full every night." Lara started praying that God would give them five new male believers. Matthias recalls, "I didn't think this was realistic, but eventually I started praying with her, and it happened, five men got saved." Andraus came to faith in the early nineties.

The church started to grow and according to Matthias, "the problem was leadership." In that denomination there is a tradition emphasizing empowering, training and investing in laity—indeed, the theme resurfaced often in interviews with foreigners and locals alike. So Lara and Matthias devised a strategy both to recruit new members for the church and quickly empower them and develop them into capable leaders. The three aspects of the plan were as follows: 1) Everything the church did would be evangelistic, meaning aimed at making new converts, including children's meetings and the ladies' group. 2) Anyone who came to faith would be trained for leadership. "We did some stupid things, but people were empowered," he commented. 3) Every leader trained would be trained in and told to engage in Muslim evangelism.

They prayed for leaders and in 1991 the church found a pastor named "Bilal," also from the Arab world, from the country where Matthias and Lara had spent their first years as missionaries. By the late nineties Andraus had completed seminary in the Philippines and had returned to serve as the pastor of the Juduur church. He held that position from about 1997 through 2011. During one of our interviews he mentioned that his time in the Philippines was important in helping him to realize the "possibilities" of ministry to Muslims.[8] In coordinating and funding the seminary training of Andraus this denomination showed its commitment to leadership development. An experienced pastor and educator from another evangelical denomination reflected on this difference and recalled how during his earlier years he was working with university students and desired ministry training, yet his denomination, considerably larger and wealthier than Andraus's, never even mentioned the possibility. Eventually he paid his own way through a local religious college, and had to wait decades before being able to complete a

---

8. The Philippines' population is about 5 percent Muslim, many of them in the Mindanao region.

master's degree in theology through a European institution, all of this with little help and no initiative from his own denomination.

The strategy seems to have been successful, in that the church went from a handful of elderly people in the eighties to dozens of indigenous adult members today—including the leaders mentioned above, all of whom became evangelical Christians through the ministry of the Juduur church (in part, at least) during this time. The church did experience a number of departures at one point, and some of the families left to form another evangelical church in Juduur which is still meeting today, although the precise reasons are unclear. When I asked Iskander about why his church was engaged in Muslim evangelism and the others were not, he responded, "When Matthias and Lara came [in the mid-eighties] they were really passionate about this and people were laughing at them," implying that at least some of the leaders formed during this time adopted the intended outlook on Muslim evangelism. Iskander then comments that today "Many leaders know that if Muslims don't come to faith . . . the church [here] will go extinct."

The Birth of the Church in Kitma

Around the year 2000 two important projects were started by the Juduur church. The first was a partnership with an international NGO whereby Bilal, who had essential technical training which enabled him to do this work, was able to lead a team to engage in some infrastructure improvements and repairs in the region of Kitma, which is almost entirely Muslim and much poorer than Juduur. This created relationships with the Muslim people of the area. The second was that during a period of political, social, and economic turmoil, the already difficult circumstances of the villages in the Kitma region became devastating. Pastor Andraus and his wife went to visit some villages to see about distributing aid. They intended to avoid two errors: the first corruption, as UN money given to the government allegedly largely vanishes into the bank accounts of the politicians and the second bias by only distributing aid to Christian families. This last is pragmatic as their numbers are so few that it does not make a big enough impact. Leaders from the Juduur church would visit village elders and ask them for the names of local poor families, and then they would go to visit those families to verify that they were poor. They believed that the elders would give them the names of poor families but also the names of their relatives, even if they were not poor. Having verified that the families were indeed poor they would assist them with food or food coupons. As the difficult economic and political situation showed no signs of improvement, a Christian NGO and other local churches started to support this effort. Laity from the church went out to the villages periodically to distribute the aid. With foreign funding the relief effort was able to hire a couple of employees. Pastor Andraus started devoting more time to fundraising, while Atallah started doing more of the actual distribution.

Not a single interviewee explained these efforts as being directed towards church planting. One person said that the groups would go out "with their antennas up." In an interview with Andraus and Atallah they mentioned the "person of peace" concept that was mentioned in chapter 3.[9] In spite of these two comments it seems clear that nobody had conceived that an actual MBC would be born of the relief effort. Being on the lookout for the chance to have a conversation about Jesus or the Bible (having one's "antenna up") is a relatively common aspect of evangelical piety; it is not, however, a comprehensive strategy for planting a new church. Seeking a person of peace—someone who can introduce the Christian to the wider community—is a strategy for forming relationships and gaining a hearing in a community. That may be an important step *towards* evangelism, but it is a preliminary one at that, and cannot be considered a coherent church-planting strategy. The *intention* was to help people in need, and in doing so share their experience of the love of God which they had found in Jesus, that this resulted in the founding of a church appears to have been a surprise to all involved.

As the relief work continued the families in the villages eventually got to know the Christians from Juduur and as one participant put it, started asking questions like, "We're Muslims, we'd never help you with food, why are you helping us?" The Christians offered to study the Bible with them and so explain their charity to non-Christians. In some cases entire families accepted the invitation to study Scripture. In other cases just one person from a household accepted, but *with the permission of the patriarch or matriarch* who knew and trusted the Christians. This is important because it meant that studying the Bible would probably not be considered deviant or dangerous activity by the head of the family. People came to faith in Christ, sometimes as individuals but sometimes as several people from one family.

---

9. In missiology a "person of peace" refers to a local who is open to the Christian message and will introduce the missionary/evangelist to other locals, including family members. The woman at the well in John 4 is such a person. The phrase originates with Jesus in Luke 10:6. The context is his instructions to a large group of his disciples regarding their impending evangelistic mission. They were sent out two-by-two and told to rely on the hospitality of people in villages and towns. People who extended hospitality to the disciples were the "persons of peace." The practice is recommended in the *Camel Training Manual* and also in Patterson and Scoggins, *Church Multiplication*.

Ayya recalls the first time they gathered together the Kitma believers in one place; it was for an Easter meal. As an ex-Muslim herself she explains that holy days may be some of the most difficult times of the year. During the Christian holy days one may well be alone, as one's fellow Christians are with their (Christian) families. During the Muslim holy days, one must try to discern to what extent they can participate in family events and meals which clearly have an Islamic origin and meaning. This is a complex question relating to identity: how should the believer act so as not to violate his own sense of new identity, while also preserving his relationship with his family and friends? In an effort to help these believers to navigate this difficult time, it was decided that there should be an Easter meal, and there were about 30 people present. At one point they were asked to say their names by way of introduction, and she recalls that she thought people would just share their first names (which would probably not pose any risk to their security), but they started saying their full names and what town or village in Kitma they were from, and how they had come to faith in Christ.[10] This meeting was the first meeting of all the Kitma believers, and afterwards some requested to continue meeting as a large group which they did. "In [one city in Kitma], after five years, we had seven believers. We saw entire families coming to faith. In 2005, *they* said, why can't we have our own church?" recalls Matthias. The lay elders requested recognition from the denomination, and after some time to meet the denomination's requirements, the Kitma church was recognized as an official congregation of the denomination under the leadership of three lay elders, who were (and are) under the supervision of the regional leadership board. Receiving legal recognition from the government is not an option, and the denomination was making a daring move by recognizing this church as a member congregation.

There were at least three other factors that contributed new believers to the Kitma community since its formation. First, according to Andraus, by simply being a Christian presence in Kitma, which is almost entirely Muslim, they started to meet people who had been interested in the Christian message for some time and secret Christians. These people had come to faith independently of the work of the Juduur Christians but, having no way to discern who were fellow believers, and no local church in their area that could or would welcome them, they kept their faith to themselves. Second, people were added to the Kitma community through collaboration with Christian media. With evangelistic satellite programs and websites there is often a way to contact the ministry in charge, who then try to form

10. Kraft, who researched MBBs in Lebanon and Egypt, points out that there is "a strong desire among members of disadvantaged groups to be a part of a group, but a group that distinguishes itself from others" (*Faith Is Lived*, 958).

relationships with local ministries so that they can connect a new believer or enquirer with someone who can then provide instruction, baptism, and, where it exists, an introduction to a local congregation. Third, new believers have been added via the evangelistic "booth witness" ministry of Khalil. (Note how all of these overlap with the factors facilitating conversion from the previous chapter.)

The order of worship at the church services was conventional—a time of fellowship, an extended period of "Friday School" on topics like "theology of God" or "the nearness of God," then some hymns or songs, and time for prayer and a sermon. I asked if they take an offering and Iskander replied that, "Until now we do not take an offering. I want to make sure new believers don't get influenced by this . . . it was a mistake." In other words, he is concerned that the Kitma believers will grow accustomed to receiving from the church but never having to contribute to its life, even though any financial contribution from them would presumably be rather small.

Since its inception the church in Kitma has shifted the format of meetings a number of times. For a while there was a weekly meeting of 40 to 50 believers, and a couple of times a year a conference for all the CMBs in the region attended by about 100. The estimate for the number of CMBs in the area was about 200, but due to opposition the church did need to relocate a couple of times. Another key difficulty was transportation. Due to the poverty of the CMBs and enquirers in Kitma it is difficult for them to all come together at one place every week, as many of them do not have access to a vehicle and cannot afford to hire a taxi. This is one of the main factors that led to disbanding the weekly congregation and splitting into local cell churches. The intention is to gather all the believers together in one "mother church" once a month, but as of my last knowledge of the Kitma church this had not yet started.

The leaders had mixed feelings about the shift to cell churches in Kitma. One of them commented that it had long been their vision to have multiple cell churches. Another was critical of the shift, and she observed that when you break into cell churches, it is very easy to cease meeting over a holiday, or while the host family is traveling, and then never resume meeting. Another commented that the cell church model was difficult because they did not have enough leaders to visit them all, whereas with one congregation they could make sure that at least one or two of the lay pastors were present. This preoccupation about having more work than the leadership could handle was mentioned by several people, sometimes more than once. According to Iskander one does not even need to intentionally engage in evangelism in the villages around Kitma, saying to me, "You go with your Arabic to these villages and in no time people will be asking you about religion." All the leaders agreed that there is more work than they can cover, and there are not enough people to follow up with the various believers in the area. Questions of leadership and empowerment recurred during the interviews as key areas of concern for the present and the future of the Kitma church, and it is necessary to look at this topic in greater depth.

EMPOWERMENT THROUGH INCULTURATION

Inculturation provides a useful lens which can help us better understand what is taking place in Kitma in terms of power. Recalling the material from chapter 1, inculturation represents the encounter between the gospel and culture, "when faith challenges culture . . . not in formulaic terms but in the lives and encounters of actual people."[11] In order to answer this question, we must describe the "old" of Kitman society from which these believers have turned, as well as the "new" exercise of power, embodied in the Christian faith as lived out by the Juduurians, to which they have converted. And since empowerment and the exercise of power are often related to leadership of some form, the attempts of the Juduur leaders to form leaders among the Kitma believers will be described.

The "Old" Concept of Power: Mosques and Imams

In this short history one salient issue is leadership. Matthias was intent on deliberately forming new leaders for the Juduur church, and claims that this has always been part of the ethos of his denomination. The focus on identifying potential leaders and training them is, by contrast, notably absent in many of the other evangelical churches in the area, even though they are doctrinally quite similar. The lack of leaders, as noted above, was a difficulty mentioned by several interviewees. The Kitma believers are coming to the Christian faith with the template of mosque leadership already familiar to them. This is part of their context and their background, and this requires our attention.

Since the early days of Islam, specifically since the flight of the Prophet to Yathrib (Medina), the mosque has been central to the life of the Muslim community. Many hadiths are related to Muhammad being at the mosque, which was by no means considered to be only a religious building. It appears that the Yathrib mosque had a courtyard around it where women were allowed, though the actual prayer room itself appears to have been for

11. Gittins, "Deep Structures," 59.

men only. Many activities were carried out in the mosque and its courtyard: playing games, doing commerce, detaining prisoners, caring for wounded soldiers, napping, and so on.[12]

In Kitma, mosques continue to be, primarily, prayer rooms. The Arabic word is *masjid* (of which the English word *mosque* is a corruption), which literally means a place of kneeling. The prayer room is only for men, though some mosques may have a room apart for women. In general, women are expected to pray at home. Islamic tradition teaches that praying with other Muslims (presumably at a mosque though not necessarily) is more meritorious than praying alone. A common feature of mosques today are minarets, though there is nothing in the shari'a that makes the presence of a minaret obligatory. Five times a day (in Kitma) the call to prayer is issued through loud speakers. If possible this should be done by a muezzin who is, in Kitma, always a man. The men gather to pray and the prayer leader is the imam. The imam need *only* be a prayer leader and need not know how to preach, interpret, teach, or council Muslims—his only obligation is that he must know the Qur'an well enough to lead the prayers in Arabic.[13]

Once in Juduur I was passing by a mosque and the call to prayer sounded and I decided to attend. I signed to some men inside and told them I am a Christian and asked if I may observe the prayers. The imam, a slight, young man, said yes. I took off my shoes at the entrance and sat in the back to watch. Afterwards I conversed with the imam and his father and upon asking some questions about interpreting the Qur'an I was told that there was no one who could answer those questions. They wondered if perhaps the senior cleric in Juduur (a very influential person) might have the authority to engage in new interpretation (*ijtihaad*),[14] but they were not sure.

A sermon (*xutba*) is given on Friday by a preacher (*xatiib*), who need not be the same person as the imam, and is usually broadcast over loudspeakers. From a religious point of view, the purpose of the mosque is to be a place for the daily prayers to be carried out by men. Central mosques in big cities may have schools or charities attached to them, but that is not mandatory. Similarly, while some imams have a high level of training in the Qur'an and Islam, that is not necessary—one only has to know how to lead prayers in Arabic. It does not matter if the imam *understands* the Arabic.[15]

12. These examples are all drawn from *Sahiih Al Bukhari*, Volume 1, Book 8.

13. Ali and Leaman, *Key Concepts*, 54.

14. According to Groff, *Islamic Philosophy*, 105, ijtihaad is "Etymologically related to the term jihad (effort, striving), ijtihad is a legal concept that has to do with exerting oneself or exercising independent judgement." Muslims debate whether or not ijtihaad is possible or desirable anymore.

15. Rippin, *Muslims*, 107–11.

The "New" Concept of Power: "Mak[ing] Them Brave to Ask Questions . . ."

Having described briefly the leadership role of the imam in the mosques in Kitma, and having outlined the roots of the Kitma church(es), we are now prepared to examine the problematic issue of leadership formation and empowerment so important to the Juduur leaders. At first the responsibilities of a leader-in-training would be quite simple, but the final goal would be to have someone who can do the work the lay pastors do: teach, evangelize, give advice, read and interpret Scripture, and perhaps even take part in the regional denominational leadership as well.

Given that the Juduur community had produced some dedicated and reliable leaders, I asked about training new leaders from the Kitma church/churches: the responses were mixed. All the leaders, local and foreign, seemed to firmly believe in the denominational tradition of empowering lay leaders which appears to have worked well in reviving the Juduur church, but working with CMBs led to some pronounced challenges. According to one interviewee, there was difficulty related to understanding and interpreting Scripture, since CMBs bring to Christianity their Islamic background of how to read Scripture.

Recalling the material from chapter 1 on the relation of power to the Scripture, Islam as practiced in Kitma does not permit, much less encourage, local Muslims to engage in critical, inductive study of the Qur'an. Muslims are taught that the Qur'an was dictated, word for word, to Muhammad through the mediation of an angel. This dictation theory is different from the inspiration theory espoused by the evangelicals in Juduur and Kitma, which finds in Scripture a text that is held be to divine but also human, and thus requiring a creative and critical interaction with the text in relation to personal spirituality and the life of the church. According to Andraus, some new believers from a Muslim background have a difficult time learning how to read and interpret the Bible. In effect, they have been told not to ask questions about the Qur'an and to respect the absolute hermeneutical authority of the local Islamic tradition.

Within the context of the church, however, they are being told that they can and should ask questions about the Bible, and that if done with faith and humility, they will be able to discern God's guidance and direction for their own lives. This skill is all the more important for leaders to cultivate because personal interpretation of Scripture can go wrong, so part of the office of the leader is to communicate the hermeneutical boundaries placed on personal interpretation which emerge from a normative tradition indicating forbidden interpretations of the Bible. In other words, while actions have been taken to deliberately empower some CMBs, one of the key avenues to that empowerment, personal interpretation of Scripture, is reportedly sometimes very challenging to them—it represents discontinuity with the well-ingrained Qur'anic hermeneutic (or anti-hermeneutic perhaps) which they had known. Or as Andraus put it, "Muslims are not brought up to think—to analyze things . . . this is not the Muslim mentality." One lay pastor remarked, "You have to make them brave to ask questions."[16]

It is possible to interpret this act of empowerment using Lukes's three dimensions of power. Power can be used to prevent an issue from being discussed or addressed, and in their previous experience in Kitman Islam, power was so used to foreclose the discussion of certain questions. In their approach to leadership development, the Kitma believers are encouraged to reclaim that facet of power in relation to the Bible.

Matthias, in comparing the leadership that emerged in the Juduur church with the perceived difficulties in finding new leaders from the CMBs, said:

> The leadership that has emerged in [Juduur] has been miraculous. They are second to none. The Lord has done a deep work in the lives of some of them . . . that's what we're looking for in [Kitma . . .]. We'd like to see such a deep work done in the lives of some of these MBBs that they will emerge and we'll recognize them for who they are. There are certain qualities, though, that are required: boldness, risk-taking, surviving suffering, understanding the broader issues of unity, and biblical truth that are not influenced by some of these Islamic thoughts and background.

He continued by saying that many of the believers backslide, which Iskander confirmed separately.

Andraus described an additional problem: that once other Christian groups hear about a local being trained for leadership they hire them. Since the Juduur and Kitma churches do not have funds to pay someone a salary, while other Christian NGOs and missions do, the leader-in-formation is lost.[17] They may continue to *attend* church, but their involvement is limited to attendance.

16. A missionary from a different region made a similar comment to me, saying that the converts in his country read the Bible as if it were "flat text," that "they read [present tense] the Bible like they read [past tense] the Qur'an." His proposed solution to this was to design a course on hermeneutics and biblical interpretation and early church history—that is, how the early church developed its interpretation of Scripture.

17. These NGOs are, for the most part, devoted to various sorts of relief and development work, and not dedicated to evangelism or church-planting, even though some

A dissenting voice here was that of Ayya, who did think that there were people ready for initial leadership positions in the Kitma region. She felt that a double-standard was being used in relation to the CMBs in Kitma, and that they were being held to a higher standard than new leaders from a Christian background. She relates an experience from her own life as an example: after she had become a Christian and was involved in a small local church she took part in the Lord's Supper, and she was critically asked by a Christian there if she really understood what she was doing. When she said she did, she was told to explain the Lord's Supper as verification. She did not believe that a new church member from a Catholic or Orthodox background would undergo the same scrutiny. She also stated that if a new evangelical from a traditional church still had, say, an icon of Mary in his house (frowned upon by local evangelicals), it would not be considered a barrier to leadership. According to her, the same patience and acceptance of gradual conversion and maturation is not accorded to Muslims, and this is one reason for the lack of new leadership among the Kitma believers. That having been said, she did not say that the other reasons given above are irrelevant or incorrect. While she clearly stated that the Christians from the Juduur church were probably the best-equipped in terms of ministry to Muslims in the larger area, she did feel that in the end Muslim converts were being held to a higher standard than evangelicals who had come from the traditional churches.

Why might this be the case? If CMBs are indeed being held to a higher standard than other new evangelicals—and I have no way to know if that is indeed the case—it is probably because Islam is seen as the rival, the Other, by Christians (and probably vice-versa as well). If we recall centuries of precarious existence under Muslim rule, the divinely-sanctioned treatment of Christians as second-rate citizens by Muslims under the shari'a, and the very real danger related to doing ministry in an Islamic context, we start to see some significant factors that might account for the alleged hesitancy on the part of leaders other than Ayya to give leadership positions to CMBs. The Orthodox Christian who became evangelical presumably already believed in, or at least assented to, doctrines like the Incarnation, the Atonement, and so on. When he became evangelical he did not turn away from these things as old and wrong, although he may have turned away from the veneration of icons and other practices not permitted by evangelicals, and he turned *to* something new and right, in his eyes, which is a personal relationship with God through Jesus Christ. The gulf this Christian had crossed

---

of them may identify themselves as Christian or being affiliated with some church or denomination.

is much less wide than the one the ex-Muslim convert has crossed, thus the evidence needed to verify the transition is also less rigorous. In spite of all of this, all the leaders emphasized trust in the Muslim enquirer. When I asked Andraus what he does when a Muslim asks about baptism, he replied, "The same thing I do when a Christian [from a traditional church] asks for baptism." Moreover, seekers are put in touch with their local cell church quickly, and the minister does not examine them to discern if they are truly sincere or not.

Power and Muslim Evangelism in Juduur: The Ministry of Khalil

The difficulties faced in Kitma in relation to empowering new leaders should be balanced by noting that in quite a few situations the denomination has been rather successful in empowering and forming new leaders to engage in ministry. During my field research with the Juduur Christians I was able to meet Khalil. He was not originally involved in the Kitma ministry, but in Muslim evangelism in Juduur, and more recently in cities near Kitma. Thus some of the enquirers and converts that are the fruit of his ministry may have recently been channeled into the cell churches in Kitma. The creation of his innovative evangelistic ministry is a successful example of the sort of empowerment that Matthias and Andraus advocate. Following is a summary of how Khalil became the full-time lay evangelist for the Juduur church focused primarily on Muslims.

Around 2005 a group led by one of the former pastors of the Juduur church was going to a European country to evangelize. During the summer vacation in Europe many Muslim families with relatives in North Africa drive south to the ferry ports and take a car ferry to North Africa. This reportedly offers a good occasion for evangelism and distribution of Christian-themed media,[18] especially while families are waiting in their cars to board the ferry. Khalil was invited and decided to use his vacation time from his secular job and go. He left hoping for a vacation in Spain with fellow Christians and returned with a passion for Muslim evangelism. He asked Matthias how to go about this sort of ministry, and Matthias told him, "I'm not going to tell you what to do, but they need to hear the Gospel—they need love. How you're going to do that, it's between you and the Lord." Some months later Khalil devised a way to engage in Muslim evangelism and his ministry called "booth witness" was born. His idea was to have a portable booth with evangelistic material which he could set up in parts of the city where he could distribute material and engage in conversations with pass-

18. Such as booklets, Bibles, CDs, and DVDs.

ers-by, most of them Muslims. He started to do this on the weekends. The next year he went on the European mission again, and upon his return his manager informed him that he had been fired.[19] Matthias encouraged him to continue to do the booth witness during the week when he had breaks from looking for new employment. As locals and foreigners heard about his ministry they started giving contributions to support him, and now he does it full time. So he is not an employee of the Juduur church, but his ministry is supervised by some of the people from the denomination, which means there is a system to maintain accountability.

I asked to accompany Khalil to see how he engaged in this ministry and was able to spend the entire day with him. We went to a street with a busy intersection and a wide sidewalk. He had several different brochures and pamphlets with him, all in Arabic, but he did not set up the booth that day. He greeted some passersby with the customary *marhaba*[20] and asked them if they would like some material about *sayyidna al masiih*. The title is carefully chosen because in Arabic there are two different versions of the name "Jesus." Christians use *yasuu3* and Muslims use *3iisa*. Khalil used a title acceptable to both Muslims and Christians which roughly translates as, "our master the Messiah." He had varied material which he gave to different people based on age and gender and religion. Some people accepted his offer, others did not. Some people stood and read the material and then asked him questions. At one point two young Muslims asked him about the corruption of Scripture (*tahriif*), and if the Torah and Gospel are not corrupt.[21] This resulted in a lengthy conversation. Later, he complained that it is sometimes socially awkward for him to speak with Muslim women, and how he needs a woman to help him in this evangelistic activity. He explained that he would do this for about one to four hours a day. As we departed to get some water he picked up some of the material that people had discarded. He then remarked about how expensive it was to buy the pamphlets. He noted that very few people discard the material because he tells them what it is before he gives it to them. I asked him if he faces any opposition and he said that once when he had his booth set up near a busy plaza a Muslim man started yelling at him *mahattat al kufr!* ("Base of disbelief!" roughly translated.)

19. It does not appear this had anything to do with his evangelistic work.

20. *Marhaba* is a religiously neutral greeting. The well-known *al salaamu 3alaykum* is, in Juduur, mostly used by Muslims who are greeting fellow Muslims. That having been said, few Muslims would object to being greeted with that phrase by a Christian, though some might not return the peace with the customary response—*wa 3alaykum al salaam*.

21. Many Muslims believe that the Torah and the Gospel *texts* have been corrupted, but this teaching is not found in the Qur'an.

Since his phone number and email are on the material he distributes he also gets a few calls or emails each month from people who warn him that what he is doing is bad. Beyond this, it does not appear that he or his family has ever been harmed. I asked him what he teaches Muslim enquirers about and he answered, "The love of God; the God of the Qur'an is not loving." During his evangelistic conversations he referenced the Sermon on the Mount often, and especially the verse, "Love your enemies . . ." (Matt 5:44).

We departed and had lunch with his family. During lunch he received a text message from an MBB who was "in a very bad state," saying that by this time next year he wanted to change his job, his family, and his citizenship. One source of difficulty for the convert according to Khalil was his wife, who was angry about his conversion to Christianity.

In the afternoon Khalil and his family and his neighbor, Amjad, and his family all piled into a large van and we departed for Kitma. We eventually arrived at a very poor village, to visit a family with large bags full of clothes for them. The children greeted us with the typical Islamic greeting *salaamu 3alaykum*. We met Abu Ali there, a gaunt old man who was the head of the household. He lived there with his wife and children and some of their children. I learned that two of his sons were in jail, which meant they had no money. The men were led to one sitting room, and the women to a separate one. Before long Abu Ali brought up the topic of religion and an hour-long conversation (all in Arabic) ensued, in which topics from the relation of Christianity to Islam to original sin were discussed. Abu Ali had informed Khalil that if he converts to Christianity then his whole household will too. Abu Ali struck me as quite astute, but it emerged that he was not able to read, so Khalil told him that he would bring him an mp3 player with recordings of the Gospels in Arabic. On the way back I was able to speak with the Christian women and was informed that Abu Ali's family didn't even have sugar, flour or oil, which explains why we were served tea without sugar, which is extremely odd. I asked the women what they talked about, and they said the women in Abu Ali's house were not CMBs, so they talked about life in general: one of the Juduur women talked about how she had overcome cancer, one of the Kitma women wondered why God allows for a man to have four wives when a woman can only have one husband, and so on. Khalil called a missionary and explained that Abu Ali's family was in a bad situation, and could he get them some food tomorrow? The answer was yes. By the time we got back to Juduur it was night and I returned to my hostel.

The material above offers a landscape demonstrating the complexities involved in leadership formation and evangelism in Kitma. On the one hand, there were multiple difficulties forming leaders for Kitma, but on the other hand, leaders were still emerging, as can be seen with the example of Khalil. Indeed, I never heard of any other church that had a full-time evangelist (again, a lay person) attached to it. By the end of my research Khalil felt he may have found a young woman to help him in his ministry (herself a CMB, unlike Khalil), and wanted to branch out to other cities beyond Juduur.

Evangelism as seen here is a use of power. First, in that it calls the Muslim to an awareness of his possible interest in conversion, it empowers that Muslim to consider a future he may not have been aware of. Additionally, the very act of evangelizing announces that the traditional use of power by Muslims to prevent the spread of the Christian message is not as effective as it once was. The *form* of the expression is also significant, because it does not rely on coercion at all, for neither the Juduur nor the Kitma Christians have such power. This form of power is, ironically perhaps, effective precisely because it lacks any coercive power. While nobody quoted this verse to me in reference to his or her evangelism and ministry, it appears that this theology of power is similar to what Paul envisioned when he wrote, "But we have this treasure in earthen vessels, so that the surpassing greatness of the power will be of God and not from ourselves."[22] This message is subversive because it implies that the *sort* of power wielded by Islam to contain apostasy (which may indeed be coercive, as seen with John's narrative above) is in fact an inferior type of power that comes from men, and not from God.

Summary

Inculturation is taking place as the message of Christ, as practiced and taught by the Juduur Christians, meets the culture and context of the Kitma believers, and many challenges surface. For instance, there are practical limitations that make teaching and meeting difficult, including persecution and transportation issues, and the time constraints of the key leaders, who also work in the secular world. Andraus mentioned that NGOs and other groups quickly hire leaders-in-training as the denomination focuses on unpaid lay leadership and cannot offer a paid salary. Thus involvement in the local church beyond attendance ends as their time is now devoted to their paid profession. Then there is the difficulty related to what appear to be the high standards associated with putting someone in a leadership position—seeking someone with qualities of "risk-taking, surviving suffering, understanding the broader issues of unity, and biblical truth that are not influenced by some of these Islamic thoughts and background." Qur'an-hermeneutics and

22. 2 Cor 4:7

mosque-leadership are major parts of that background. Ayya argues that the standards being set for potential leaders are too high, and if she is right that is a barrier created by the leadership and not the Kitma believers. One of the key methods of empowering people is encouraging them to engage thoughtfully and hermeneutically with the Bible, and this is all the more difficult because it directly contradicts what they had previously practiced. Finally, even if someone from Kitma did emerge as a leader with all these qualities, they could not be officially ordained. The government would not recognize them as a Christian, much less a pastor, and thus the minister would be unable to issue any official church documents, like certificates related to marriage, baptism, or burial, or ever represent the church in an official capacity before the government. All in all, it appears that there is an intentional attempt to treat Muslim converts and Christian converts the same, but on a practical level the Muslima, in her turning from the old and wrong of Islam to the new and right of Christ, must unlearn and relearn many more things than the Christian convert. And this tension, apparently unresolved, has made forming elders and pastors from Kitma an especially problematic endeavor.

Returning to the title of this section—*Empowerment through Inculturation*—it is the meeting of the Christian message with the local context and culture of Kitma that offers, or demands, an arena for empowerment. As the missionaries and then the Juduur believers related the Christian message to that context, empowerment came to be seen as imperative. This took place both as lay-leaders were empowered and as people were taught to read, interpret and apply the Bible to their own situations. Both of these represented departures from the "old" of the Islamic Kitman culture, and a turning towards the "new" of Christ as he had been communicated to them. This particular denominational ethos of lay empowerment, having originated over a hundred years ago in North America in a foreign context, touched something deep in Juduur and then in Kitma—something that differentiated these communities from their Muslim neighbors and, in Juduur, their evangelical Christian neighbors too. It was not the doctrine of evangelicalism that resulted in the birth of the Kitma church. Rather, the *denominational* ethos of lay-empowerment which was linked to an explicit encouragement to invite Muslims to faith appears to have been a decisive factor in the birth of the Kitma church.

TOWARDS A NEW IDENTITY IN KITMA

In light of the difficulties faced in forming new leaders from the Kitma churches with the concurrent need for new leaders, and also the apparent decline of the ability of the mission to assist the indigenous church in terms of experienced missionaries, it is appropriate to consider the strategy of the pastors of the Kitma believers. With new and existing converts, what would a successful end game look like? Lewis Rambo offers us a helpful template for examining these questions.

The Advocate's Strategy

As mentioned in chapter 2, Rambo emphasizes the *intent* of the evangelizing agent during the phase of encounter, or what he calls "The Advocate's Strategy."[23] He proposes four main components to be analyzed when trying to describe a given strategy. Those are the degree of proselytizing, the strategic style, the mode of contact, and the potential benefits of the new religion. The modes of contact have already been described above—the meetings in the context of the relief program, being approached by secret believers or secret enquirers, contacts from Internet or satellite ministries, and Khalil's evangelistic ministry. Likewise, the degree of proselytizing has been covered already: the Juduur church is an evangelistic church, and members are encouraged to share their faith with others, including non-Christians, and the church maintains a number of activities that give the church members opportunities to interact with non-evangelicals and, specifically, Muslims. All of this leads to the conclusion that the degree of proselytism is high. In relation to such communities, Rambo comments, "It should come as no surprise that these are the groups that continue to grow numerically in the United States and around the world."[24]

The two other factors that Rambo specifies—strategic style and potential benefits—warrant further exploration. Multiple studies have already been done on why Muslims convert to Christianity,[25] and these provide some background in relation to why some Muslims in Kitma became Christians. In relation to Rambo's category of potential benefits, I did explore the possible charge of proselytism in some of the interviews—asking, "How would you respond to someone who says that you are proselytizing by giving food to poor Muslims?" Andraus replied very clearly that receipt of help

---

23. Rambo, *Religious Conversion*, 76.

24. Rambo, *Religious Conversion*, 78.

25. A survey of these is present in chapter 2.

was never contingent on receptivity to the Christian message or studying the Bible. Atallah smiled when I asked him about this and said, "We love each other, and we help each other. Pray that we will continue to do so." He seemed to be implying that since the relief effort was born out of simple charity for isolated people in impoverished villages, that it was above such accusations, or that if such ministry is considered proselytism, then it is a good practice. As I pointed out earlier, the commencement of the church's involvement in Kitma was not related to an intentional strategy to plant a church there. Insofar as this information is reliable there were no material benefits or rewards for conversion, rather is the opposite true, that there was a real possibility of loss, punishment or persecution for becoming a Christian.

The fourth point, that of the strategy, is the main factor I wish to focus on now. What is the goal of the Juduur Christians in reference to the Kitma Christians? What *sort* of congregations and Christians do they desire to see formed? As one veteran missionary in the Middle East wrote, "Muslims will usually adopt the form of ecclesiology of the one who wins them to the Lord and disciples them."[26] That observation may often times be accurate, but Kitma is different from Juduur, and the very fact that the Kitma believers are ex-Muslims means that complete imitation of the Juduur church is impossible. Their context is quite different, as exemplified in the discussions on the Qur'an-hermeneutics (chapter 2) and the mosque (above).

Negotiating Identity: The Lord's Supper

As outlined in chapter 2, evangelicals generally understand involvement with a local church to be a characteristic of "genuine" conversion. Because of this, we should not be surprised to find that one identifiable aspect of the strategy is to create an empowered church that produces its own leaders, though to date that goal has not been reached. Another aspect of the strategy of the Juduur Christians for Kitma, especially Iskander and Atallah, is that of creating a *new community* with a new identity. That is to say, not only is there an intention to see people as individuals converting to Christ, but becoming a *church*, a congregation.

Among the leaders the sort of new identity to be formed among the Kitma Christians was itself contested, and this became apparent in the issue of ritual boundaries. Rituals such as the Lord's Supper can shed light on identity questions, for it is often in such rituals that the community identifies

26. Register, "Discipling," 28.

who and what it is, and, equally important, who they are not.[27] A question related to identity boundaries arose in relation to the possible use of wine during Communion. The drinking of wine is generally forbidden in Islam, for it is inextricably polluting. This is different from the traditional evangelical ethic one finds at the Juduur church, which is that there is nothing wrong with wine itself, rather that drunkenness is forbidden. These constitute two different boundaries regarding acceptable behavior. In this context, the use of wine during the Lord's Supper would constitute a blatant and observable violation of the Islamic boundary in favor of a new one.

Given such a small quantity there is no risk of drunkenness and thus imbibing at Communion is within evangelical boundaries, but it marks one as clearly being beyond the boundaries of Islam which, as it is practiced in Kitma and Juduur, teaches that no alcohol is permitted at all. Iskander advocated the use of real wine, which would emphasize the new identity of the believers. Ultimately though, the decision was made to use grape juice. Ayya outlined the reasons for this position. First, for young women in a traditional Muslim society the consumption of *any* alcohol at all is connected in the popular mind with promiscuity. Second, there was a concern that people would accuse the Kitma Christians of converting simply so that they could consume alcohol. Thus wine is not used for communion because it was deemed both that the risks are greater than the benefits and that Kitma believers can express their new identity as Christians in different and more constructive manners.

Negotiating Identity: Gender Roles

One such expression of new identity is the mixing of genders in church and the presence of a woman lay pastor. This is likewise an important identity marker. I was struck by how unproblematic the leaders found it. With other issues, such as music and baptism, my questions would often lead to lengthy comments on what was being done, and why this or that was the practice, or how something had been tried and then changed. This was not the case when I enquired if a woman in a visible leadership position, within the context of a patriarchal society, had led to problems. There was no mention that excluding women from leadership roles might be preferable or an option. As Iskander said, "The way [the Kitma believers] deal with women has to break," and so he teaches men "how to treat their wives" and about the Christian concept of a family.[28] The active role of women in leadership in

27. Bell, *Ritual*; Karecki, "Roots of Ritual," 169–77.

28. Within the evangelical context of the place this means that the man is seen

the Kitma church, including teaching and pastoral care, represents a break in identity from the Islamic past where women are expected to worship at home apart from men or, in the case that the local mosque has a room for the women, may pray at the mosque but must remain out of the sight of the men lest the men be distracted.

Negotiating Identity: Accountability and Baptism

The concept of leadership itself, as practiced by both Christians and Muslims, in the region also appeared to be a locus of discontinuity, for the leadership concepts of the Juduur team differed from those of Muslim mosques, but also other *evangelical* communities. Indeed, some of the strongest denunciations found in my interview notes were directed against the leadership practices of fellow evangelicals: "The situation of the evangelical churches in this land is disastrous. They are full of corruption and the pastor is like a big dictator . . . Fundraising is like the twentieth century heresy!" Here Iskander is denouncing the practice of inflating numbers and missionary progress by local evangelical ministers to procure money from sympathetic Western Christians. One egregious example of this I heard of was a charismatic woman missionary in a city near Kitma who would hold a preaching event and "share the Gospel" with a large room full of impoverished locals, mostly Muslims: on the way out they would be given basic foodstuffs and also a Bible. She was then able to show how she had "preached the Good News" to so many Muslims who now had Bibles, and use this claim to raise funds. One Christian living in that city told me that after these events one would find the Bibles tossed on the street or in trashcans. This is the sort of thing that Iskander called "the twentieth century heresy." While that example is in reference to a foreigner, similar, if less dramatic, allegations are made against indigenous Christians.

To counteract these practices, inflated numbers and funds that vanish into the pastor's pocket (whether local or foreign), the denomination has rules about declaring church income and reporting regular attendance at the churches. The Kitma church was led by three lay pastors, and the whole church in the area is under a board of elders, which includes men and women, pastors and laity, foreigners (missionaries) and indigenous Christians. The indigenous denomination is autonomous, but has *voluntarily*

---

as the primary authority in the house, but that family decisions are to be made consensually if at all possible and spousal corporal punishment is forbidden, which is a departure from the "old" and "wrong" of Kitman Islam where the Qur'an is understood as explicitly sanctioning hitting wives.

invited missionaries (like Matthias) to serve on the denominational leadership board. In other words, there are multiple checks and balances to ensure that one person or group does not have all the influence, decision-making power, or money. According to Iskander and Matthias, this is a deeply countercultural teaching, not only to Muslims but even to evangelicals, and represents one more aspect of discontinuity present in the strategy for the Kitma church.

Moreover, this emphasis on accountability has translated itself into the ritual language of the Kitma church, notably in their preferred practice of baptizing people two or three at a time. When I asked about baptism this was often mentioned. The explanation given was that when two converts participated in this rite of initiation together, after having been catechized together as well, a bond was formed between them, and they would tend to take up the responsibility of making sure that the other person was growing as a Christian, or at least had not reverted to Islam. This is part of the power of initiatory rites like baptism. Utilizing the three-step progression of Van Gennep[29] from chapter 2, baptism represents the assimilation or incorporation of the believer into the congregation, and thus the conclusion of the phase of liminality. Indeed, incorporation into *a community* of believers appears to be extremely important in relation to the formation and stabilization of a new convert identity.[30]

One of the aspects of the briefly liminal phase, emphasized by Turner,[31] is that of *communitas*, which refers to a community based on solidarity and equality, which is relatively structureless and may oppose the accepted societal norms. Strong social bonds can be formed through *communitas* that last long after it is concluded. For instance, one might experience *communitas* with his fellow students preparing for Confirmation, or a soldier may form close and lasting bonds with the cadets in her basic training course. According to an anthropological reading, it is not unreasonable to expect long-lasting relationships characterized by accountability and mutual encouragement and affection to be the outcome of the *communitas* of group catechesis and ritual initiation.[32]

---

29. Separation, liminality, reassimilation.

30. Other studies of MBBs have come to similar conclusions in different cultural contexts (see Syrjänen, *Meaning and Identity* for Pakistan and Kraft, "Community and Identity," for Egypt and Lebanon).

31. Turner, *Forest of Symbols*.

32. Other MBB communities also appear to prefer group baptism. For an example from the Lucknow region in India see Miller and C. M., "Villages around Lucknow," 485.

The concept of accountability—of assuring that power is not abused by diffusing or sharing it—is thus a feature, or at least a feature aspired to, of this denomination, and is seen in the organization of the church government and pre-Baptismal catechesis. In terms of the rite of initiation being performed in groups, it is also a strategy for helping to ensure that the new identity of the believer as a Christian is able to mature and become stable.

Negotiating Identity: The Teaching Office and Overcoming Patronage

We have so far seen an example of an Islamic boundary marker being retained in forming a new identity (no wine in the Lord's Supper), and an Islamic boundary marker that was (it appears) rejected without problem, in the active role of a woman in leadership. Baptism accompanied by accountability (born out of *communitas*) has also been utilized to assist the new believer/church member in forming a stable identity.

But without examining the role of teaching the picture is incomplete. Indeed, the Kitma Christians may gather without celebrating the Lord's Supper or a baptism, but teaching is *always* a part of their gatherings. Because of this, one of the questions I asked most of the interviewees involved with the Kitma church was, "In your view, what is the main thing [the Kitma] Christians need to learn about." Atallah's answer was "the nature of God—then they will understand the love of God, redemption, incarnation, et cetera." To accomplish this formidable endeavor the use of sermons alone is insufficient, so "we teach them systematic theology." The teaching on systematic theology lasts about 90 minutes and, at the time of our interview, was being done by an American missionary whom I contacted, but was not able to interview.

The teaching strategy of these ministers, both local and foreign, was not based on the idea of building the truth on Islamic concepts, but rather on the conviction that as Christian teaching was presented that Islamic doctrines would become self-evidently false. Matthias recalled the seventies and the eighties when his fellow missionaries were trying to use the Qur'an as a basis for exploring the Gospel, which to this day is found in much evangelical missionary strategy.[33] Matthias' opinion of this is negative, "I don't

---

33. See CAMEL method, which uses Qur'anic verses about Jesus to discern if a Muslim is willing to study Jesus's life as presented in the four gospels. There is also a Qur'an-Bible study called "The Seven Signs" which examines the lives of seven prophets from the Qur'an and the Bible together, culminating in a study of Jesus (available in Gustafson and CGC, *Insider View*).

believe you can pull the gospel out of the Qur'an." He refers me to Don Richardson's book *Secrets of the Koran: Revealing Insights into Islam's Holy Book*.[34] Matthias summarizes Richardson's critical view, that there are no bridges between Islam and Christianity because Islam has taken all the Christian terms and emptied them of their meaning.[35] This conviction, shared by other interviewees, entails a rigorous and exhaustive deconstruction of the entire vocabulary of Islam (turning away from the old) and a reconstruction of that vocabulary but within an evangelical-biblical framework (turning to the new).

Examples of what this looks like in practice were provided by Iskander, who does much of the teaching. At one point he preached on *tawhiid*, which is a very Islamic term meaning the oneness of God and, as understood by most Muslims, entails a monadic oneness and precludes a Trinitarian oneness. He also preached on *shirk*, which is a technical Islamic term meaning "association": Christians are sometimes accused of *shirk* for associating Jesus with God. He redefined *shirk* in terms of idolatry: when we have an idol we are setting something up in God's place, and thus we are associating it with God. He asked, what are your idols? And then he redefined "idol" as well, in terms of attitudes and goals in life, rather than what most Muslims think of when they hear the word, which is an actual stone figure that someone bows down before, a meaning of the word which he says is "not relevant at all" to their contemporary situation. He summarizes his strategy: "I do not damage Islam. But I like to destroy it with the truth." Iskander has taken words that are very clearly Islamic and has redefined them within the context of a new identity, community, and book.

What is the goal of this teaching strategy? To answer this question it is helpful to examine the relationship between the Juduur and the Kitma believers which is currently that of a patron-client which, according to Eisenstadt and Roniger, is usually characterized by an inequality of power.[36] Callum Johnson, who studied a group of MBBs in South Asia, describes patronage as follows:

---

34. Richardson, *Secrets of the Qur'an*.

35. Several examples of this have been mentioned: through the tradition of *tahriif* (corruption), the Muslim can say "Yes, we believe in the Gospel, but the text you have now is not it and no one has it," or "Yes, Jesus was a prophet, born of a virgin and did miracles, but he was only a prophet to the Jews and his message (which has been lost) is superfluous now we have the Qur'an." These two key Christian concepts—the Gospel as Jesus's message, and Jesus as God's messenger—have been retained, but what they signify in their Islamized meaning is relatively unimportant, for they have been "emptied of their meaning."

36. Eisenstadt and Roniger, "Patron-Client Relationship," 15–24.

The core of the patron-client model is that of a hierarchical and deeply personal bond between the patron and client that is rooted in an unequal distribution of resources and which facilitates an exchange of differing kinds of resources. The Patron offers access to scarce resources (e.g., goods, protection, influence, employment) that may be economic, political, or indeed, spiritual . . . The client on the other hand, offers thanks and honour to the patron, avoiding situations that may dishonour him, working to increase his reputation, providing service when requested (rent-a-crowd, labour etc.), acting with loyalty and faithfulness.[37]

The patron-client framework describes accurately much of the economic and political framework of Kitma. Thus, it is what the Kitma believers are accustomed to, but it appears that the Juduur leaders find this way of ordering church life deficient, being part of the "old" and "wrong" which must be rejected in favor of the "new" and "right," a regional church model *not* marked by inequality of power and which emphasizes self-sufficiency for the basic functions of the church.

Nor was this "wrongness" isolated to Muslims in Kitma and Juduur, according to my interviewees. Christian churches, including evangelical ones, also operated according to this principal, and one person likened churches to "fiefdoms" or "little kingdoms," where the pastor was emperor. The discipline of accountability, in finances and government, is, in part at least, an effort to uproot the bad habit of patron-client church polity. The denominational leadership structure, which distributes power between locals and foreigners, clergy and laity, men and women, also appears to be a deliberate attempt to see the Gospel (as they understand it) transform their culture (and not just Islam, for local Christians too have the same unhealthy tendency towards patron-client relationality). Not taking an offering, seen by the leader as a mistake, actually reinforced this patron-client relationship, this inequality of power. Likewise, the empowering activity of interpreting Scripture has been emphasized. That some MBBs in Kitma and Juduur have apparently had difficulty accessing this avenue of power has perpetuated this "inequality of power." "[P]ower liberates people from social and normative pressures, leading them to shift their focus inward and toward their own goals and dispositions,"[38] and the Juduur leaders *want* leaders who will be able to assertively focus on their own goals for ministry in spite of "social and normative pressures."

37. Johnson, "Patronage, Reconciliation and Salvation," 3. This article by Johnson is one of the very few existing case studies of theology by MBBs.

38. Blader and Chen, "Status of Power," 3.

The patronal model of power, therefore, is not viewed favorably by the lay pastors and Juduur leaders. In other words, it has hindered them as they turned away from the old and wrong towards the new and correct, and, in their view, a patronal church is not the sort of community where a new empowered identity can come into being and become stable and fruitful. Such an empowering environment is important because "Identity redefinition for religious converts is a complicated and long process."[39] Forming such a community is very difficult though, and the Kitma church has experienced significant challenges, specifically backsliding, persecution, and the stress of the converts of being forced to maintain two identities which are interpreted as mutually exclusive. One identity, as Christians, is considered to be deviant, polluting, and dangerous by their Islamic society but in which they have experienced hope and closeness to God. The other identity is that of a Muslim which must be maintained for the sake of safety.

The formation of such a non-patronal church requires training and forming indigenous Kitman leaders. However, while the denominational framework of leadership training and empowering new members for leadership roles appears to have succeeded in Juduur, it has not yet been successful in Kitma. Some reasons like being risk-averse are related to the danger of religious conversion while others, like the inability to engage in the empowering evangelical hermeneutical practice of finding practical solutions to problems in the Bible, require a critical creativity in relation to the text which is foreign to how Muslims in Kitma approach the Qur'an. Finally, the inability of the denomination to pay new leaders means that sometimes NGOs will hire them, and then they will direct their time and energy to that work, and their involvement with the Kitma church will be at the level of attendance only. One might call it the problem of success—the Juduur church emphasized lay leadership and produced a group of dedicated, dynamic leaders. These leaders are now responsible for the Kitma churches, but as lay people they have businesses to run and do not have the time to provide the quality and scope of pastoral care that the Kitma believers need.

KITMA AND THE BEGINNINGS
OF THEOLOGY-MAKING?

Inculturation, Contextualization and Theology-making

We have in Kitma an example of inculturation—the gospel and a culture meeting each other—in which the gospel itself is already clothed in a specific

39. Kraft, "Community and Identity," 176.

cultural setting in which the Juduur believers received it from missionaries and then developed it for their own setting. This three-way meeting is apparent in a number of the instances seen here. The assertion of Islamic Kitman culture in refraining from using wine during the Lord's Supper, the focus on lay leadership and accountability, which is a facet of the North American historical roots of the denomination (and they would say based on the Bible), the surprise and joy of the Kitma believers at being joined together with people who were strangers at that first Easter meal, and in that meal becoming a church—people from different families and villages, who now had names, and a new family, and were Christians, and could say it. The three strands are not easy to separate from each other sometimes, but that is not important—for that inculturation in some form is happening seems clear.

But the research question of this book is related specifically to the question of theology-making. Is theology-making happening among the Kitma believers? Theology-making is *one* activity or process that can (and perhaps must, eventually) occur as inculturation is happening. In chapter 1 two different forms of contextualization were outlined. One is directed contextualization which was described as doing theology *for*, and is another name for missionary adaptation. Directed contextualization is not to be confused with organic contextualization, which is what Shoki Coe endorsed and spoke of, which can be called *theology by* and *theology with*. It entails the indigenous church discerning what God is doing, or what God desires to see done, and then reflecting on the Word of God, which involves discerning what path forward is faithful to God's revelation regarding mission, the church, and Christ himself. The process of contextualization is worked out as the church carries out the course of action and evaluates its success. Coe does allow for foreign agents to have a place in the process of organic contextualization, but their role is one of assistance and cooperation, not of directing the process.

According to Coe, contextuality—wrestling with God's world—is the beginning of the process of producing contextual theology. Contextuality is "the missiological discernment of the signs of the times, seeing where God is at work and calling us to participate in it."[40] Because of this I tried to ask questions about what the believers in Kitma were concerned with, their worries, concerns and problems when wrestling with God's world and their place in it. Two related issues emerged that imply that the Kitma believers have identified their contextuality, which is a necessary precursor to the theology-making process of contextualization. Furthermore, both of

40. Coe, "Renewal," 241.

these issues are related to identity and specifically to the challenge of communicating their new identity to the larger Kitma society, and then how that society reacts to the new (Christian) identity of the converts.

Identity Advocacy as a Possible Arena for Theology-making

This topic of being able to communicate to and live out their new identity in the Kitma community emerged during a lengthy interview with Iskander. I asked him how he would feel if it became legal for the Kitma Christians to convert. His answer was complex, and he drew upon the anthropological concept of liminality to explain himself. However, he was not using the concept of liminality to refer to individuals (and this will be revisited in relation to baptism and ICs in chapter 6), but to the Kitma community of Christian ex-Muslims as a whole. In his view, the Kitma believers had, by becoming Christians, *separated* themselves from the larger society and were thus a liminal community. But since religious conversion from Islam to Christianity is taboo—a polluting, deviant activity—the larger society of Kitma either cannot or will not allow them to be reassimilated as a community of Kitman Christians even if their status were legal. He wondered if it would take an entire generation before a new (non-liminal) identity could emerge. Andraus echoed this concern, saying that some of the Kitma believers were frustrated because with the church they are Christians, but with their extended families they must identify themselves as Muslims. This represents a state of coerced, extended liminality, whereby the decision of the individual (or community) to leave Islam and embrace the Christian faith is dismissed as not only polluting, deviant behavior, but a legal impossibility. Such a state of coerced liminality is also experienced by other MBBs in the Middle East.[41]

Iskander became rather animated as he discussed the impossibility of the recognition of the conversion of Kitma believers. He soundly rejected the idea of being a "Muslim-follower of Jesus" (as did all of the Juduur interviewees, categorically) and insisted that God created humans with free will, and that Islamic society in refusing to acknowledge the valid, non-coerced use of free will of the Kitma believers in their decision to convert, was being unjust and inhumane. "You need to break the system somehow," he said, "the system is not broken yet." He wondered if eventually enough people,

41. Kraft, "Community and Identity," and, "Faith is Lived," note something similar. Note that since this double identity is coerced and not voluntary it is not appropriate to refer to this as double religious belonging according the definition proposed in chapter 2.

acting together, would eventually insist on their right to have their conversions legally recognized. On the other hand, he does not see it as his place to make that happen.[42]

What Andraus and Iskander were talking about is the question of identity insofar as it related to religious conversion. Henri Gooren writes that religious conversion is "a comprehensive personal change of religious worldview and identity, based on both self-report and attribution by others."[43] Gooren's linkage of conversion to attributed identity is helpful here, because the implication is that these Kitma believers, insofar as their society will not *attribute* to them the identity which they attribute to themselves, do not have a real religious conversion. In reference to the church and other believers, they are Christians and so identify themselves, but in relation to the larger society that is to invite danger. It appears that the Kitma believers, in identifying this locus as a place where God wants to work and be active in the world, are engaging in what Coe refers to as identifying their contextuality. When the Kitma believers start to "wrestle with God's Word" (Coe's phrase) and propose and try out possible solutions, that could indicate that they are producing their own contextual theology. Recalling Ayya's narrative of the first gathering of the Kitma Christians for the Easter meal, she was surprised at their openness and willingness to share their stories with each other. It is reasonable to surmise that this was at least partially due to the fact that they were, perhaps for the first time ever for some of them, with people "like me" (Kitman CMBs). Advocating for the government, families and society to acknowledge and respect their new identities as Christians appears to be potentially an arena for theology-making among the Kitma believers.

Persecution as a Possible Arena for Theology-making

A second way that the issue of identity in relation to the larger society (and especially families) is at play is persecution. Sometimes it becomes known

---

42. Jeff Nelson, "Lessons from Esther," discusses the issue of "going public" with faith in Christ in a Muslim context. He looks for insights from the book of Esther, who under the guidance of her mentor, Mordecai, kept her Jewish faith and ethnicity secret for a time, and then at a strategic moment, risked her life by disclosing that she was a Jewess. On page 193 Nelson describes how Esther's disclosure gave courage to "a critical mass" to "reveal their devotion to God." This appears to be what Iskander is speaking of—a critical mass of MBBs announcing their faith in Christ, one large and visible enough that the traditional uses of coercion to silence the voice of the converts is not feasible.

43. Gooren, *Conversion and Disaffiliation*, 3.

to their families that a member has become a Christian, and at times this results in persecution, as was the case in the account of John earlier in this chapter. John did not want to leave Kitma, but eventually he felt he had no other choice. Other options had been tested, like staying at a safe house (where I first met him, and from which he was turned out for talking about his faith too much with local Muslims), and staying in the Middle East in a neighboring country. He also tried to go back to his family and show respect for his father, while also not renouncing his Christian faith, which did not work in the long run. So he fled to the West.

During one interview with Ayya, I asked her if there was anything else I should know about, but which I had not asked about, and she brought up this topic of safety for the converts, and specifically for young women who are her responsibility. She described different ways of dealing with persecution. She would visit the family, which itself might make an impact on them by showing that their activities do not inspire fear, and thus may not be effective. She would explain, "Look, your daughter is tired, let her come stay with me for a few days," during which time they would pray and help the Christian to forgive her family, which was described as important. They had also tried out safe houses, but for a single woman in Kitma or Juduur, staying alone is not considered to be socially acceptable.

On one occasion she said that it came to a point where a young lady's life was in danger and it was not an option for her to remain with her family, even after a period of time for them to cool off and for the convert to get some rest. In that case, the young woman did have to leave the country, and she was sent to a Western country for an educational program, and the family was informed that eventually she would return. What is remarkable about this instance of contextualization is that it pays respect to the Kitman culture by allowing the convert's family to save face. They can say, honestly, "Our daughter has gone to the West to study. She will return when she is done." Indeed, rather than harming the family's status by revealing that they failed to compel the convert to return to Islam, it enhances their honor, in that their daughter has been able to engage in a praiseworthy and respectable educational endeavor which is out of reach to most families in Kitma. This is contextualization related to identity questions, and the church's leaders were able to find a path that was neither the so-called "extractionism" that missionaries are accused of, nor was it an "insider movement" wherein the woman is not allowed to reinterpret her new identity in terms of the word "Christian." If and when the woman does return, it is unlikely that her family will harm her, for she has brought them honor. By the time of her return, there is the hope that her family will have come to accept her new identity as a Christian, though there is no guarantee of that.

In this instance the believer's new identity was preserved intact, as a Kitman Christian. The Kitma church was faced with a crisis, possible bodily harm of one of their sisters, so they were compelled to take action. Their wrestling with the word of God led them to the conclusion that the title "Christian" and belonging to the "church" were not merely Euro-American accretions to the faith portrayed in the New Testament, but were part and parcel of that faith itself. They were not to be concealed or denied, even for the sake of security. On the other hand, their reading of their own context in relation to her family grasped that her life would be very difficult if she were estranged from them to the point of never being able to return home (which may be the case with a convert like John). Thus two tropes common to Western missiology are avoided. She is not the heroic believer who has left "the darkness of Islam" for "the light of Christ," and who was persecuted by her unbelieving family. Nor is she the devout Qur'an-believing Muslima who wants nothing to do with the "pork-eating, wine-drinking, mini-skirt wearing, three-god-worshiping, Crusade-waging Christians and their church, but who really loves Jesus." Rather, she is a persecuted Christian Kitman maiden, and a path has been found for her to preserve her family's honor, and allow them some time to come to terms with the reality and sincerity of her conversion (and thus her new identity), but also for her to hopefully return home some day on good terms, and as a devout Christian. In such encounters with persecution, the Juduur-Kitma Christians have found a demanding field wherein they could make their own theology, one that might be described as a pastoral theology of persecution.

In concluding this section I want to reiterate that, insofar as I understand the situation correctly, the Kitma believers themselves are not engaged in the production of their own theology, though they have started that process, insofar as they have identified an important issue which they desire to address, namely that their new identities as Christians be accepted by their larger community. The birth of their church, the strategy of the advocates, and their struggle in the area of identity, which includes the possibility of persecution—all of these are key facets related to their contextuality as potential CMB theology-makers. For Coe, though, contextualization is a step *after* indigenization, and, as we have seen, the efforts of the Juduur leaders to indigenize the leadership and move away from a system of patronage are still ongoing.

It is possible that the individual CMBs are engaging in the process of theology-making in their own lives, on a personal level, for there is no requirement that a theology-maker be a leader or have a specific level of education, even though that is somewhat common. Are these CMBs perhaps writing their own poems or songs, and how are they answering questions about contentious topics like *tahriif* and the Trinity when Muslims ask them to defend the concept—these may well be areas for personal theology-making. Due to the limitations of my research though, I do not have the knowledge to answer these questions.

CONCLUSION

Due to the limitations inherent in this research a complete account of the life of the Kitma church cannot be provided. The information I was able to gather though portrays a community undergoing very significant challenges, whose continued existence is itself as surprising as its birth was. When the Juduur Christians sought to create an empowered, non-patronal church in which stable identities could be formed through the ministry of indigenous Kitma leaders, they found that some of the methods of empowerment which had been successful in Juduur are harder to apply in Kitma. Similarly, the poverty and persecution present in Kitma were practical difficulties that, coupled with the fact that all three lay pastors had full-time jobs and families, made the need for indigenous Kitman leadership all the more urgent. Any of the topics mentioned in this chapter could be an occasion for theology-making—baptism, the Lord's Supper, the nature of leadership, preaching sermons, gender relations, church order/polity—but after studying the context of Kitma and the mother church of Juduur, I have suggested two specific areas which appear to be ripe for theology-making by the Kitma believers—identity advocacy and persecution.

It does appear that for the Kitma believers an area of concern is the tension between their desire to be acknowledged by their community in their new Christian identity, and the insistence of the shari'a (and some of their families) that conversion from Islam to Christianity is a form of "pollution" to be silenced or ignored. But other ex-Muslim Christians have felt that same tension and sense of injustice and shared the conviction that "the system must break," and they have started working towards making that happen. That is the topic of the next chapter.

5

Liberation and Wisdom in the Texts
of Ex-Muslim Christians

Obedience through love is worth more than obedience through fear.
—RAMON LLULL[1]

Human beings automatically think of God as someone who pos-
sesses and wields power. Jesus forces people to consider whether that
deeply rooted conviction is true or not. In historical terms it is readily
apparent that power, left to its own inertial tendencies, tends to be
oppressive in fact. So it cannot be the ultimate meditation of God,
though human beings might tend to think so.
—JON SOBRINO[2]

In chapter 3 some suggestions were made regarding the factors present in the second half of the twentieth century that facilitated the creation of an environment wherein unprecedented numbers of Muslims could, and did, apostatize. Sometimes this resulted in isolated believers, and sometimes in the creation of Muslim-background congregations. Chapter 4 then gave one concrete example of how that process took place in the Middle East. Those chapters sought to provide a description of the contexts wherein ex-Muslim Christians might go about theology-making.

1. Llull, *Raymond's Proverbs,* 53:9.
2. Sobrino, *Christology,* 213, 214.

With that background in place we are prepared to examine some of the texts composed by ex-Muslim Christians. This chapter is a case study, not of a group of ex-Muslims in a specific place (chapter 4) or CMBs connected by common ethnicity (chapter 4, chapter 6), but of the texts of CMBs who have written down their own experiences and thoughts and shared them with the world. The texts to be examined here are mostly autobiographical and address, to some degree, the authors' conversions from Islam to Christianity. These texts speak to us of God, how the authors came to the conclusion that the Christian portrayal of God is correct, and that the Muslim understanding is flawed. The texts speak of Jesus, politics, salvation, Scripture, work, family, relationships and migration. With the understanding that theology is broader than "certain knowledge," these texts will be examined with the goal of discerning and describing any theological content they may have.

THEOLOGY AS LIBERATING PRAXIS

Empowerment

Poetry and conversion-persecution narratives are two of the most common forms of text that are composed by ex-Muslim Christians. One striking example of poetry is from Fatima al-Mutayri,[3] a convert to Christianity (*mutanassira*) and subject of the Kingdom of Saudi Arabia until her martyrdom at the hands of a family member in 2008. She was 26:

> *The ode that Fatima Al-Mutayri wrote before her martyrdom*[4]
> May the Lord Jesus guide you, O Muslims
> And enlighten your hearts that you might love others
> The online forum[5] does not revile the master of the prophets
> It is for the display of truth to you and for you it was revealed
> This is the truth which you do not know
> And what we say are the words of the master of the prophets
> And we do not worship the cross and we are not insane
> We worship the Lord Jesus, the light of the world
> We left Mohammed and we are no longer on his path
> And we follow Jesus the Messiah, the clear truth

3. Translator unknown.

4. *The Way of Fatima*, 8–9. This title was given to the poem by the unknown editor and translator of the document.

5. It appears that Al Mutayri (sometimes spelled Al Matayri) wrote this poem as a response to a poem posted on an online forum for Christians in the Gulf. That message threatened Christians with death and accused them of several evils, some of which Fatima refutes here.

And truly we love our homeland and we are not traitors
We take pride that we are Saudi citizens
How could we betray our homeland and our dear people??
How could we, when for death for Saudi, we are ready???
The homeland of my grandfathers and their glories for which I
am writing these odes
And we say, "proud, proud, proud, we are to be Saudis"
We chose our way, the way of the guided
And every man is free to choose which religion
Be content to leave us alone to be believers in Jesus
Leave us to live in grace until our time comes
My tears are on my cheek and, oh! the heart is sad
On those who became Christians,[6] how you are so cruel
And the Messiah says: blessed are all the persecuted
And we, for the sake of the Messiah bear all things
And what is it to you that we are [considered] infidels?
You will not enter our graves or be buried with us
Enough, your swords do not concern me at all
Your threats do not concern me and we are not afraid
By God, I am for death, a Christian, oh my eye
Cry for what has passed in a sad life
I was far from the Lord Jesus for many years
Oh history record and bear witness, Oh witnesses!
We are Christians walking on the path of the Messiah
And take from me this information and note it well
You see Jesus is my Lord and he the best protector
I advise you to pity yourself and clap hands [in resignation]
And see your look of ugly hatred
Man is brother of man, oh learned ones!!!!!
Where is the humanity, and love, and where are you
And my last words I pray to the Lord of the worlds
Jesus the Messiah, the light of the clear guidance,
That he changes your notions and set right the scales of justice
And spreads love among you oh Muslims.

There are several important things that must be noted regarding this poem. First, is that the author has no reservation about using divine titles for Jesus Christ, specifically "Lord of the Worlds," which is a well-known Islamic title for God[7] but certainly not for Jesus. Second, the author is very aware of the reality of violence, but appears to follow the ethic outlined in the

---

6. The word translated here "those who became Christians" is *mutanassiriin* in the Arabic.

7. Qur'an 1:2.

Sermon on the Mount,[8] praying for her enemy to repent and, presumably, join her in embracing the Christian faith. Third, the author has no problem calling herself a Christian (*ana masiihiyya*). Fourth, we see something like what we have in the early church in that the Christians were accused of being bad citizens because of their religion. Similarly, in a country like Saudi Arabia, embracing Christianity is often seen as an act of treason against the state. The author here follows (probably without knowing it) the pattern of Tertullian[9] who argues that Christians are not bad citizens, but perhaps the best of all citizens. Fifth, there is a strong emphasis on the love of God being the heart of the Christian faith. That resurfaces again and again in other conversion narratives as diverse as the Pakistani Bilqis Sheikh's *I Dared to Call him Father* and the Egyptian Emir Rishawi's *A Struggle that led to Conversion: Motives for a Gospel-based Faith*[10] and the Pakistani Gulshan Esther's *The Torn Veil*. Lastly, there is an unabashedly evangelistic tone here. This comes across better in the Arabic of the final line: *wa yubashshir al mahabba baynakum ya muslimiin*. The word translated "spread" can also mean *evangelize* in Arabic.

Recalling Nock's emphasis on the old and the new in religious conversion, we might say that the something new has attracted her in what she perceives as a religion of peace and love (Christianity). She has also come to the conclusion that the "old" of Islam is lacking because it lacks those qualities. Her opinion is that

> Muslims claim that Islam is a religion of peace and love and to this day Muslims never hesitate to mention this in their media to the extent that they drive us crazy with it. When I was a Muslim and sleepwalking through my days, I repeated the same words. I used to claim that Islam does not attack others, but after doing a study about Islam, I discovered the opposite is true.[11]

Such sentiments are not uncommon in apostasy narratives—whether the apostate turns to agnosticism, atheism, Christianity or deism. Specifically I am referring to the trope of the Muslim wanting to defend Islam or the Prophet from "unjust" accusations, studying the original sources like the *ahaadiith* and the life of the Prophet by Ibn Ishaq,[12] and coming to the

8. Matt 5–7.

9. See for example Tertullian, *Apologia*, 42–43.

10. Originally published in Arabic under the title *saraa3 'adda 'ila al ihtida': dawaafi3 lil imaan al injiili*.

11. *Way of Fatima*, 12.

12. Ibn Ishaq is the earliest known biographer of the Prophet. He was born ca. 704 and died some time between 761–770. Born in Medina, he was the grandson of an

conclusion that Islam is fundamentally violent and that the Prophet was misogynistic and cruel.[13] Ayya, from chapter 4, became disgusted with Islam as she learned about how the Qur'an tells men that women should be treated.

We find these themes of coercion and evangelism surface again in the following text:

Selections from "Steadfast"[14]

Advance! With the streams of living water. . .it's the time for evangelism
Don't be afraid . . . it's a dangerous time
Fill your heart with love . . . the revolution of love drives away fear
Any other god is evil
Opium for people and naïveté of the mind
Your Christ is a path of reformation and a sun of enlightenment
Don't be afraid. . .all the enemy's wells are dry
Whitened tombs . . . decorated . . . papers on which death is written

Steadfast . . . steadfast
We'll evangelize
In our cells, we'll evangelize
In solitary confinement, we'll evangelize our body cells
We'll evangelize the particles of the air . . . we'll baptize the steel bars
We'll save the walls . . . we'll light the tombs with your light
We won't keep silent[15]

Here, persecution and evangelism are closely and directly linked to each other: "it's time for evangelism . . . it's a dangerous time." Also, the centrality of love is again present: "the revolution of love drives fear away." The liberation motif—mentioned by Rambo in his conversion model—is formulated in terms of transitioning from being in a drugged state to clarity of sight and to light radiating from Messiah who is "a sun of enlightenment." The image of the sun is especially important for anyone who has spent time in a jail or prison in the Muslim world, since the cells there usually have no

---

enslaved Christian, and upon conversion to Islam was granted his freedom. His *Siirat Rasuul Allah (Life of the Messenger of God)* has been enormously influential through the centuries.

13. Ibn Warraq, *Leaving Islam*; Khalil and Bilici, "Conversion out of Islam."

14. In Copeland, *Den of Infidels*, 171–72.

15. The poem was written in Arabic originally, by an author using the name Mozafar. His entire conversion narrative can be read in Copeland, *Den of Infidels*.

ventilation or windows and the prisoner can go for months without seeing the light of day.[16]

"[L]anguage-use plays a critical role in the attainment and/or exercise of power,"[17] and here we have a rhetoric of empowerment. Al Mutayri says, "your swords do not concern me at all" and she is announcing that, while the reality of physical punishment remains, the psychological fear that once made this exercise of power effective in stopping the spread of the Christian message is now powerless. The poem "Steadfast" carries a similar message, that while the power of the state to imprison the apostate is still real, that coercive act of imprisonment is in fact powerless to stop the spread of the Christian message because "we'll evangelize in our cells . . ."[18] Paradoxically, in their powerlessness, these two poets have found an empowering message, and announce that while coercion is still a reality it is meaningless. I doubt these ex-Muslim Christians were aware of and echoing Latin American liberation theology, but it is noteworthy that their texts invoke a similar critique of power to that enunciated by Jon Sobrino in his discussion of Latin American liberation theology, which is contained in the epigraph of this chapter.

In many of these texts we find individuals who have experienced a new source of power, which "allows the grip of social norms and standards to lose their hold on regulating behavior."[19] These texts contain a subversive message—that the use of coercion which historically was relatively effective in containing the "pollution" of the Christian message is now powerless against the converts' sense of empowerment.

Baptism

Some of the language used is provocative, like Al Mutayri calling Jesus "Lord of the Worlds" or Mozafar's reference to "papers on which death is written," which the Muslim reader may understand to be a veiled reference to the Qur'an. The explicit mention of baptism ("we'll baptize the steel bars . . .") also puts forth a contentious topic with no sense of timidity. Having examined baptism as a rite of initiation in chapter 2, it is helpful to see what

16. See, for instance, the Egyptian prison experience in Robinson and Botross, *Defying Death*.

17. Kedar, *Power through Discourse*, v.

18. The theme of the hidden power of the Kingdom of God being greater than the coercive power of the state (or Empire) is prevalent in the Apostolic and early church (Acts 16:23–40, *Martyrdom of Polycarp*, *The Martyrdom of Saints Perpetua and Felicitas*).

19. Galinsky, "Power to Action," 454.

ex-Muslim Christians say about baptism, and how it is related to this rhetoric of empowerment.

Bilquis Sheikh, an ex-Muslim from Pakistan, explains how baptism is seen by Muslims:

> I knew that the significance of baptism is not lost on the Muslim world. A person can read the Bible without arousing too much hostility. But the sacrament of baptism is a different matter. To the Muslim this is the one unmistakable sign that a convert has renounced his Islamic faith to become a Christian. To the Muslim, baptism is apostasy.[20]

The implication is that there is some finality to the physical ritual of baptism which is not lost on the larger Muslim community, and I have found this to be equally true in the Middle East. Attending a church physically may be seen as odd or even polluting, but the ritual of baptism itself has a sense of finality to it (recall Tertullian's metaphor of crossing the Red Sea) and after that the Muslim community has little hope of winning the convert back. Baptism opens the convert to additional persecution.

Baptism is not interpreted merely as an individual's commitment to Jesus, but as a commitment to his church as well. One ex-Muslim pastor strongly connects baptism and the church, writing,

> In the process of baptism one should take oaths like, "I have received Jesus Christ as my Savior and Lord. I will lead my life according to the teachings of the Bible, and I will do whatever the Church instructs me to do consistent with it," etc. How can a person dare to leave Christ after receiving instruction and taking oaths of this kind?!"[21]

Similarly, when Steven Masood is told by the Western pastor at a Methodist church in Pakistan that he should be baptized in private, he resists, insisting on a public baptism during the Sunday worship.[22]

In what may well be the earliest autobiography of a Muslim convert to Christianity, John Avetaranian,[23] born Muhammad Shukri Efendi, explicitly criticizes the weakness (from his point of view) of the theology of the Protestant missionaries in the Ottoman Empire. The missionaries are afraid to baptize him or want to baptize him in private.

---

20. Sheikh, *Call Him Father*, 61.

21. Emphasis added, Ayub, "Observations and reactions," 30.

22. Masood, *Into the Light*, 150.

23. 1861–1919.

> I read many writings about baptism, which for the most part held the view that baptism was only a symbol or a sign. However, they did not convince me since I had gained a different view from the Gospel. This view was that *baptism, for me and for everyone who is not born a Christian, is a confession of Jesus before men and an act of faith through which a person is received into the Kingdom of Christ.*[24]

He concludes that *"the missionaries did not take baptism as seriously as I did"* (ibid.).

Baptism in the writing of some CMBs is held to be more central to the Christian life than for Western evangelical missionaries who helped, in some cases at least, to evangelize them. It is not clear precisely what the source of this difference is regarding baptism. American anthropologist Edwin Zehner, who has studied conversion from both Buddhism and Islam to evangelical Christianity, offers one suggestion:

> I personally suspect that new MBBs value baptism more than even the missionaries do, because they are already used to the notion of a "ritual of entry" (two of them, in fact—the *shahada* and circumcision). The missionaries, on the other hand, almost all come from backgrounds that [regard] baptism as a symbol, delaying it, and even . . . shifting some of its New Testament symbolic resources to other "acts of entry" such as the "prayer of conversion."[25]

It is striking to see how Mozafar relates evangelism and baptism in his empowering rhetoric. Like al Mutayri, he has disarmed his persecutors. Their power has become null and void. Even when they put him in jail he will continue to preach and, not only that, deploy the most powerful ritual resource he can conceive—baptism. And as shown above, baptism is indeed a very powerful (and subversive) resource. His imprisonment, intended to eliminate his polluting, subversive rhetoric, is not and cannot be effective. His theology of persecution, probably taken straight from the Sermon on the Mount, guarantees this. Baptism is a clear connection in terms of praxis, or theology as action, to the rhetoric of empowerment just described.[26]

24. Avetaranian, *Muslim who became a Christian*, 45, italics in original.

25. Correspondence with author, March 2010.

26. Llull makes a similar point, though it is unlikely that these converts know of him. "If you give yourself to Our Lord Jesus Christ what have you to fear from those who would incarcerate you?" (*Raymond's Proverbs* 34:15).

Praxis

Several of these themes are reminiscent of liberation theology, which understands the outcome of theology-making not as certain knowledge, but as praxis. It appears that the themes of liberation and parallels to other forms of liberation theology are so strong that it may be accurate to identify some of these writings as liberation theology. Let us submit the claim to scrutiny.

We must ask if these texts lead to praxis, which is " . . . the ensemble of social relationships that include and determine the structures of social conscience."[27] In relating praxis to liberation we read further, "Since oppressive relations occur in every society, and in many societies characterize the larger part of social life, praxis can come to be defined as revolutionary or transformative practice, aimed at the changing of those patterns."[28]

The main oppressive pattern here is not economic as was often the case with the Latin American varieties of liberation theology. Nor is the oppressive pattern the institutional racism denounced by black theology, nor the prolonged and illegal occupation of the West Bank and Gaza which Naim Ateek[29] targets in his Palestinian liberation theology.[30] Each of these liberation theologies read their contextuality in a different way, identifying different unjust structures which, they felt, were incongruent with the justice and liberty revealed in the Kingdom of God. In the texts of ex-Muslim Christians it is possible to identify different unjust structures which the authors are targeting, trying to undermine, transform, or redeem.

One of the most common "unjust structures" identifiable in the literature is the Islamic shari'a. This is especially true for converts whose conversion took place within an Islamic state. Shari'a stipulates death for these apostates, but the empowered Fatima commands, "Leave us to live in grace, until our time comes." The shari'a puts them in jail, but even there they will "baptize the steel bars." To the efforts of the shari'a to silence the propagation of the Gospel, Mozafar announces to God, "We'll light the tombs with your light." These statements are indicative of liberating praxis—an aim to subvert unjust social structures.

Another subversive aspect of praxis has already been noted—baptism. And baptism is the ritual culmination and enactment of religious

27. Schreiter, *Local Theologies*, 91.

28. Ibid.

29. It is worth noting that Ateek does not support efforts to evangelize Muslims, as he told me in 2012 during an interview.

30. Key sources on Latin American liberation theology are Boff, *Jesus Christ Liberator*; Boff and Boff, *Liberation Theology*; Gutierrez, *Liberación*. For Black theology of liberation see Cone, *Black Theology*. On Palestinian liberation theology, see Ateek, *Justice*.

conversion, the goal (or at least a goal) of evangelism. Both of the texts mentioned above are explicitly evangelistic. Daniel Ali, a Kurdish convert, originally from Iraq, offers a good example of how pronounced this emphasis can be: "In terms of all He has done for me, I cannot, and will not, shut my mouth and keep Christ to myself! . . . We cease to be Christians if we keep the faith to ourselves."[31] Many other conversion narratives of ex-Muslim Christians likewise are explicit in advocating Muslim evangelism and inviting the Muslim reader to leave Islam and embrace Christianity.

Perhaps the most successful living evangelist of Muslims is the Coptic priest Zakaria Boutros.[32] He was mentioned by several of the missionaries and CMBs whom I met and interviewed. While he himself did not come from a Muslim family, in many ways he exemplifies the subversive praxis of evangelism, and in him some CMBs find an example for their own witness. Without going into great detail, the systematic theology of Boutros, which appears to be a form of Coptic Orthodoxy with evangelical sensitivities, is not the issue. He has influenced many CMBs through the theological message that he is communicating, not so much in his words, but in the very *act* of engaging in overt, unapologetic, bold evangelization of Muslims. Equally scandalous to many Muslims is his success.[33] His apologetic ministry, which is broadcast on satellite TV all over the Muslim world, enables a Copt to challenge Muslims regarding everything from the Qur'an to the Prophet to shari'a. This state of affairs represents a huge reversal of the order envisioned in the Qur'an (at least as many Muslims interpret it) wherein Muslims ("the best of all peoples")[34] enjoy a privileged position above the People of the Book, who "pay the jizya with willing submission, and they are subdued" (9:29). It is significant that Boutros is often accompanied by his assistant, Rashid, who is a CMB. The very act of engaging in Muslim evangelism, even if it does not result in large numbers of conversions, is in itself subversive. This is all the more the case when substantial numbers of Muslims do in fact convert, which has taken place through Boutros's ministry and his "short, sharp, shocking" approach to Christian witness.[35]

The texts of CMBs vary widely in how explicit they are in inviting the Muslim reader to convert. Sometimes the possibility of religious conversion is only implied as the author narrates how and why they themselves

31. Ali, *Out of Islam*, 149.

32. Sometimes spelled Botros.

33. During a conversation with him in 2006 he told me he had baptized over 500 Muslims himself.

34. Qur'an 7:89.

35. This is how he described his technique to me during a conversation in 2006.

converted.[36] At other times the author makes an explicit invitation to the Muslim reader to consider the Christian faith and convert,[37] including even a form of the sinner's prayer so the Muslim can convert right then and there by himself.[38]

This desire for liberation, accompanied by a praxis that aims to transform or subvert unjust social structures, is not limited to the Arab world. We also see it enunciated in "A Letter from the Afghan Persecuted Church in Christ," an address to then-US President George W. Bush.[39] The background was the new constitution that was going to be passed which would have no provision for religious freedom for Afghan Christians. They were writing to President Bush to ask him to intervene because, "The sword of Islam should be removed from Afghanistan and Afghanistan should be a democratic country instead of Islamic, where all the sects have freedom."[40] The Afghan Christians ask, "if it is possible to make mosques in US and Rome, why could there [not] be a church in Afghanistan???"[41] The letter alleges around 3,000 Christian Afghans at the time of its writing in 2003.

But what is it about the shari'a that has led some ex-Muslim Christians to identify it is an unjust structure which must be undermined through the liberating praxis of the Gospel?

Perceived Injustices Related to the Shari'a

The status of the apostate in a Muslim society was outlined in chapter 2, but here it is appropriate to add some additional examples of specific difficulties that converts living in many Muslim countries mention and have written about as they try to live out their lives as Christians. These are all the "consequences" of conversion in Rambo's model, and they help us to understand why the shari'a has been identified by some CMBs as an unjust structure to be subverted, and also the nature of the rights they would like to have in a new (liberated) society.

Historically, " . . . as Islam elaborated, it was Canon Law (*Shari'ah*) rather than theology that was most rigorously protected and applied."[42]

---

36. Shah, *Imam's Daughter*; Saleem, *Blood of Lambs*.

37. Rabiipour, *Farewell to Islam*.

38. Alam, *Out of Islam*.

39. Found in an appendix of Andrew and Janssen, *Secret Believers*, 265–68.

40. Ibid., 267.

41. Ibid., 268.

42. Badeau, *Arab Role*, 10.

From the point of view of Islam the shari'a is God's benevolent will for humankind, and it touches on almost every aspect of life:

> The shari'ah has always held a central place in Muslim life and Islamic thought. As God's revealed law to guide humanity on the proper path, it is meant to govern both individual and communal life, from matters of worship to commerce to warfare to family relationships.[43]

For some people detailed guidance from Allah for the most quotidian actions is reassuring, but many ex-Muslims claim that aspects of the shari'a are de-humanizing and identify it as a humiliating system of oppression. Beyond the punishment for apostasy, it is helpful to explore in more detail other aspects of the shari'a which are identified as inhumane and unjust.

One of the most difficult situations relates to marriage.[44] One CMB from Egypt described to me the following difficulties: A man whose documents show him to be Muslim may marry a Christian woman, but many Christian parents will not agree to have their daughter marry such a man. This is because if the two wed, their children will inherit the status of Muslim from their father, in accordance with the shari'a. This means that even if they are baptized and raised in the church, they will probably have to take classes on Islam periodically during their schooling under a Muslim teacher. It would also mean that in all questions of family law, like divorce, custody, and inheritance, cases will be handled according to the principles of Islamic shari'a, and not by Christian church courts.

In the case of an ex-Muslima, it is likely she cannot be married to a Christian, as the shari'a prohibits anyone other than a Muslim to take a Muslim wife. Unless she can legally change her religion, she will always live with this limitation in her home country. Her options are either a Muslim man (which most Christians understand as being contrary to Scripture and/ or culturally reprehensible) or a fellow ex-Muslim. If she assents/agrees to marrying a Muslim man who has little or no sympathy for Christianity, she may well be pressured constantly to "revert" to Islam, and/or be beaten, and she may be rejected by the local Christian community—that is if she is even able to visit them anymore. If she marries a foreigner then she will probably leave the country, facing all the challenges of a new society in a new country.[45] Moreover her ability to evangelize her friends and family is drastically

---

43. Ali and Leaman, *Key Concepts*, 122.

44. Green, "Identity Issues for ex-Muslim Christians"; Meral, *No Place to Call Home.*

45. It is this path that is often found in the texts written by converts—that of emigrating and marrying a foreigner. See for instance Lotfi, *Iranian Christian*; Rabiipour,

diminished. Yet this option may be preferred. Moreover it represents a successful use of power to eliminate the polluting presence of the apostate: by not permitting her to marry a local she has to marry a foreigner (if she is going to marry anyone at all), and this will rid the Muslim country of her presence.[46]

"Childrearing can be one of the biggest challenges for apostates from Islam."[47] For converts living in many Muslim countries, their children will be Muslim in the eye of the law. This means raising children who are taught Islam at school, have Muslim extended family, and yet who attend church and who call themselves Christians. The shari'a makes it impossible for converts to experience a new and stable identity that respects their various social identities—ex-Muslim Christian, member of this family, citizen of this state, and so on.

The taboo on religious conversion, the use of violence to punish converts, and the restrictions just mentioned all help to account for why the very legal system of Islamic society is often a key object of subversion in these texts.[48] In many of these texts, theology-making leads to liberating praxis and an affirmation of the possession of an interior power, superior to the coercive power of the Umma. Evangelism, exposing what the converts consider to be the inhumane nature of the shari'a, and a refutation of the efficacy of persecution to silence their voices appear to be a long-term strategy to transform the Islamic societies of the converts into tolerant societies with something resembling freedom of religion.

" . . . How Do We Fight for Our Rights?"

Nevertheless, it would be incorrect to picture this sought-for liberation in solely negative terms of liberation *from* the shari'a. It is a recurring theme,

---

Farewell to Islam; Saada, *Arafat Man*; Saleem, *Blood of Lambs*.

46. One Iranian convert I interviewed related to me that her bishop told her she could be baptized, but that she would probably never get married then, as there were no marriageable Christian male converts in Iran at that time (Miller, "Secret World of God," 1–14). Andrew and Janssen, in *Secret Believers*, include a number of dramatized examples of CMBs trying to have a Christian marriage within an Egyptian context (wherein legal conversions are impossible).

47. Meral, *No Place to Call Home*, 70.

48. For more detailed information on the difficulties faced by converts as they seek to form their new religious identity see chapter 8 of Kraft, "Community and Identity." Kraft, who interviewed numerous converts in Egypt and Lebanon, argues that converts face anomie, disappointment with other Christians, both local and foreign, and are especially challenged by the issue of how to raise Christian children who are treated as Muslims by the state.

but it is with the goal of reaching something else, of constructing a new society. As Timothy Abraham, from chapter 2, wrote in an email, "We are done with Islam and good riddance to bad rubbish, and the question that remains is, how do we fight for our rights and not yield to that Eastern fatalism in resignation to persecution?"[49] This liberation theology is thus not only critical but seeks to build a new and just social order, one influenced by the teachings and ethics of Jesus Christ and found in the Gospels.

But in the meanwhile, until liberation is achieved, how are they to live and negotiate the difficulties presented above regarding difficult issues like marriage, children and identity-formation? The sought for liberation appears to be deeply related to identity-formation. These believers are trying to live out a new identity amid structures and traditions related to the Islamic shari'a which appear to forbid this. This question—*how do we fight for our rights?*—leads to theology-making in the form of praxis. But the texts of CMBs do not *only* understand theology as liberating praxis, they also see it as wisdom for daily life in a very complex and sometimes dispiriting context.

THEOLOGY AS WISDOM

Conversion Narratives as Evangelistic Texts

Different communities communicate what they know about God in different ways (chapter 2). One of them, praxis, has already been mentioned. There is, however, another form of communicating what is known about God and our relation to him that surfaces in the texts written by ex-Muslim Christians: wisdom. In Christianity (and other religions as well) there is a strong tradition differentiating wisdom from analytical knowledge, and seeing wisdom as "[applying] knowledge and experience to life with a view to living it wholesomely and harmoniously."[50] Wisdom is also understood as "the ability to discern the divinely ordained pattern within nature and experience, and then to follow the prescribed way of living well so as to be in right relationship with God."[51]

Perhaps the most common theological texts of CMBs are conversion narratives. Through the use of narrative these texts tell one *how* to go about converting to Christianity, and then how to live as a Christian, and within the narrative answer complex questions about relating to hostile family

49. Personal correspondence, 2010.

50. Atkinson, *Ethics and Pastoral Theology*, 896.

51. Sheldrake, *Dictionary of Christian Spirituality*, 643.

members, evangelism, persecution, imprisonment, employment, how to interact with unsympathetic Islamic governmental authorities, how to interpret visions and dreams, and so on. Shorter conversion narratives can be found on the Internet[52] and in print,[53] but it is the book-length ones that offer the fullest treatment. Significantly, sometimes the convert will relate what he or she did, and then explain why it was not the best thing to do, and what they should have done. There is clearly a pedagogical element in these narratives. Thus we should not interpret them as auto-hagiographies, but as genuine attempts of ex-Muslims to communicate how they dealt with the difficulties associated with their conversions Two examples of such texts were mentioned above (Sheikh and Rishawi), but we could also point to books like *Once an Arafat Man* by Tass Saada (2008), *Jumping through Fires* by David Nasser (2009), and *Secret Believers: What Happens when Muslims Turn to Christ?* by Brother Andrew and Al Janssen (2007).

The Paradoxical Reality of Persecution and a Loving God

The reality of persecution was a common concern in Jesus's own teaching, and remains one today for CMBs. Persecution is used against individual believers, and entire communities, and a key concern for a community of believers is how it can avoid closing itself off to the world in a protective cocoon, or what Shirley Madany calls "the stifling of the spirit."[54] The questions addressed by this wisdom theology are varied and difficult. The answers appear as common sense advice at times, but wisdom theology goes beyond such advice as it brings together the invisible benevolent and sometimes hidden love and will of God with a sometimes violent and oppressive world that rejects that divine love and wisdom. As such it represents knowledge about God, perhaps not "certain knowledge," but a personal knowledge, or more precisely, a knowledge about the personality of the God who reveals himself in his Messiah and whose acts are recorded in the Bible.

The intersection of this knowledge of God's personality and the reality of persecution provides a fertile area for the theology-making. For instance, to interact with Muslim enquirers can be dangerous business for the local church and the local pastor or priest. Assisting an apostate is often seen as colluding in her polluting activity. Gulshan Esther[55] gives an account of

---

52. Probably the largest single repository of such narratives is online at http://www.answering-islam.org/Testimonies/index.html.

53. For instance, Copeland, *Den of Infidels*.

54. Madany, *Muslims Meeting Christ*, 7.

55. Esther, *Torn Veil*.

how difficult it was to convince a Pakistani Christian to give her a Bible. He was clear that it was a dangerous activity both for him, and for her. Monsignor Paul Hinder, auxiliary bishop of Arabia, gave the following answer to the question "What pushes a Christian to embrace Islam [in Arabia]?"

> Not so much conviction, as a desire to get a job, a promotion, a higher salary, or even to marry a Muslim woman. When it does happen it becomes front page news. By contrast, we would not dare accept a Muslim's conversion to Christianity. It would just be too dangerous not only for the person involved but for the Church as such.[56]

Unlike Bishop Hinder, there are evangelical and Pentecostal believers who will "dare accept a Muslim's conversion to Christianity" but understand that such an action requires a great deal of shrewdness. Two of the elements suggested by this wisdom theology in relation to surviving, and perhaps even thriving, in a context of persecution, are forgiving enemies and a devotion to the Bible, which we will explore in that order.

Love, Reconciliation and Peace

Some conversion texts display a particular interest in reconciliation and a hope for peace. An example of this is found in *Once an Arafat Man* (2008). Tass Abu Saada was born in Gaza and, according to his autobiography, was raised there and in the Gulf. He was a defiant youth, who had been a sniper for the Palestinian Liberation Organization, and eventually moved to the USA where he married an American woman. His conversion narrative contains several lessons that could fit in most any Sunday school class throughout the world, like work hard, be honest and success will follow. But of interest here is what he identifies as the moment of his turning, when, in the famous words of William James, "a self hitherto divided and consciously wrong and unhappy, becomes unified and consciously right, superior and happy, in consequence of its firmer hold upon religious realities."[57] He identifies that particular "turning" as the point when he is able to love a Jew—Jesus of Nazareth. The setting is a living room in the USA, with an evangelical friend and business colleague:

> And then I heard myself praying something totally out of character for me. "O God, bless your people Israel. O Lord, lead them back to their Promised Land. Let them see you as their

56. Caffulli, "Catacomb Church," n.p.

57. James, *Varieties of Religious Experience*, 189.

God." . . . I clapped my hand over my mouth. I had never wished a single good thing for the Jews in my entire life.[58]

Using Rambo's terminology, this was his surrender, his turning. Conversion generally entails a reinterpretation and restructuring of past events, even if over a lengthy period.[59] In reflecting on this moment years later, he writes, "The Jew, Jesus Christ, had drained out of me my long-standing hatred for all other Jews. These people were no longer my foes. They were instead my cousins, going back to Abraham."[60] For Saada, his moment of conversion, of commitment, was the same moment when he learned to "love his enemies" (Matt 5:44), perhaps the single verse I heard most quoted by ex-Muslims during the course of this entire research. Saada had become reconciled to God precisely insofar as God had reconciled him to his enemies, and indeed, had made his enemies into his own family, his "cousins, going back to Abraham." Love, in this narrative, *is* the conversion. Finally, Saada's theology translates into action, into praxis, and the last chapter of his book is a proposed peace plan for the Israel-Palestine conflict.[61] Love, it appears, is coterminous with power in his theology. But love/power can only be identified by its ability to reconcile warring parties (the Israelis and Palestinians, the author and Jesus the Jew). Because love and power are coterminous there is no room for compulsion or coercion.

The Bible

Another recurrent wisdom theme in these conversion narratives is the centrality of the Bible, specifically how important it is to the inquirer or the convert, and how multifaceted its role is in these conversion narratives. One example of that was seen in the conversion narrative of Timothy Abraham, from chapter 2. Steven Masood, a convert from Ahmadiyya Islam from Pakistan, was surprised to find the Gospel of John written in his native language. He asks his Pakistani Christian friend, "If this is the Injil given to Jesus the Prophet . . . why is it written in Urdu and not in Arabic, our holy language?"[62] The very translatability of the Bible becomes a powerful factor

---

58. Saada, *Arafat Man*, 108.

59. Gooren, *Conversion and Disaffiliation*, 17.

60. Saada, *Arafat Man*, 118.

61. Note that the connection of love to liberating praxis is clearly enunciated by Gustavo Gutierrez in one of the foundational texts of liberation theology: "Real Christian love is founded on commitment to a more just society and action to bring it about" (*Liberation*, 278).

62. Masood, *Into the Light*, 31.

in his conversion narrative, and even as a child he was discontented with the monolingual nature of Islamic worship: " 'O Allah,' I said scornfully to him, 'can't you understand any language except Arabic? Is that why you do not understand a prayer in Urdu or Pashtu?'"[63]

Another example is found in *Into the Den of Infidels*, a collection of multiple conversion narratives. In it we find the rather lengthy narrative of "Paul." He relates how anxious he was when he first brought a Bible into his house. His religious teacher had given him a special task to read the Bible and reveal all its errors:

> The first day was the most difficult. I was under the impression that the Bible was not from God, and that it might bring demons into my house so I wouldn't be able to pray. Therefore, I kept it outside my bedroom. For many days I was paranoid. Whenever I heard a sound in the house, I thought God had sent demons to punish me for having this book around.[64]

But as he read the book he experienced a change of heart: "I finished reading the Gospel of Matthew . . . I read the rest of the Gospels and the Epistles and was amazed to find philosophy and rhetoric superior to those of the Qur'an. Since the Bible was written 630 years before Islam, how could we say that the Qur'an was unique in rhetoric?"[65] The implication (for the Muslim reader, at least) is that there is no danger in having or reading the Bible, and that the "philosophy and rhetoric" of the Bible are at least equal to those of the Qur'an. He later goes on to learn more about the life of the Prophet and becomes disillusioned with him. Near the end of his narrative he reminds readers that as a Christian he now loves his Middle Eastern country more than he ever did before, another recurring motif in these texts, an attempt to affirm his social identity as citizen *and* Christian. One key theme, then, is the centrality of God's love and the conviction that God's love is present in the midst of suffering, and that "Perhaps we could say that such sufferings are 'Christ's sufferings in my flesh.'"[66] If the rather sacramental theology of baptism represents discontinuity with some forms of evangelical piety, the affection for and reliance upon the Bible at all times appears to be in continuity with much of evangelicalism.

The texts are written with the awareness that different people are facing different circumstances. The life of an Iranian youth growing up in the

63. Ibid., 21.

64. Copeland, *Den of Infidels*, 91.

65. Ibid., 99. Ayya from chapter 4 made a similar comment, saying that the teaching of Jesus was, in her opinion, superior to that of the Qur'an.

66. Arthur, "Out on a Limb," 5.

USA (David Nasser) is different from the life of a Lebanese terrorist (Kamal Saleem). The authors put forth their own circumstances, including what *not* to do. So Nasser tells us about hanging out in a car with a Christian buddy and smoking pot and talking religion, without recommending that particular approach. Bilquis Sheikh tells us about how she baptized herself, but clarifies that this is not the normal or preferred practice. Saada tells us that one reason why he got married (before his conversion) was to secure residency in the USA. Steven Masood tells us about how he stood up in his local Ahmadiyya mosque in Pakistan and, as a young man, confronted the religious leader with some of the problems surrounding the claims of the Ahmadiyya movement's founding figure, but then tells us that he had been motivated by pride, with the implication that the beating he subsequently received was not genuine persecution.

Recurring Themes of Wisdom Theology

Taking into account the great variety found in the conversion narratives of CMBs, we are able to nonetheless identify some recurring tendencies, which I have outlined above. Many of the authors are clearly *evangelistic*, meaning that they are writing for a Muslim audience (in part at least), and they invite Muslims to embrace the Christian faith. Second, I have argued that *one reason* for this is that by converting Muslims to Christianity the oppressive structures which they believe are related to Islam, the Qur'an, and the Prophet, can be replaced with structures that are just and right (*liberation*). Third, in this wisdom literature there is a concern with *persecution* and ample advice is given regarding how to handle thorny issues related to government, the mosque, and family, all the while not compromising one's new identity in Christ. Fourth, there is a recurring return to the theme of *reconciliation*, with the conviction (sometimes explicit) that love and forgiveness can be accessed only in the person of Jesus Christ, and not Muhammad. Fifth, there is a recurring teaching that the Bible is a perpetual source of encouragement, strength, and sometimes, answers.

Wisdom aims to "discern the divinely ordained pattern within nature and experience . . ."[67] These texts are attempting to do this—to discern the hidden order of God's work in relation to politics, history, family, persecution, migration, and marriage.

---

67. Holder, "Wisdom," 643.

EXAMPLES OF THEOLOGY AS LIBERATION AND WISDOM: GULSHAN ESTHER AND HANNAH SHAH

In exploring the wisdom themes found in these texts, we encounter a number of different concerns. This section will explore two conversion narratives and give some examples of how CMBs utilize their own experiences—both positive and negative—to communicate a wisdom theology to their readers, and specifically to persons who have converted to Christianity, or may be open to such a religious conversion.

One of the most widely-distributed conversion narratives of an ex-Muslim Christian is *The Torn Veil* by Gulshan Esther, as told to Thelma Sangster.[68] This is the story of a privileged Pakistani lady who claims she was miraculously healed of paralysis. In addition to the healing miracle there are visions of Jesus with the twelve Apostles,[69] an audible message from God instructing her to read about Jesus in the Qur'an,[70] and a recurring devotion to the Bible. Part of the gradual development that led to her religious conversion was a visit to a medical doctor in England when she was a teenager. Several of the factors facilitating conversion from chapter 3 are present in her own conversion narrative—travel, visions, a miracle, availability of the Bible in the local language, etc.

Two of the key concerns common to many CMBs surface repeatedly in this book relate to work and family. After her miraculous healing, which she insists was from Jesus, her family becomes upset with her: " . . . it made my brothers restless."[71] One brother recommends she revise her narrative: "We would respect you more if you said that Mohammed had healed you. This Jesus is not very important to us."[72] Things go from bad to worse as she will not stop telling people about Jesus who miraculously healed her. Eventually the same brother informs her that "For the sake of Islam we can murder you. It says so in the Holy Koran."[73] This change in her brother causes her to ask,

---

68. The book, first published in 1984, has been re-issued in multiple editions. I am using the 2010 edition from CLC Publications (Fort Washington, Pennsylvania).

69. Esther, *Torn Veil*, 75.

70. Ibid., 60, 76.

71. Ibid., 85.

72. Ibid.

73. Ibid., 91. One might respond that the Qur'an says no such thing. But that is not important in the story—her brother believes the Qur'an says so, and it is unlikely that in Pakistan he would suffer any repercussion for such an action since it would be seen as a necessary way of maintaining his family's honor by stopping the spread of Esther's polluting influence.

"How could religion breed such hatred that they would rather see me dead than telling a truth they didn't agree with?" She is threatened with all of her substantial properties and income being taken away from her if she will not stop talking about how Jesus healed her. And here we find her wisdom theology, for in her response to this serious ultimatum she says:

> I've listened to you at length, and of course, I understand your concern . . . I can't answer all the points you've made because I am waiting for the answer of Jesus to me. He will tell me what to do next. When I hear the order I'll obey Him, and even if you kill me, I'll do it . . . I promise I won't dishonor the family in what I do . . . [74]

There is a delicate and dangerous balance here. She is trying to honor her family, but also honor God. She is trying to live out her two identities, as a follower of Jesus but also as a loyal member of her family. From the point of view of some of her family members though, these two identities are mutually exclusive. For a while she is able to continue in this precarious situation, but when her family forces her to choose between them and Jesus, she chooses Jesus, and goes from a life of wealth and ease to one of poverty. She is informed by Jesus (in another vision) to find a local Christian (up to this point she does not know there are Pakistani Christians) and that he will give her a Bible. She makes careful plans and escapes from her family before they harm her. The Christian, a Pakistani major in the Salvation Army, instructs her not to bring any money or jewelry, lest someone sue the Christians or the church and accuse them of having converted her for the sake of financial gain.

Here we find a theological statement about wisdom in reference to a harmonious life. Esther has tried to maintain harmony and balance by loving her family but also by sharing the miracle that Jesus has done in her life—a miracle that did not take place during her pilgrimage to Mecca, Medina, and Jerusalem, as her father had so hoped. But eventually she is stymied in her attempt at the harmonious and balanced life. She is forced to choose between obeying Jesus and the prospect of great loss—losing her family, her wealth, and possibly her very life. The bold statement recorded above, accompanied by her stealthy escape, provide the convert or enquirer with a possible pattern of action should they be faced with a similar situation. The message is that while you must try to honor your family, you must never do so at the expense of confessing Jesus Christ.

Bryson Arthur, a Scottish theologian, made a similar point with these words in which he laid out a theology of risk, suffering and persecution:

74. Ibid., 92.

> The suffering involved in risk is anxiety of a particularly acute form. And anxiety is a profound care and worry that we are going to encounter loss . . . Faith is the only remedy for anxiety and so it is the counterbalance of risk. Faith is the healing dynamic in the suffering of risk.[75]

It appears that both Arthur and Esther are proposing a similar theological idea. But Esther's narrative style and wisdom theology (as compared to Arthur's more systematic approach) make her content accessible to a very different audience, which would probably never read a theological journal or essay. As is the case with so many conversion narratives, the story ends in exile, with Esther teaching and ministering in the UK.

A more recent book published both in the UK and the USA is that of Hannah Shah. She provides another example of wisdom theology in her book *The Imam's Daughter*. She tells of being raised in a Pakistani home in the UK. Her father is the imam at the local mosque and receives disability payments from the government. She is taught that white people are dirty and immoral but her later experience calls this into question. Her father, who periodically rapes her from age six up with no opposition from her mother or siblings, is very unlike the father figure in Esther's book—a pious and caring man. Multiple wisdom lessons emerge as she shares her experiences with other young ladies from a British-Asian background. For instance, at one point she talks with a social worker named Omar and starts to open up to him about what is going on at her home. She arrives home one day and finds Omar speaking with her father, who is kind, humble, and welcoming to Omar, who is also an Asian Muslim. Omar leaves and Hannah is beaten, raped, and locked in the cellar for days. Omar later comments to Hannah that, "It's not right to betray your community."[76] Hannah is communicating an important message here: beware of Muslims in government positions, because they may well put the honor of the (ethnic Muslim) community before your well-being. Omar thought he was doing the right thing by concealing the shame of an imam mistreating his daughter, but Hannah reprimands him saying, "You're shit at your job."[77]

In Shah's book the wisdom and liberation motifs are closely related to each other. A number of factors combine in Shah's life that result in her conversion to Christianity and to starting a ministry to provide safe-houses for young Muslim women who are being abused or are afraid of being forced to marry someone, as almost happened to her. Her audience is not just Muslim

---

75. Arthur, "Out on a Limb," 22.

76. Shah, *Imam's Daughter*, 160.

77. Ibid.

women in the UK but also the British population as a whole, urging them to realize that forced marriages are not just a quaint and curious custom of certain Asians that should be respected under the guise of non-judgmental multi-culturalism, but are a genuine injustice against young women:

> At school our politically correct lessons had avoided the dark and misogynistic side of forced marriages. It was presented as a cultural and religious practice that, while seeming strange to most British people, should be treated with respect and under-standing. The reality—that this was often a shocking and brutal abuse of women—was left unreported.[78]

In the Father of Jesus Shah says that she found genuine love, and in the church of Jesus she found a man who genuinely loved her and now they are married. In breaking free of the confines of Pakistani culture where honor is more important than justice (as she conveys it) and in marrying "for love," she has experienced her liberation. She invites other young Asian women to consider her experience with the implication that they too can experience the same liberation, though she is less overtly evangelistic than some authors such as Rabiipour or Alam. She has identified an unjust social structure in the Pakistani Muslim community—the abuse of young women which includes forced marriages.[79] In the Christian religion she claims she has found an ethical system that values justice above honor, and it was the honor- and shame-based ethic of her Pakistani community that created the oppressive environment in which the abuse of girls and women is prevalent, if rarely acknowledged. This sense of justice has empowered her to take a stand against the abuse of women which she claims to be prevalent among Indian and Pakistani Muslims in the UK.

---

78. Ibid., 163.

79. It is important to note that Shah does not claim that all Islamic societies have these same unjust practices. She clearly states that she is talking about the form of Islam which she experienced as she grew up in the UK. The Qur'an itself is mute on the topic of arranged/forced marriages, though it does call marriage a "sign" from God (30:21). The example of the Prophet includes the consummation of his marriage to Aisha who was given to him as a wife by her father, and the union was consummated when she was nine, according to her own narration: "'Aisha (Allah be pleased with her) reported that Allah's Apostle (PBUH) married her when she was seven years old, and she was taken to his house as a bride when she was nine, and her dolls were with her; and when he (the Holy Prophet) died she was eighteen years old" (*Sahiih Muslim* Book 8, No 3311). Thus arranged marriages are permitted. Forced marriage is seen as forbidden due to *Sahiih Muslim* Book 8, No 3303: "A woman without a husband (or divorced or a widow) must not be married until she is consulted, and a virgin must not be married until her permission is sought. They asked the Prophet of Allah (PBUH): How her (the virgin's) consent can be solicited? He (the Holy Prophet) said: That she keeps silence."

CONCLUSION: CONTEXTUALITY AND CONTEXTUALIZATION

Coe's model of contextualization offers a framework to understand how theology-making might take place. Schreiter's sociology of theological knowledge describes what the outcome of the theology-making process might look like. Insofar as Coe's model of theology-making is adequate, and Schreiter's forms of theological knowledge are adequate, it is logical to conclude that ex-Muslim Christians are indeed engaged in theology-making.

A critical discernment of contextuality is the pre-requisite for the process of contextualization. Based on the texts described here, in evaluating their contextuality, some ex-Muslim Christians have discerned that God is active in the world in terms of liberating Muslims from the "darkness" of Islam, and also liberating entire Islamic societies from that "darkness." Their active response to this discernment of their contextuality is multifaceted.

First, the composition of conversion narratives constitutes a de facto invitation to convert for the Muslim reader, even if that invitation may not be spelled out explicitly in the text.

Second, reacting to the state or family persecution of converts in many Muslim lands (or even in the UK, in the case of Hannah Shah), the texts advocate religious freedom and tolerance—a subversive and risky form of praxis. The acts of writing, publishing, distributing, advocating, conversing, evangelizing are all praxis and they *are* theology. Recalling Schreiter's theory, we should not construe theology only as "certain knowledge," for in liberation theology by its very nature God-knowledge must express itself in and lead to praxis. When an ex-Muslim Christian writes a text, describing their own experiences and communicating their wisdom, they are engaged in praxis and in the very choice of the medium of poetry or conversion narrative they have already made a theological judgment. Contextualization, here, means aiming and working towards a transformed society where "man is the brother of man," as Fatima al Mutayri wrote.

Third, these theology-makers know first-hand the difficulties that people face as they walk the long road of religious conversion, and then live with its consequences (contextuality, "God's world"). They have the resource of their own experiences—the resource of wisdom—and their theological knowledge is transmitted in their own narratives. That is contextualization. It is organic, growing from the discernment of the ex-Muslims themselves. It is *theology by*, in that the authors are selecting their own questions and topics and audiences, and then addressing them according to their own chosen method and format.

What is the shape of the liberation sought? For converts in the Muslim world it is acceptance as co-citizens, acknowledgment of their conversion by the instruments of mosque/state, and an open public square wherein religious agreements and disagreements can be discussed with security and respect and without recourse to coercion, imprisonment, torture, exile or execution. In a word, they want a *home*—a place where they will be accepted, secure and safe. This goal comes across in the title of Ziya Meral's survey of persecution of CMBs around the world: *No Place to Call Home*.

Furthermore, this contextual theology-making is organic. While there are influences from and interactions with certain outsiders, like Andrew and Boutros, the texts here are born from the context of the ex-Muslims and seek to address the questions that originate in that context—persecution, family relations, citizenship, migration and so on. For converts in the diaspora it is likewise a subversion of activities that are interpreted to be linked to Islam and also unjust or dangerous.[80]

Many ex-Muslims believe that the only thing holding hundreds of thousands of people—maybe millions—from leaving Islam for Christianity is fear of punishment and persecution. Some have crossed that threshold, and their message is "now is the time for evangelism," and "Love alone can remove grudges, and forgiveness alone can blot out transgression. To die for the killer is the only way to annul killing,"[81] and "A man who can disagree and yet remain gracious with you is a hundred times greater than a god who cannot bear divergence of opinion or criticism—the dictator's fragile throne."[82] The dictator's fragile throne is the entire oppressive system of the Islamic shari'a, and in the words of Fatima al-Mutayri, the goal is "civility that is transparent in appearance // and a new civilization in all measures and laws . . ."[83] It is this "new civilization" which is the Promised Land to which these exiles are traveling, to use a favorite image from Latin American liberation theology.

80. Shah is an obvious example of this, but see also Kamal Saleem's book *The Blood of Lambs*. By his own account he was a terrorist with the Muslim Brotherhood for many years who immigrated to the USA as a *daa3i* or Muslim missionary. After a car accident he was welcomed into the home of a Christian family who helped him recover and a group of Christian businessmen paid for his medical bills. This experience of hospitality and kindness occasioned the crisis (to use Rambo's term) that eventually led to his conversion. His mission now is to warn the West about the dangers that Islamists pose to their freedoms and security, in his view. Like Shah, he wants people to "wake up" to the realities he has experienced in contemporary Islam, however politically incorrect they may be.

81. Rishawi, *Struggle that led to Conversion*, 175.

82. Quoted in Andrew and Janssen, *Secret Believers*, 15.

83. *Way of Fatima*, 18.

The research question of this book first asks if ex-Muslim Christians are engaged in making their own theology, or to use a more technical term, are engaged in the process of organic contextualization. In this chapter I have argued that answer is *yes*. It is now possible to move on to the second part of the research question: what sort of theology is being produced and what knowledge about God is proposed? I have argued that in these texts one can identify theological knowledge as wisdom and a praxis that aims at liberation and is motivated substantially by the sense of God's love being revealed in Christ.

But the sources used here are, admittedly, from all over the world. In order to more fully explore how CMBs are engaging in contextualization and making their own theology, it is helpful to focus on a specific community of CMBs and see what theology-making looks like not in the format of written texts (as here), but lived experience as a church. With that goal in mind we can now turn to an examination of Iranian Diaspora Christians in the USA and UK, which is the focus of chapter 6.

6

Iranian Christians in the American and British Diaspora

Using texts written by CMBs, the previous chapter examined aspects of the theologies authors from many different countries and backgrounds have produced and are producing. This chapter is a case study of Iranian Christian (IC) churches in the American and British diaspora, almost all of whom come from a Shi'a Muslim background as opposed to the Sunni Islam of much of the Ottoman Empire. By examining the life of such congregations and the Christians that constitute them, it may be possible to identify some key loci of theology-making.

This chapter will begin with a description of some of the historical events and changes that appear to have fostered an environment in which hundreds of thousands of Iranians, both in Iran and in the Diaspora, have made a decision to convert to Christianity and leave Islam. In the next section, a brief description of the groups I researched will be presented. The rest of the chapter will consist of an exploration of questions related to identity, ritual, and teaching within the context of the churches. Finally, examples of why some Iranians find Christian churches attractive will be provided.

THE GROWTH OF IRANIAN CHRISTIANITY SINCE 1979[1]

Chapter 3 presented some key reasons why, according to my respondents, the number of reported conversions from Islam to Christ had increased. In this section some specific examples of those factors facilitating conversion in reference specifically to Iranian Christianity will be provided. The

1. Portions of this chapter appeared in Miller, "Power, Personalities, and Politics: The Growth of Iranian Christianity since 1979," *Mission Studies* 32 (2015) 66–86, and are used with permission.

examples are the result of my own interviews as well as what little literature has been written on the topic.

Krikor Markarian proposes a number of political, religious, and economic factors that appear to have contributed to the creation of an environment in which hundreds of thousands of Iranians from a Shi'a background, both within and outside of Iran, have converted to Christianity.[2] The first factor Markarian suggests is the ministry of the Assemblies of God bishop Haik Hovsepian. Hovsepian, an Armenian, is a rare example of the Great Experiment (belatedly) functioning as hoped. Hovsepian began to evangelize Muslims in the late sixties and, by 1976, had founded five house churches among whom were about 20 Muslim-background Christians: by 1981 that number had increased to around 60. Two years after the revolution, in 1981, Hovsepian became the leader of the Council of Protestant Ministers in Iran. From this position of influence he shared his methods and experience with other leaders and some of them began to experiment in conducting worship in Farsi rather than Armenian, meaning that the Christian worship in these churches could now be understood by the majority Shi'a Muslim population without translation. Hovsepian made himself odious to the Iranian regime by protesting the imprisonment of a fellow pastor, Mehdi Dibaj, a CMB who had been a Christian for over 40 years. After calling international attention to Dibaj's apostasy trial, the latter was eventually released from custody. Four months later Dibaj was assassinated, and is considered a martyr by ICs. His written testimony to the court that heard his case has become an influential document for ICs because of its bold tone:

> The eternal God who sees the end from the beginning and who has chosen me to belong to Him, knew from the beginning those whose heart would be drawn to Him and also those who would be willing to sell their faith and eternity for a pot of porridge. I would rather have the whole world against me, but know that the Almighty God is with me. I would rather be called an apostate, but know that I have the approval of the God of glory, because man looks at the outward appearance but God looks at the heart. For Him who is God for all eternity nothing is impossible. All power in heaven and on earth is in His hands.[3]

This written defense is signed "Your Christian Prisoner."

Three days after Dibaj's release in 1994, Hovsepian was abducted and assassinated. According to Markarian, this emboldened large numbers of

---

2. Markarian, "Cyrus to Ayatollah," 15–17; "Spiritual Vacuum," 10–13; and "Today's Iranian Revolution," 6–13.

3. Dibaj, "Written Defense," n.p.

Armenian and ethnic-Iranian Christians: "At Haik's funeral, hundreds of Persian MBBs turned out to honor him despite the presence of government agents documenting all who were present."[4]

During this time, after the Revolution, there was also a growing sense of disappointment with the new regime. Members of non-Shi'a religious communities including Sunni Muslims, Baha'is, Jews, and Christians experienced a loss of freedom and rights, as did women.[5] This was the case even for those communities which had supported the actions of the Ayatollah Khomeini against the Shah. "Once it became clear that Ayatollah Khomeini was going to successfully set up a Muslim religious dictatorship, both Assyrians and Armenians swiftly came to the conclusion that Iran was not the place for them."[6] Since then a considerable number of Christians, Jews, and Baha'i have emigrated.

Prior to the Revolution much had been promised in the way of economic development and freedom, but the perception was that the new Islamic government, assuring all that Iran was governed according to the divinely revealed Shari'a which had its source directly in God and not in man, did not deliver. Rather than prosperity and growth, the economy stagnated for an extended period of time, and when there was economic growth it was unevenly distributed—with the proceeds, according to those opposing the new way, often going to allies of the Ayatollah.[7] Another source of deep disappointment was the unprovoked Iran-Iraq war (1980–1988). Both sides claimed to be engaging in the sacramental, divinely-sanctioned violence of jihad, notwithstanding the fact that their opponents were Muslims. Bradley, who has written the only book-length treatment[8] of contemporary Iranian Christianity, arrives at the conclusion that "Since 1979 Shia Islam and the rule of the government have been one, so Shia Islam's reputation was bound to be weakened . . ."[9] Or as another observer writes,

> The Iranian revolution seemed an answer to the prayers of so many faithful throughout the Muslim world . . . However, the years of forced consolidation of clerical power, the devastating war with Iraq, and the debilitating isolation imposed by a hostile

4. Markarian, "Today's Iranian Revolution," 8.

5. Mahdi, "Iranian Women's Movement," 434.

6. Bradley, *Iran and Christianity*, 167.

7. Zangeneh, "Socioeconomic Trends," 481–94.

8. Bradley's main work is his 2008 *Iran and Christianity: Historical Identity and Present Relevance*. His 2007 book *Iran: Open Hearts in a Closed Land*, is a popularized version of the longer, better documented 2008 book.

9. Bradley, *Iran and Christianity*, x.

outside world have taken much of the shine off the Islamic Republic.[10]

This sense that strong Islamic rule was essential to the development of Iranian Christianity was also mentioned by several of the people interviewed during the research. Recalling the analysis from chapter 2 on why Muslims convert to Christ, this can be identified as "disappointment with Islam," and utilizing Rambo's conversion model, may correspond to the crisis phase. Utilizing the analogy of the religious marketplace, the Islamic rule of the Ayatollahs causes people to become disillusioned with "their brand," and seek some alternative. Furthermore, the use of Farsi in worship in some churches (among other factors) has made a new product, Christianity, more easily available to Farsi-speaking Iranians.

Bradley proposes that there are also some historical aspects of Iranian culture that make the Christian message attractive to some Iranian Muslims. He points to the fact that Shi'a Islam has within it, unlike Sunni Islam, the concept of redemptive suffering, meaning that the Christian doctrine of Jesus's atoning death is readily comprehensible. There is also the deep conviction expressed in many of my interviews with ICs that Islam is a form of socio-religious colonialism unjustly imposed by Arabs (an "unaccomplished and uncultured" group of warriors) on the rich and great culture of Persia. As one interviewee said, "Islam was a step up for the Arabs, because they moved from fighting with each other to unity; but for Iran it was a step down." Another told me that after he completed his asylum process in the UK, he would legally change his Arabic name to a Persian one. Moreover, the Bible paints a largely positive image of Persia/Persians, going so far as to portray God as referring to Cyrus as "my messiah" or "my anointed one," in reference to his role in having the exiled Jews return to and resettle Palestine.[11] The story of Esther takes place in Persia. It has also been suggested that the Magi whom Luke has worshipping the infant Jesus are from Persia. While the Bible paints a respectful picture of Persians,[12] concomitant with the status of the powerful Medo-Persian Empire, the Qur'an says little to nothing about Persia.[13]

10. Abdo, *No God but God*, 193.

11. Isa 45:1. Other passages deal with Elam, which is southern Iran today, like Jer 49:34–39.

12. Huntzinger, *Persians in the Bible*.

13. Multiple apostates from Islam have made similar observations; this includes non-Iranians and people who did not convert to Christianity. For instance, " . . . Islam has been cleverly devised on the principle of divide and rule, and its purpose is to enable the Arabs to dominate the rest of the world" (Anwar Sheikh in Ibn Warraq, *Leaving Islam*, 288). The 30th surah of the Qur'an is titled "al rum" which means "the Romans"

One interviewee, Gloria, lamented that in history class in Iran, everything started with the advent of Islam, without any mention of the illustrious history of Persia in the ancient world. She explained that insofar as Islamic historiography is concerned, everything before the birth of Islam is *jahiliyya*, an Arabic word which means both *ignorance* and the entirety of pre-Islamic history. The founder of Farsinet, which hosts the worldwide list of Iranian congregations,[14] told me that the first document he ever placed on the Internet (when it was little more than an assortment of message boards) was a document on "Persians in the Bible." Pastor Hashim explained that he was talking with a relative in Iran by phone and he used the common phrase *in sha' allah*. It is a well-known Arabic phrase meaning "if God wills it," but is used by people all over the world without translation. Hashim was corrected by his cousin, and told not to use the Arabic phrase, but the Persian phrase of the same meaning: *be omida khoda*. Sufyan is an Iranian convert who has a PhD in a field of natural science and pastored a refugee Iranian church in a large Turkish city for about ten years. He commented that more and more people in Iran are choosing Persian names for their children rather than Arabic names. One Iranian pastor told me that he had given all of his children names starting with "p," since many Arabs cannot make this sound.[15]

In sum, Islam has come to be regarded by a substantial number of Iranians as a sort of pollution that corrupts their otherwise great culture. Once Christianity moved beyond the ethno-linguistic boundaries of the Armenian and Assyrian churches to the larger ethnic-Persian, Farsi-speaking population, it too became an avenue for recovering what was lost. This evangelical Christianity is perceived as being affirmative of Persian-ness, however one defines that term, because it affirms the history of the Persians in its holy book, permits (and in the evangelical version requires) the use of the local vernacular for worship, and translates itself into Persian—in its liturgy, and holy book, and even in the act of naming children. In addition to newer and better translations, the communications revolution, especially the Internet and satellite TV, have made the Christian message easily accessible to Iranians who may have never even met a Christian. Christian

---

but actually refers to the Byzantine Greeks. The opening verses lament the victory of the Persians over the Greeks (who are monotheists, unlike the Zoroastrian Persians). In this surah the Prophet predicts that in another battle they will soon be victorious and on that day the "believers will rejoice" (30:4).

14. Online: www.farsinet.com/icc/.

15. The basic Arabic alphabet does not have a sound for "p" or "v." Iranians use a modified alphabet that does have signs for these two letters.

satellite broadcasting in Farsi started in 2000,[16] and diaspora ICs have been active in broadcasting Christian content to Iranians still in country.[17]

All of these factors appear to have been important in creating an atmosphere in which Iranian Muslims could hear and embrace the Christian faith against the background in which key claims of Islam were seen as compromised by the Islamic state.

RESEARCH BACKGROUND

Four congregations were examined during the research for this chapter. The two in the USA were Southern City (now defunct) and Plateau City (the most successful of the four during my research). In the UK there was Bay City, a mature church with a website, a sign outside, and trained leaders. There was also an embryonic congregation in Castle City. All four of these congregations share a number of characteristics. For one, they were all formed mostly of Iranian CMBs. Additionally, all of them also had some tie to non-CMBs in terms of leadership—one had a leader who was a converted Zoroastrian, another had a link to an Assyrian Christian born in Iran, and some had white Farsophone leaders who served in different capacities. Finally, none of these churches owned their own property—they either borrowed/rented room from established churches or met in homes.

Plateau City: A Growing Church

One congregation I researched in the United States is in a Mid-Western state. This congregation grew over the course of my research, unlike the church in Southern City. I interviewed the pastor and assistant pastor on several occasions, attended the Sunday meeting, and interacted with the congregants both in church and, a few times, over coffee where more extensive interviews took place. This church will be called Plateau City church. It was founded in the nineties by an evangelical Assyrian Christian from Iran, assisted by a retired missionary, a woman who was fluent in Farsi, neither of whom currently live in the state. Around 2001 the Assyrian pastor was offered a position at a church in California. He and the assistant pastor prayed and the senior pastor accepted the position. The assistant pastor, a layman, Hisham, (who also has a full-time job) led the church services. Originally the church was meeting in between the two main Iranian population

16. Markarian, "Today's Iranian Revolution," 9.
17. Lewis, "Primetime in Iran."

centers, two cities which are over an hour away from each other by car, and this became impractical. So the church moved to Plateau City, and the Iranians from the other, smaller, city mostly began to attend English-language churches. I am told by the assistant pastor that new refugees from Iran are sent to the smaller city, so Plateau City church does not have any such people.

The senior pastor of the church is Thad. He grew up in Iran as the child of missionaries, as did his wife. He eventually came to the US for college and, after getting married and receiving a Master of Divinity, was commissioned by veteran missionary William McElwee Miller[18] to return to Iran as a missionary. He and his wife did so and stayed there until shortly after the Islamic Revolution in 1979. After a lengthy period of ministry on the American East Coast he moved to this Mid-Western state. The import of this background is pluriform. His Farsi was acquired as a child and then an adolescent living in Iran. Another significant point is that this man knew Iranian life and culture before the Islamic Revolution, a period of time which surfaces often in conversion narratives of older Iranians as a key turning point in terms of their understanding of their own identity as Iranians and the nature of Islam. Eventually, as a former missionary to Iran, Thad and his wife moved to Plateau City for reasons unrelated to the church and, since he was already ordained and had ample experience with Iranian Christianity, was asked to be one of the church's pastors.

Southern City: A Defunct Church

In Southern City in the USA, the website which contains a list of many Iranian churches throughout the world indicated the contact information for the pastor of an Iranian church. I contacted him, Matt, and we met twice for extended interviews, and interacted by email and phone as well. In brief, he explained that the Iranian church in the city had been started around 2005 or 2006. For some time, some non-Farsophone Americans were pastoring the group and Matt met them in 2007, but the congregants were not content with their leadership style, and specifically their emphasis on narrative teaching (as opposed to didactic teaching, apparently) and lack of Farsi. Pastor Matt was then a domestic missionary working in a neighboring city. He did speak Farsi and in July 2007 was asked to come and take a leadership

18. Miller published *Ten Muslims Meet Christ*, one of the earliest collections of testimonies of converts from Islam which according to Pastor Thad "made quite a stir" when it was published in 1984. Gaudeul incorporated these conversion narratives into his research findings.

role in the church. He started attending the church in December, and served as pastor beginning spring of 2008.

The high point of attendance as he recalls it was around May of 2009, when they had 24 or so attendants. Up to this point the church had been meeting in people's homes. This became a source of tension for the home-owners though, as people would stay late after church to socialize, and the hosts had children who needed to be put to bed. So in spring of 2009 the church started meeting in a room on loan from a local Baptist church. Also, during this period Matt was commuting an hour or so each way from his home to the Southern City. He and his family discussed the matter and they decided that to be a pastor of this church and help it to flourish and grow it would be necessary to live in Southern City rather than commute. So in the summer of 2009 he and his wife and their daughter moved.

During this busy time of moving two of the main families in the church had a falling out and by the fall of 2009, when he had settled in Southern City, he described the church as "falling apart." According to Matt, the two families would not even sit down together to discuss the problem. One of the main families stopped attending, and attendance, small to begin with, declined further. At the time of our first meeting in the fall of 2009 he expressed a sense of failure. In his recollection there were some sources of tension. The question of what church they should relocate to was significant: some preferred to use a charismatic church, while Matt felt that a Baptist church would be better. The matter was settled by a congregational vote. He also mentioned on several occasions a theme that would resurface on several occasions during this research—the tension between charismatic and non-charismatic evangelicalism. Some of the church members, and indeed, the original founder of the home church, were involved in what are often called the Word of Faith movement and the Prosperity Gospel.[19] When asked about the origin of this Muslim-background congregation (MBC) Matt explained that it had been founded by an Iranian layperson and the church met in his home. As time went on the leader of the church appeared to become convinced that he was receiving messages directly from the Holy Spirit, and would do things like address a person and say, "You have a spirit of pride." This behavior was considered odd and disruptive by enough people that the church decided to find new leadership.

When describing the state of the church during our first interview, he said that he still went to the church every Sunday and that a handful of

19. " . . . a theological current that states that if certain principles are followed, the expiatory work of Christ guarantees to all who believe, divine healing, the riches of this world, and happiness without suffering." "Prosperity theology," in Corrie, *Dictionary of Missionary Theology*, 322.

people, around six, would come. They would pray and study the Bible. During our last interview (June 2011), Matt was stoic about the experience. Was there anything he could have done differently? He wondered, did God have a purpose in all of this, or did this represent a real failure of the church, and by implication, "a victory of Satan"? Furthermore, he wondered if his career as a domestic missionary would need to come to an end, as the financial downturn had made raising funds for such ministry more difficult. While he continued to pastor the tiny group of Iranians on Sundays, he was directing most of his efforts at training evangelical Latinos in the area of mission and witness to Muslims. Requests to be put in contact with former members of his church did not produce any contacts so the narrative here could not be verified by other sources.

Castle City: An Embryonic Church

The other two congregations researched were in Scotland. One of them was what might be called with more accuracy an embryonic congregation. It did not meet every Sunday, but did have a weekly Bible study in Farsi. The person who had taken the initiative to form and care for this group has been living in the United Kingdom for decades, and in addition to being a (retired) physician also holds a degree in theology. Unlike the other Iranians who form the core of this group, he himself comes from a Zoroastrian background. Having been in the UK for so long he is apologetic about how weak his Farsi-language skills have become. On the other hand, he is a good example of the sort of highly-skilled émigré from Iran which have been so important in the formation and growth of Iranian Christianity in the diaspora. This MBC came into being after this leader started to offer the Alpha course in Farsi at a local church in Castle City.

My first experience with the IC community in Castle City was a day-long series of lectures and discussions, accompanied by a Persian meal, which took place in a Baptist church in an upscale neighborhood. The visiting speaker was a minister from the Church of England, herself an IC. Before the conference I chatted with some of the people present and learned that some were seeking refugee status, or had been accepted as refugees, and that not all had good English-language skills.

The ICs in Castle City have demonstrated significant flexibility in dealing with their situation. There are enough of them to have a Bible study and to come together for occasional meetings like this (always accompanied by a meal of some sort, it seems). But on Sundays they attend regular Anglophone churches of various stripes—Baptist, Episcopal, independent,

Presbyterian. They stay in touch with the well-established congregation in Bay City.

Bay City: An Established Church

The final congregation, also in Scotland, is in Bay City. This congregation meets every Sunday afternoon in the sanctuary of an evangelical church rather than in a classroom, as in Plateau City. They have a well-defined leadership structure with an Iranian pastor and several elders and deacons, some Iranians, and some Farsophone Westerners. I interviewed the pastor of this church (Faris), and two of the elders. Of the four groups researched, this was the one where I spent more time with the congregants—eating with them, sleeping at their flats, getting my hair cut by them, and so on—than at any other. The congregation is a mix of refugees and asylum-seekers and well-established Iranians who have been in the UK for years. Also, there are single people and married people, young and old, and a few children as well. Of the four congregations explored here this is the only one that has a visible sign outside the church, in English and Farsi, with the name of the church on it. All four of the MBCs studied here were either started by Iranians or by Iranians assisted by non-Iranian leaders.

In addition to research connected to these four churches, I interviewed various people with experience of Iranian Christianity, including one IC who had served as a missionary and pastor to a refugee church in Turkey (Sufyan), as well as an American couple who are domestic missionaries working with an Iranian church in a major city in the Northeast of the USA. Having described the congregations where the research was carried out, we can now examine some aspects of their communal life, beginning with the key rituals of the Christian religion—baptism and Communion.

RITUAL, ANTISYNCRETISM AND PERSIANNESS

This section will analyze some aspects of ritual among the ICs whom I interviewed. Conclusions will be drawn both from reports of how the rituals are carried out.

Baptism and the Lord's Supper

During an interview with Thad, the Iranian-born child of missionaries, missionary in Iran and then pastor at the church in Plateau City, we discussed the topic of baptism. The following interview excerpts[20] touch on important topics:

> DM: . . . tell me about baptism, preparation for baptism and indeed what does the actual baptism look like? [Tell me] what it would look like for an un-churched guy who comes in and starts going to church here and says, "Pastor I like this, I read through your catechism . . . and I'd like to be baptized." . . .
>
> Thad: Well it all varies from church to church but there are a couple common components. Most Iranian churches will not baptize a new believer in less than six months or a year. Western churches of course will baptize them very quickly and it's a huge mistake. The first thing we tell a new person is that baptism does not make you a Christian, I mean it does not save you. Baptism is. . .we use the marriage symbol: you know, you can love your bride even if you don't have the ring yet, it doesn't mean that you don't love them and doesn't mean you don't have a love relationship, what formalizes it is the wedding.
>
> So, what we do is, we make a note of the person's first confession of faith, and we ask them then to attend the regular programs of the church. A house church meeting once a week perhaps and the public worship. We first off want to get to know this person inside and out. If the person is in a hurry to get baptized it's a huge red flag. It could mean there's an immigration issue, it could mean that there's some other issue and so we are never in a hurry. And we say to them, well, we use the Persian word which is really prettier and nicer, it's for the church to decide when you're ready to be baptized, not for you to say . . . it is the church's responsibility, and I say the church has the responsibility from God to baptize you in a proper way.
>
> And I say to them also, look once you become baptized your Muslim friends are going to come up to you and they're gonna challenge you with lots of questions and how embarrassed are you gonna be when you don't have enough answers from the Bible, enough answers from your faith? They're gonna say, look you just got brainwashed into being a Christian, you're not a real Christian. So take my word. So we put them through this and we begin to watch: does this person pray in meetings, does this person begin to show some signs of a Christian, the fruit of the Spirit so to speak. When I can I visit the person's family, I visit them at work, I kinda find out more about them.

---

20. All interview excerpts in this section are from 2009.

> So let's say the six months are up and we're very convinced that the person is genuine, so we ask them to write their testimony. And their testimony consists of three points: what my life was like before Christ, what I believed in; the second question is what specifically convinced me that Jesus Christ is the Son of God?

Regarding preparation for baptism, then, we find a few common elements. 1) There is a waiting period of six to twelve months wherein regular attendance is required and spiritual growth is evaluated. 2) There is the teaching that baptism does not effectuate salvation, but is a vital, public formalization of it. 3) It is a time of scrutiny in relation to the motives of the person requesting baptism. 4) It is a test to see if the person requesting baptism has the humility and patience to submit to the judgment of the church regarding her readiness for the rite. 5) It is a time of apologetic preparation, making sure the enquirer will be able to answer the objections of his Muslim friends and family. And finally, 6) if the enquirer meets these conditions, they are asked to write their testimony, which itself reflects back on the theology of baptism as formalizing and presenting publically one's faith in Messiah and incorporation into the church and, specifically, this or that specific congregation.

The emphasis on the title *Son of God* was surprising to me: not only that is was used in the baptismal liturgy, but that it was emphasized to the point where the confession of faith of those being baptized was "how I came to believe that Jesus is the Son of God." This is *not* the common practice of American or European evangelicals. Indeed, while Messianic titles like Lord and Savior are still used in this liturgy, the primacy of place is given to the title that is *most* scandalous to Muslims, not least. Compound this with the fact that the people being baptized were supposed to invite their relatives and friends, including Muslims, to the baptism, and this becomes all the more striking. It appeared to me, initially, quite illogical. It seemed like making this sort of confession utilizing the title Son of God for Jesus might be provocative for Muslim family-members and friends in attendance, so I asked for more detail:

> DM: And you use *Son of God*? Just as an aside, so you're not sympathetic with things like using *xaliifat allah* or the caliph of God....[21]

---

21. Recall that for many Muslims the title "Son of God" is deemed to be offensive, so some Christians ministering to Muslims engage in directed contextualization by editing that title out of the Bible, either in practice by not using it, or by actually printing Bibles that use some other title to translate the Greek *huios theou*, such as "the vice-regent

Thad: No, no let's get right to the heart of it. The Bible calls him the Son of God and . . . we make them confess that repeatedly and hopefully believe it. Then, the third question is: how has Christ changed your life? So they write their testimony. They write it and they present a written report to us and we look it over—with them of course—and we say: oh, this is good here but you have, for example, you have not alluded in any way to what Christ did on the cross or forgiveness of sin or anything.

And then, once they've shared it with the elders . . . we set their baptismal date. And we tell them that we want their whole family and all their relatives and friends in the city to be there. Now we will present them with a nice invitation from the church if they want to send an invitation. And we're asking them all to be there for a couple reasons: we don't want this to be a secret baptism, I mean we're in America now, we're not in Iran; and we want all these Muslims to come and hear a testimony, because there's nothing like hearing a testimony to convince others.

He then went on to relate his experience at one baptism that has some interesting similarities to the initial Easter meeting of the Kitma believers. The Kitma believers were asked to mention their names but they went beyond that sharing the names of their villages and, in some cases, how they converted. Similarly, these initiates were asked to present a brief testimony. But that did not happen:

I remember one service where we had five candidates, Duane, and each of these guys and gals [shared] testimonies, we told them to talk ten minutes but most of them talked for about a half an hour. It turned out to be a three-hour service. I mean people got out and went to the bathroom and came back but it was dramatic. Five people telling about their story, I mean we don't believe in immersion [as a necessity, so when] I baptize, I have them kneel in front of the church with the sprinkling format . . .

If some of the aspects of how baptism is understood and how a request for baptism is considered by church leaders seem quite different than what

of God" (*xaliifat allah*) or "beloved of God" (*habiib allah*). The motive behind such a translation is to make the Christian message more palatable to Muslims and not as scandalous by using a "dynamic equivalent." Rick Brown supports this approach with reservations ("Son of God," "Biblical Muslims"). The counter-position, that the title "Son of God" must be retained even if it may be initially repugnant to some Muslims, is embodied by these Iranian Christians, as well as the ex-Muslim Christians studied in chapters 4 and 5. Indeed, I do not recall ever meeting a CMB who did not strongly condemn the use of any title other than "Son of God" to translate the Greek *huios theou*.

one would expect at an evangelical church in the USA, there are also important strains of continuity, as with the liturgy used:

> DM: But you do use a modified version of the traditional Presbyterian [baptismal liturgy]?
>
> Thad: Right. But we add a couple things. We ask them to renounce all false religions and all superstitions. So that they renounce: in their confession they say, "Today I renounce,"—we don't use the word Islam—"all false religion and all superstitious practice to embrace Christ." And we add another question, that they accept the authority of the leadership of the church, and we have one other question, that they embrace the principle of Matthew 18. So if they have a problem with another believer they will either try to go personally and work it out or bring another believer. Because in the Iranian culture, because of the honor society and honor/shame principle, it's very difficult to confront each other over problems. So what you do is you just gossip: I got a problem with Duane, I don't go to Duane and say "Hey Duane, why'd you say that?" I just go around badmouthing you.[22]
>
> So . . . we at least make them say, "I understand that according to Matthew 18, if my brother has sinned against me I'm responsible to go talk to him and work it out." Which is totally against their culture to do.

This difficulty in relation to gossip was corroborated by Iranian contacts who admitted that it was a cultural problem which was not healthy. In this instance of inculturation, then, we have an example of how sometimes the Gospel confronts cultural practices, demanding that they be changed or reformed. This summary of baptism is an example of how powerfully a ritual of initiation can interact with and communicate about ethics (gossip, humility, patience), spirituality (do they pray?), theology (the language of Son of God, the relation of the rite to salvation and the church), and community (having family present, being initiated into a particular congregation). It is difficult to imagine any other single instance of Christian life that more deeply informs and is informed by such a broad array of forces and beliefs and practices.

Nor was this rite of baptism the only example of emphasizing the title "Son of God." Sufyan is one of the early converts, from the first cohort who found themselves in the West during the Revolution and never returned to Iran. This first wave of migrants was, in general, wealthy and/or highly

---

22. Compare this to the experience of Matt in Southern City, where a similar problem surfaced.

skilled.[23] Sufyan became a Christian while in university in the USA and eventually went on to receive a PhD in science. He and his American wife served as missionaries in a large Turkish city for over a decade, where he pastored an Iranian church consisting mostly of Iranian refugees. When asked to describe the Lord's Supper as they practiced it, he said that they took the Lord's Supper once a month, and they would use a very simple call-and-response liturgy, something of his own creation:

> I say *Jesus Christ* and they respond *God*. (The Farsi word *Khoda*, not *Allah* in Arabic.) There is a question and response, a loose liturgy: I ask, what does Jesus mean? and they respond Savior. What does Messiah mean? The anointed one. Why is he God? We read some passages from the Bible then, like the baptism [of Jesus][24] and the transfiguration.[25] I say, these three words— Jesus, Christ, God—are written on the gate of heaven. If you believe these things you can enter in, it doesn't matter what church or ethnicity you belong to. I also read the passage from John about, "makes himself equal to God."[26] Sometimes I also read from the Qur'an—the passages about Jesus.[27] If people believe these three things (Jesus Christ God) then you can take communion, there is no requirement of baptism. We normally use a simple Turkish bread loaf and good grape juice, though cherry juice is used every now and then if needed.[28] We are not so quick to baptize.

Here again, but in the context of the Lord's Supper rather than baptism, is a strong emphasis on the divinity of Jesus. The very question, "Why is he God?" would sound either ridiculous or blasphemous (the sin of *shirk*) to most Muslim audiences. And again, the insistence on the "Jesus Christ [is] God" language goes far beyond the regular practice of the Lord's Supper in Western evangelicalism,[29] which sees the ritual mostly as a memorial of Christ's death on the cross, and is dominated not by the Son of God motif seen here, but the exclamation of Jesus's cousin John, "Behold, the Lamb of God who takes away the sin of the world!" (John 1:29)

23. Hakimzadeh, "Vast Disapora."

24. Matt 3:13–17.

25. Mark 9; Matt 17.

26. John 5:18 and surrounding.

27. For instance 2:87, 2:253, 3:45ff, 4:171, 5:46, 19:19ff, etc.

28. On asking about the cherry juice I was told that until recently grape juice was just not widely available, whereas cherry juice was.

29. One might even say this about the whole of Western Christianity, including Roman Catholicism.

Jesus Saves (Persianness)

How can all of this be interpreted? This does not appear to be an instance of directed contextualization or "theology for." Indeed, many missionaries who advocate directed contextualization would be offended at what they would perceive as alienating, polemical language that needlessly erects barriers between Muslims and Christians. Rather there appear to be two dynamics at play in this recurring mention of Jesus's divinity/sonship in ritual. The first is that the rituals clearly distinguish who is in and who is out, serving as conservative boundary markers. The language about Jesus reminds the congregation (and those who do not belong to it yet) of who they are, and who they are not—they are not Muslims. In other words, the ritual and its vocabulary are instances of anti-syncretism. That is, they keep the influence of Islam out and maintain a strong and unequivocal affirmation of orthodox Christology.

Secondly, the ritual situated within the context of the larger worship serves to communicate to all involved that an explicit embrace of what is, by Islamic standards, an affront to God and a heresy (*shirk*), in no way diminishes the Persian-ness of the Christians. In fact, it augments it. In rejecting Islam and giving a prominent place to Christ's divinity and sonship, they are asserting that they are more authentic Iranians than Muslim Iranians are. That Persian-ness is a cornerstone of Iranian Christianity can be seen in the following examples.

There are so many Iranian elements in the larger setting of the church service that it is impossible to interpret it as anything other than an exuberant celebration of Persian culture, though that is not its *only* goal. I observed women wearing Persian scarves, the reading of Christian Persian poetry, and as always, unlike with Islamic worship, everything was in Farsi, from the prayers to the sermon to the songs. A festivity like Nowruz, the Persian New Year, is celebrated by all ICs. The IC pastor from the Church of England commented that she liked Nowruz because it was close to Easter, bringing two celebrations of new life together in her mind. The church in Plateau City held a big party for all Iranians on Nowruz, complete with food, traditional Persian music and poetry, and a short talk from the pastor. Nowruz has its origins in Zoroastrianism, and while some Muslim rulers and scholars frowned upon it as a pagan holdover, it was so deeply engrained in Persian culture that alone of the ancient Zoroastrian holy days it has been preserved.[30] Some evangelicals may feel uncomfortable with this, but

---

30. Shahbazi, "Nowruz."

historically Christianity's ability to syncretize local, pre-Christian festivities into its holy calendar has sometimes aided in its expansion.

During Nowruz, a table is set with items that symbolize the aspirations of the celebrants for the new year—like coins for wealth and eggs for fertility. Muslims added a Qur'an in effort to own the celebration. One IC in Castle City explained that she placed the Bible on the Nowruz table rather than the Qur'an, and another IC who had apparently not reflected on this option nodded in approval at this ritual modification. Though its roots were in Zoroastrianism, today Nowruz is more a celebration of Persian identity and heritage. ICs unapologetically recognize its roots in Zoroastrianism while also confessing "Jesus Christ, Son of God, and Savior."

In sum, it appears that these ICs see Christianity's flexibility as one of its great strengths. Christianity is able to preserve and sanctify Iranian culture in a way that Islam has not and cannot. So within the context of a vigorous affirmation of Iranian culture and heritage, the affirmation of the divinity/sonship of Jesus communicates the message that not only are ICs true Iranians, but they are better Iranians than are Muslims, and that by confessing that Jesus is God one simultaneously leaves Islam and enters into a new and more authentic form of being Persian, innocent of the "corruption" of the ayatollahs and purified of Arab-Islamic "pollution." Another way to put this is argued by the converts: Iranian identity and Islamic identity cannot only be separated but, in the interest of the former, *they should be*.[31]

Furthermore, baptism among these ICs can be understood not only as a symbol for regeneration and a dedication to Jesus who is "Lord and Savior" and his church, but also an effort to reconstitute Iranian identity; baptism means leaving a violent, Arab-contaminated Persian-ness and entering a pure and irenic Persian-ness.

The concept of liminality can help us to interpret this ritual from the point of view of CMBs *in* Iran. On one level, ICs will always be liminal figures in relation to Iranian culture as traditionally constructed, because Iranian identity is Shi'a Muslim identity. This does not preclude a transformation in that construction of identity, indeed ICs and other apostates are actively working towards such a reconstitution. The IC in Iran is a polluting figure because of her apostasy, and she is a permanently liminal figure because of her refusal to engage in certain practices and agree with (or at

---

31. Because of this, it is difficult to identify this contextual theology with Schreiter's ethno-graphic model (or Bevans's anthropological model). Such a form of contextual theology-making would presumably start with the presupposition of the "value and goodness" (Bevans, *Models*, 55) of the traditional Iranian Shi'a culture, and try to discern God's activity there. These Iranian believers find little of value in the Shi'a component of the traditional construction of Iranian identity that they had known.

least not disagree with vocally) certain political foundational mythologies. But the baptism and Nowruz celebration here criticize that identification of Iranian-ness with Shi'a Islam. The Iranian who is exploring Christianity by meeting with Christians is engaging in a dangerous and deviant activity.[32] That exploration usually must usually take place in a secretive manner as a liminal seeker distant from society. During the exploration the person cannot have the status of being a good Shi'a Muslim, but nor can they lay claim to being a Christian in the fullest sense of the word, as they have not undergone ritual initiation. The rite of baptism as practiced by most evangelicals features some additional marks of liminality, like de-gendering, since both males and females wear the same androgynous white robes.

According to the dominant (or once-dominant) construction of Iranian identity, once the baptism has been carried out the bridge has been burned, and, as the Prophet said, *whosoever changes his religion, slay him.* The "pollution" has likely become irreversible at this point, and execution or exile is possible, especially if the person is identified as one who is actively evangelizing, spreading her "pollution." But baptism and the Lord's Supper as practiced by the Iranians I studied appear to directly repudiate this construction of Iranian identity, as if saying, "It is we who have an authentic Iranian identity, and you Muslims do not." The final stage of Van Gennep's ritual process is reincorporation. The Shi'a construction of identity will not allow for these figures to be re-aggregated as Christians. But the church does re-aggregate the baptized and those who participate in the Lord's Supper into a community where Persian language, culture, and heritage are vigorously celebrated—in the name of Jesus Christ whom they confess as Son of God. These questions of identity will be revisited in greater detail in the next chapter.

CONTEXTUALIZATION OF THE TEACHING MINISTRY AND MESSAGE

Teaching, the Inquirer and the New Believer

But re-aggregating individuals into a new, allegedly more authentically Persian, community, is not only a matter of purging Arabo-Islamic elements, like words and rituals and names, and replacing them with Persian-Christian ones. The IC critique of the Revolution and the ensuing Islamic state go deeper than that, and the teachers I spoke with appeared to have the strong conviction that a fundamental transformation of how Iranians viewed God,

---

32. Kraft, "Faith is Lived out in Community."

humans, and ethics was needed. That is, the new rituals and vocabulary alone that emphasized continuity with pre-Islamic Persian culture would not suffice to establish a genuine Persian church and identity.

Teaching plays a key role in the life of the IC churches. Even the "embryonic church" in Castle City met for a Bible study weekly, and when there was a larger meeting—the conference mentioned above—it was for a day of *teaching*. The teaching was done in Persian, but fortunately all the Power-Point slides also had translations into English, and the speaker would chime in with English phrases every now and then. Her presentation was about the personality of God. For most British evangelicals it was the sort of material that people learn when they are children: God is love, he is loving, he does not give up on us, we can always go back to him and confess our sins, we do not need to stop sinning before we come to God, we are in a genuine relationship with God, and so on. It was odd for me seeing people listening attentively to what struck me as such rudimentary lessons. This was my first meeting with the ICs in the UK. I eventually realized that these lessons were being presented as a corrective. Having come from an Islamic background, these people already believed in an omnipotent Creator who reveals his will to humanity, but the personality of God which they had learned in Iranian Shi'a Islam was, in their view, radically flawed, and in dire need of correction. This day of teaching was part of such a strategy.

The content of the teaching in Bay City was similar. Leaders took turns preaching on Sundays, and each preacher was free to choose his topic as he liked.[33] Two of the elders had agreed to teach through the Decalogue. On the Sunday in question, the commandment was *You shall not present false witness*.[34] He gave a preamble saying that the Commandments are not a ladder, and salvation is a gift of God related to repentance, and not earned by obeying the laws. That having been said, he explained that avoiding paying taxes was a form of lying as is flattery. God never lies, and we can trust him. That was the problem with Adam and Eve: they did not trust God. Yet we must trust in him even when life does not make sense, because God does not lie. He also referenced Ephesians 4:29 saying that in our speech we should not gossip about each other, "We should speak *to* each other, not *about* each other." So while we need to be honest in our conversation, that does not mean that we are to say everything we know about a person to someone else.

---

33. Teaching, leading worship, reading poetry and praying could be done by women, but it appeared that preaching the sermon was reserved for men.

34. Exod 23:1, 2.

This is another example of what appears to be corrective teaching, because in Shi'a Islam there is a tradition endorsing *taqiyya,* or dissimulation. In other words, under certain circumstances lying is sanctioned by God, and among the names of God are "the one who leads astray"[35] and "the schemer."[36] This sermon undermined and negated that perception of the personality of God: God is true and he is truth, and he never sanctions lying, nor does he scheme or deceive us or lead us astray. I suspect that there was no need to explicitly state that this represented a refutation of the Qur'anic teaching because the listeners already knew it.

Upon being asked about the role of teaching in the church, and specifically about preparation for baptism, the Bay City pastor Faris explained that they use Alpha, but that Alpha is not ideal for Iranian converts or enquirers because it starts directly with Jesus. That is to say, Alpha assumes that people already have a more or less Christian understanding of God, even for people who have rarely or never been to church. Such people presumably believe that God is kind, loving and forgiving. Iranians from a Muslim background did not have that same set of presumptions according to him, so his church had composed additional material to supplement Alpha. His summary of the material covered includes systematic theology with an emphasis on apologetics, the notion of *tahriif,* or that the text of the Bible is corrupted, and then what he called "basic questions," like *is religion relevant?* And *can we know God?* Then the topics of biblical inspiration, the Trinity, man, sin, and the effects of sin are addressed. The emphasis on sin is, in his words, "sin as a condition" rather than sin as individual transgressions.

Each of the topics he mentions point to an area of theology where Islam and Christianity have what appear to be mutually exclusive doctrines. For instance, in Islam there is no doctrine of original sin, but a doctrine of original innocence. Orthodox Islam, after the *mu'tazila* controversy[37] at least, has held that God himself cannot be known, but only his characteristics, and even those do not pertain to his essence, which is why God can be "truth" but also "deceiver."[38] But this position is contradicted in Christianity by the assertions that "God is love" or that Christ is "the image of the invisible God" (Col 1:15) and the doctrine of the incarnation.

The pastor went on, "We need a savior, not an imam or a prophet," implying that the ministry of Muhammad, even if it were from God, would

35. For instance 6:125.

36. *Al maakir,* used several times in the Qur'an. For instance 3:54, "They [the Jews] deceived, and God deceived, and God is the best of deceivers," though others prefer to translate the word as "God schemed."

37. Eighth through tenth centuries.

38. Rippin, *Muslims,* 84–85.

not be sufficient, because merely supplying humans with rules, however good they might be, will never actually fix the fundamental human problem, which, *pace* Islam, is not ignorance *(jahiliyya)* but the sinful condition of humanity as a whole. The series is rounded out with teachings on the gift of the Holy Spirit, Baptism, the Lord's Supper, the Church and the daily Christian life.

This is a detailed, comprehensive and rigorous program. Some individuals engaged in Muslim evangelism have seen in Islam a sort of preparation for the Gospel,[39] implying that God benevolently has prepared people to hear and understand the message of Messiah *by placing them within an Islamic context.* This point of view would see the Persians moving from their Zoroastrianism to Islam, with its one deity, biblical prophets, Scriptures, and moral laws as a progression towards the complete truth of God. In this view, Islam, far from being a destructive imposition on Iranian culture, is a divinely coordinated historical stage that prepares Persians for the message of Christ. The approach of the ICs is clearly not built on the perception of Islam as a preparation of the Gospel,[40] but on the conviction that every aspect of the religious life touched by Islam must be reformed. The structure cannot be repaired, but razed to the ground and a wholly new one built up.

The pastor concludes by pointing me to the church's website and You-Tube, where there are recordings of him teaching on these topics in Farsi. The church's website does indeed contain a veritable library of Christian material in Farsi, and the pastor assures me that this material is being used in many churches, including in Iran. Many of the articles are translations of material from well-known evangelicals like Philip Yancey and Max Lucado, which is a reminder that Iranian Christianity as it exists today is deeply influenced by global (and especially American) evangelicalism.

Near the end of the interview the pastor refers to a Persian proverb without giving any explanation of why it came to his mind: *The horse is the same, but the saddle is different.* He does not say so explicitly, but I believe that this is foundational to the teaching program: not only should the saddle be new, but you need a whole new horse. Not only should the Iranian get baptized and come to church and start calling God *Khoda* rather than *Allah*, a complete transformation of the person's weltanschauung is required.

---

39. Gustafson, *Insider View.*

40. In this, it is in continuity with the group focused on mission to Muslims at Edinburgh 1910 which did not see in Islam more than a refutation of the Gospel, much less a divine preparatory step towards it.

Teaching and Leadership Training

Because Islam is not seen as preparation for the Gospel, and because an entirely new weltanschauung is needed (a new saddle *and* a new horse) this kerygmatic strategy cannot end at baptism. Three of the leaders I interviewed were all concerned with devising some way to train leaders for the Iranian churches, whether inside of or outside of Iran. Pastor Faris, from Bay City, said that in terms of leadership the Iranian churches were facing a very large problem, for many leaders still had a "mosque mentality." My interpretation of this phrase is that many leaders among ICs operate not like Christian pastors (as he understood their ideal role) but as rulers of mosques,[41] where people would come to ask questions or request advice, and be told precisely what to do without offering any explanation as to why that was the proper course of action, much less try to help the petitioner to answer her own question through a (guided) interpretation of the Bible. Thad in Plateau City echoed these concerns and shared similar experiences, saying,

> So, when I teach the Bible, Iranians worship people and are committed to people rather than to principles or rather than even truth. So they abuse the teacher of the Bible by using, "Oh, well Pat said this, or Pat taught this" therefore you must do this. So there's a confusion at times. I worked very, very hard to teach my congregation. I would sometimes stand before my sermon and hold the Word of God above my head and say, "I want all of you to know that I answer to this. That my life must be under this . . . this is what I'm teaching. This is the Truth." Visually I was trying to show them.
>
> And so, when they would ask me questions, rather than give them an answer I would give them a verse. Let's look this up. "Can Christians marry a non-Christian?" Well, that's a good question, I wonder what God thinks about that? Let's look at 2 Corinthians . . . So I would teach by driving the facts of the Word of God because I was afraid that they would become little robots, you know, following me.[42]

According to Pastor Matt, from Southern City, this was one of the reasons that his church failed. Here is his account from an email of one of the reasons that his congregation failed:

---

41. Note that the Iranian Shi'a context of a mosque is somewhat different than what was presented in chapter 4 in relation to the Arabophone Muslims in Kitma.

42. Interview, 2009.

A second issue was leadership expectations. Of the remaining extended family (of the initial two), one member was angry at me for not dictating to her what she should have done in a particular dating situation. Instead I had taught her what the Bible taught about the situation, gave her advice and counsel, and said I would pray she would make the right decision. In the end, the situation resulted in significant pain for her, and she blamed me for not being a strong enough leader. The man she was seeing was a seeker who blamed me for the eventual break-up, so he quit the group. She had also begun meeting with a doctrinally aberrant group, and was apparently leaning toward leaving our group, although she had not yet.[43]

Pastor Matt's approach would generally be seen as empowering and pastorally laudable by contemporary standards. Rather than simply telling the woman what she should do (the "mosque mentality" as Pastor Faris called it), he tried to empower her to use appropriate biblical resources to answer her own question. But regardless of whether his approach was right or wrong, it contributed to the decline of his congregation. Building on what Pastor Faris said, that some leaders have a "mosque mentality," in this example we find a Christian who leaves the church because the leader (American-trained, but fluent in Farsi) does *not* operate according to her expectations of "mosque mentality."

It is significant that the believers in Kitma and Juduur (chapter 4) were wrestling with similar issues—specifically the relationship between power and the interpretation of Scripture. Matt was trying to empower the woman by leading her through the process of interpreting Scripture on her own—an empowering act. She was disappointed because her understanding of power was different from his—she wanted him to exercise power by giving her a correct answer that would solve her problem. When he did not act accordingly, she left. It seems like she was still understanding power according to the Persian mosque pattern—a divine word and command that is objective and requires only obedience—not comprehension or interpretation.

This concern with the quality and nature of leadership and training for leadership was seen as especially urgent by Sufyan, Thad and Faris, who had served the churches in Iran, Scotland, Turkey, and the USA. All three individuals devoted a substantial amount of their time to leadership training: Sufyan and his wife had returned from the mission field in Turkey to the USA where he was hoping to work on an Internet-based educational program for people training for leadership in Iran. Thad, in 2009 and 2010,

---

43. Email, December 2011.

had been helping to produce material for an interactive, online seminary which would be available to ICs in their home country. By 2011, though, he admitted that they had encountered many problems, but he was still producing television shows for and working with a well-known Farsophone satellite channel. Faris has lectures on YouTube and his church's website has what is basically an online library in Farsi.

The problems faced by ICs in relation to ministerial education are pronounced. Within Iran there are no functioning seminaries for Protestants or evangelicals, and even if there were the public act of attending a seminary would be dangerous for a person who is, legally speaking, a criminal (that is, a Christian ex-Muslim). Furthermore, such a seminary would quickly be shuttered or destroyed by the government, or thugs acting on behalf of the government. Also, most of the churches in Iran are home churches, which do not have the resources to pay a pastor's salary, much less seminary tuition. Consequently, the only options available are a combination of personal mentoring, teaching in the church, and material available by satellite and Internet. Even in the diaspora many leaders and pastors do not receive a regular salary from their congregations. While there are many ICs throughout the diaspora, the diaspora itself is genuinely global, and not concentrated in just a few cities. Also, many ICs (like the ones in Castle City and eventually the ones in Southern City as well) simply attend local churches. For those who attend Iranian congregations, with a few exceptions,[44] those congregations are not large enough to provide such an income. Therefore, even where there are evangelical seminaries, it is unlikely that a person will spend years of their life and a large sum of money so that they can take up a position that will not offer any stable income. Of the leaders I interviewed none of them received a stable, substantial income from an Iranian congregation. This was true even for people who had been in ministry for many years.

An example of the difficulties that such a scenario poses can be seen in the example of pastor Hisham, the lay pastor at Plateau City Church. The church he belongs to is Presbyterian, but he is employed full time as a technician. He works four nights a week doing vehicle maintenance, and then three days a week at the church. He often has a ten-hour overnight shift on Saturday night-Sunday morning before he comes to church to lead worship. His efforts to explore higher education so that he can be ordained have met with many obstacles. For him to be ordained in the Presbyterian Church of America he would need to obtain a Master of Divinity, a degree

---

44. According to my sources there are some large Iranian congregations in cities like Dallas and London that possess their own church building and have salaried pastors.

that normally takes two or three years of full-time study and practicum, and normally requires an undergraduate degree as a prerequisite. There are ways to earn this degree through part-time, non-residential study, but that would take about seven years by his calculation. He contacted a local seminary about such a possibility and they informed him that he would first need to prove his proficiency in English. In the meantime he is able to listen to Bible lessons and sermons from his workplace and he seems content with this.

Pastor Faris goes so far as to say that a Bible college (or seminary) is not a good format for forming leaders, because it is an "artificial environment" and "we will not get good leaders from there." All in all, among the people I interviewed, and especially leaders, there was a consensus that this was a main challenge for the future of Iranian Christianity. There seemed also to be a general consensus that the traditional seminary model was either unrealistic or undesirable, and that some combination of mentorship and material delivered by Internet and/or satellite was the best path forward. To date though, no one had been able to bring those various elements together in a satisfactory way.

These believers are engaged in reading their *contextuality*—evaluating their own context and world. A number of different possible modes of contextualization have been proposed wherein the community brings what they know of God's Word to bear on their contextuality. But to date none of those proposals have proved consistently successful. In other words, the area of leadership training is clearly a work in progress, a locus of activity demanding attention that has been identified, yet for which no one solution has been found. Moreover, the question clearly has theological import because its goal is to provide precisely those people who will be responsible for the ministries of teaching, baptizing, and celebrating Communion which have been explored above.

THE ATTRACTION OF CHRISTIANITY

As argued above, Iranian Christianity seeks to provide a purified way of being Iranian, one purged of the negative influences of Islam and Arab-ness. This in itself is a powerful reason that attracts people to Iranian churches and Christianity, and it was mentioned in many interviews. But there are other factors that are also significant, though perhaps not as dominant, which will be explored here. Moreover, evangelical Christianity offers a way of life that is at once religious but fits in relatively well with the modern world, which is seen to be different than the perceived failures of the Revolution, such as the violence of the war with Iraq or the country's marginalization in many international forums. But the attraction of Christianity and the life of the church to Iranians is not merely reactionary—as if they had become Christians *only* to preserve their culture, or *only* to object to the rule of the Ayatollahs. In this section we will explore some of the specific reasons given by interviewees as to how and why they became attracted to Christianity and the church. In doing so, we pick up the threads from earlier chapters about why Muslims convert to Christianity (chapter 2) and what they do theologically when they are Christian.

Sometimes, the church was itself the reason for the conversion, or, to put it a different way, conversion occurred so the person could participate in the church community's life.[45] One refugee told the story of how he was in Lebanon working with a family business and how he would often walk by a local evangelical church, and would hear the joyful singing inside. It should be recalled that his context was Shi'a Islam, which tends to emphasize acts of penitence, like self-flagellation during Ashura to mourn the tragic death of Hussein.[46] The concept of joyful worship of God piqued his curiosity and eventually was a factor that helped lead to his conversion: he now takes part in such worship at the church in Bay City.

Especially in a city like Bay City, where there are a substantial number of refugees and people seeking asylum, the church also provides emotional and spiritual support during what is often a frustrating and frightening experience. This factor in Bay City, not present in the other three cities where research took place, led to a number of challenges for the church. During interviews leaders said that sometimes people would attend church simply to build their case before the government, since it is well known that Iran vigorously punishes apostates from Islam. It is impossible for me to discern if some of the people I interviewed in Bay City were attending the church for this reason. Their zeal for the faith and the church (and the purified Iranian culture) appeared heartfelt. Ultimately though, there is no need to suppose that both motives could not be present in the same person: both to build a case for refugee status and also to worship God in Christ and fellowship with other believers. At such junctures it is necessary to recall the observation of Marc Bloch, the great French historian, who said,

> As for *homo religiosus, homo oeconomicus, homo politicus,* and all that rigmarole of Latinized men, the list of which we could string out indefinitely, there is grave danger of mistaking them for something else than they really are: phantoms which are convenient providing they do not become nuisances. The man

45. Gaudeul, *Called from Islam.*
46. Chelkowski, "Ta'zia."

of flesh and bone, reuniting them all simultaneously, is the only real being.[47]

All the leaders interviewed were aware of the problem of people attending the church (and requesting baptism, specifically) for the sake of bolstering their immigration claim, even in places like Plateau City where the church has no one requesting refugee status from the government.

In some cases reasons for participating in the life of the local church were extraordinary. In the case of one convert, Samira, she narrated her first experience of Mary, and from then on, even as a little child, determined that she must be where Mary was, meaning, among other things, the church:

> DAM: What was your first exposure to Christianity or Jesus or the Bible or any of those things?
>
> Samira: Well, my first exposure was when I was six and had a vision of the Virgin Mary. And at the time I didn't know who Mary was or who Jesus was or who Muslims were—I didn't know anything about anything. I was in a mountain place; it was dark, I fell and I couldn't get up. And there was this huge rock; this lady came from behind the rock: she was all in white, and she held my hand and picked me up and said that she was Mary. And when she held my hand something stayed with me and I just loved her and I asked my mother who she was, and she said she was the mother of Prophet Jesus, as Muslims knew her. And I just knew since then that I wanted to be where she was, which was the Church.[48]

Samira's experience is quite unique. Even if generalized to some category like "mystical experiences" I did not find any other person who gave a similar account for their commitment to a local church. As mentioned above, not all ICs in the diaspora attend Iranian churches. Samira, for instance, is an Episcopalian in the USA, and serves at a typical congregation there. She became a Christian decades ago, before Iranian churches were common in the USA. Also, she became attracted to liturgical Anglican worship, and there are (outside of Iran) no Persian Anglican churches.[49]

For another convert, in Plateau City, the reason was a welcoming (and again joyful) community. After winning the visa lottery to come to the USA,

47. Bloch, *Historian's Craft*, 151.

48. For more on Samira's conversion and her early experiences with Christianity see Miller, "From Shi'a Islam to Mary," 81–92.

49. The Church of England does have a chaplain for Iranian Christians, but I understand there are no permanent Anglican Iranian congregations in England.

he visited two of the local mosques. One was full of people mourning the great figures of Shi'ism, and this turned him off. At the other mosque, according to him, after the doors were closed and non-Muslim visitors had left, the imam launched into a tirade against the USA and then-President Bush. This struck him as disingenuous, as he said, since all these people were there in the USA enjoying many benefits and rights they would never have in Iran. His father (not a Christian) mentioned to him that there was an Iranian church, and he had seen an advertisement for it at the local Iranian market.[50] After trying it out he decided to join as this community was able to both affirm its Iranian-ness but also interpret itself in a way that made it at home in the USA. This is a case where the church was itself the Christian message, as he had not considered conversion prior to becoming part of the MBC in Plateau City.

In Bay City one of the ICs with whom I was staying invited me to attend his other church (this one not being Iranian). On Sunday morning we attended an evangelical Presbyterian church in the city center. The church was obviously wealthy and was full of locals—everything from children to students to young families to elderly people. After the service I saw my companion shaking hands with and talking with one of the men of the church, a well-dressed British professional, and not the sort of person to chat with a poor, single man applying for refugee status. But the narrative of the IC—having suffered persecution in Iran for his faith—allowed him a certain power that the (apparently) wealthy native did not have: persecution. Persecution is a pervasive theme in the New Testament, but the British man could not be persecuted, even if he sought it out. Having been persecuted for his faith meant that this poor, unmarried refugee had a sort of power that the wealthy British Christian did not. Paradoxically, my companion's powerlessness for the sake of his faith had become a sort of power in itself.

Another example of a felt need being met in the church, but again, not an Iranian church per se, is from a convert in Scotland. Her conversion took place over many years, which is not uncommon. One of the first exposures to Christianity she mentioned was as a child living in Switzerland. The Shah had sent her father there to the work with an international medical organization and she would pass by a large Roman Catholic church while walking home. The aesthetic of this church which she would step into from time to time impacted her deeply. She described its dark spaces, flickering candles, holy smell and chanting in Latin. She says she was "beguiled . . . by this out-of-world experience," with its clerics in flowing black robes, confessionals,

---

50. Pastor Thad remarked that the owner of the market was not a Christian, but that he had no problem with the announcement being placed on his message board in the market because anything that the Ayatollah disliked was fine by the owner.

nuns, and Stations of the Cross. "It was very comforting . . . I used to envy these people." She felt an intimacy and connection to this, her own "secret world." Her parents were not happy about this, particularly they objected to the images—a classical Islamic objection to Christian piety. She clarified: "It was my world." Later she read literature in a British university, including the poetry of the Jesuit Gerard Manley Hopkins, which also influenced her. She does not regularly attend the embryonic MBC in Castle City, but she does regularly attend a local Episcopal parish. It appears that the actual aesthetic, architectural beauty of churches and liturgy, as well as the aesthetic beauty of Christians' literary output were central to her continued participation in the life of the church. And while it is possible for ICs to build a splendid, beautiful church building, it is unlikely. In general, they do not have the numbers or resources for such an endeavor, and evangelical Christianity does not emphasize investing vast resources in beautiful buildings that have no utilitarian function. But even in the case of this convert, her first actual attendance at a church was occasioned by a chaplain at her university who invited her to the local Methodist church over a holiday when everyone else was at home and she was alone in her dorm.

Finally, given the oft-mentioned disappointment with the political-religious program of the Ayatollahs in Iran, it is worth noting that I never saw any of the churches being used as a locus of political action of any kind. In addition to Christianity as a place for genuine Persian-ness, there are a great variety of reasons that Iranians give when asked why they were attracted to Christianity or why they started attending a given church: visions, aesthetics, migration, the joyfulness of musical worship, and, as was seen in the example of the church in Plateau City earlier in the chapter, mutual support through fellowship and prayer.

CONCLUSION

In this chapter I described some of the factors that facilitated the growth of Christianity among Iranians and the fieldwork I carried out for this chapter. Then the question of ritual, with special reference to baptism and Communion, was explored, and I proposed that ritual is used by some ICs both to assert their identity as Persians and also to emphasize their distance from Arabizing Islam. Ritual was identified as one element in a larger strategy of identity-formation. The patterns of teaching found among the ICs I met confirmed my conclusions regarding ritual—that the teaching that takes place likewise asserts Persian identity by thoroughly deconstructing the Islamic image of deity and replacing it with a Christian one. The program is expansive and broad, spanning from the beginning of pre-baptismal training all the way to leadership formation, and touches on ethics, theology, biblical interpretation and study, prayer, spirituality, and more. The proper method for leadership training is the locus of much activity and seen to be of great import, but a sustainable and suitable method has not yet been found. Finally, multiple examples were provided of the great variety of motives for embracing Christianity and the church among ICs—motives in addition to and beyond the reconstitution of Persian-ness, as the local church meets many of their felt needs. Beyond the church as a genuine abode of Iranian-ness, these ranged from the church being a place of emotional support (especially through prayer) to being a community that irenically reconciles life in the West with being Iranian.

Having now completed the studies of Kitma, the texts of CMBs, and this one, it is appropriate to tackle in greater detail the central question of this research regarding the contextual theologies of CMBs. That is the purpose of the next chapter.

7

Theology-Making
Context, Content, Metaphor and Purpose

CHAPTER INTRODUCTION

In this chapter I will draw together the many different themes that have been encountered within this book. First, the context of the theology-making will be examined. Following this, dominant trends in the theologies of ex-Muslim Christians will be set out and discussed, on the basis that a specific vision of love-and-power is a central theme and impetus that influences almost all of the theology-making I observed. I then will argue that identity-formation is a key aim or goal that is interwoven with the contents and themes of these theologies. Finally, I will show how the context, themes, content, and dominant metaphor examined are all related to each other in the framework of Shoki Coe's ecumenical model of (organic) contextualization.

Throughout this book some of the central symbols and identity-markers of Islam (and Christianity) have been studied. In relation to Islam we have looked at the law of apostasy, the place of the Qur'an in the community, the Qur'anic theory of *tanziil* (descent), the role of the mosque, topics relating to leadership, and, in general, the operation and theory of power present in some Muslim communities. In relation to Christianity we have looked at the ideal of "valid" evangelical religious conversion, baptism, the Bible in relation to the community, and theory of divine inspiration of the Bible, and how leadership, love, and power are experienced and understood by some CMBs. These were all issues that emerged from the research on how these CMBs understand their own contextuality.

Some of the factors in chapter 3, themselves in many cases strategic uses of globalization by evangelicals, describe how in many contexts, whether in the Muslim world or elsewhere, Muslims are encountering the claims of the Christian faith to an unprecedented extent. The reality of social change likewise implies a context wherein old symbols and values are being re-evaluated. Also significant here is the deterioration or legal restriction of the ability of some Muslim communities to effectively use power (chapter 1) to stem the "pollution" of apostasy (chapter 5 and the examples from Iran in chapter 6). This complex web of influences has translated into an unprecedented number of known conversions.

CONVERSION AND THEOLOGY-MAKING WITHIN THE FRAME OF INCULTURATION

Religious Conversion

The discussion on religious conversion and why some Muslims convert to Christ (chapter 2) gave various examples of the process. Conversion, in turning from the old to the new, usually involves the turning away from certain old symbols and values, and turning to new ones considered both authentic and superior. Examples of this were Ayya who turned away from Muhammad's treatment of women to Jesus's treatment of women or some of the ICs who discarded the (Arabic) ritual of Islam for the (Iranian) worship of Christianity.

But cultures are not discrete, easily-defined things at all. Rather they represent or contain within themselves a number of different domains related to politics, age, gender, geography, economics, religion, ethnicity, education, family, commerce and so on. These are overlapping domains, each of which influences and is influenced by the identity of the individual: Tim Green calls them social identities (chapter 2), which are intermediate between the core and the collective identity, ". . . the way a whole symbolic group is labeled and distinguished from other groups by its identity markers."[1]

The meeting of the Muslim in his specific cultural niche with the Christian message is never with an "unadulterated" message, being already mediated by some variety of (likely) American-influenced evangelical tradition. This meeting may lead to religious conversion if the Muslim determines that the symbolic order of the Christian faith (including but not limited to Jesus, God the Father, the Bible and the church) is in some way superior to the "old" symbolic order he knew in Islam. Furthermore, this meeting

---

1. Green, "Identity Issues for ex-Muslim Christians," 440.

often takes place because of the agency or "quest" (to use Rambo's term) of someone seeking answers.

But because "culture" and "identity" are so multi-faceted and complex, even after one's religious identity has changed, the question remains: what happens with the social identities of the convert? Or to put it another way, since they have changed their relation to the religious domain of their culture, how will that affect their relations with the other domains? In light of the consistent policy of some Muslims to utilize power to stymie the spread of the "pollution" of apostasy, the specific question is, having rejected their old religious identity and relation to the religious domain of their culture, is there any possibility of not rejecting one's relation to the rest of the domains of their culture and social identities? Such a decision would take place within the context of inculturation—the meeting of the culture and the Christian message.

Revisiting Inculturation

Inculturation as the meeting of a culture and the gospel encapsulates quite well what I observed in Kitma, the Iranian diaspora, and in the texts of CMBs. One of the main concerns was the formation of a new identity— Kitman Christians, ICs, Pakistani Christians. But this is a new identity not dictated by family history, in that these Christians do not come from Christian families or the ethnic minorities which are historically Christian. The shari'a and traditional constructs of identity did not allow for this sort of shift in identity. To be Kitman from *this* family meant to be Muslim. To change one's identity as a Muslim implied, by necessity, to also leave *this* family and *this* nationality.[2] So much of the activity of the Kitmans, Iranians, and authors studied here is related to the struggle to form a new identity, and to find ways to convince others to accept their new identity without persecuting the convert. Returning to Eliot's image of "living among the breakage," identities break, and new combinations of identities are being formed (and re-formed). Apostasy from Islam is social change, and many Muslims suspect that when a relative or friend has left Islam, they have "betrayed" their country, society and family. When families or states resort to persecution they are reacting to a social change by using power to assert the importance of the old symbols of the Islamic culture. For the convert the old symbolic system has been judged and found wanting; they have modified or discarded the old symbols and meanings.

2. Meral, *No Place to Call Home.*

Modernity provides an arena wherein novel combinations of social identities may emerge.[3] In parts of the world one can now be an openly-gay, non-celibate Christian cleric; a woman legally married to another woman; a feminist Muslima; or in the USA an African-Irish-American president. Similarly, many converts from Islam to Christianity are actively trying to form new constellations of social identities which previously had been seen as impossible (Saudi Christian, Catholic Turk, etc). While some examples of double belonging to Islam and Christianity at the same time were presented earlier in this book, the converts I studied were clear in not wanting to belong to Islam anymore.

Gittins notes that "We talk of an initial movement of *inculturation*, when faith challenges culture, and the reciprocal movement that causes faith to be reformulated and re-expressed, not in formulaic terms but in the lives and encounters of actual people."[4] The process of inculturation may be difficult to identify, for it is easy to mistake a mere translation or adaptation as inculturation. According to Gittins, "Visible *surface structures* may be too quickly identified with the *deep structures* assumed to underlie them . . . ."[5] A mark of inculturation is that these deep structures are being transformed and challenged by the Christian message. John Paul II wrote that inculturation requires "the intimate transformation of cultural values through their integration in Christianity . . . ."[6] The sort of evangelization required is one that, in the words of Paul VI, operates "in a vital way, in depth and to the very roots [of a culture]."[7] These statements appear to imply the creation of a new identity, both personal and communal. This might be roughly analogous to the early Christians in the Roman Empire—the Greeks and Romans were called the first race, the Jews the second race, and the Christians, who ethnically included Romans, Greeks, and Jews, came to be known as the third race, such was the depth of the transformation of their identity.[8]

The main question addressed in this work is related specifically to theology-making. It is probable that a community or assemblage of linked people with a common cultural background engaging in the process of

3. Berger, *Heretical Imperative.*

4. Gittins, "Deep Structures," 59.

5. Ibid., 56, italics in original.

6. John Paul II, *Redemptoris Missio* §52.

7. Paul VI, *Evangelii Nuntiandi* §20.

8. See Tertullian's *Ad Nationes* 1:8 and the anonymous *Epistle to Diognetus* 5, among others. Stephen Louy, "Origins of Christian Identity," is an important volume on identity-formation across ethnic boundaries in the Apostolic church drawn from Paul's epistles and explores the topic in depth.

inculturation will eventually engage in the process of theology-making. It must be noted that theology-making is just one activity that makes up the broader process of inculturation, for inculturation could also affect everything from dress to ritual to music to liturgy to political activity, and so on. The error that Gittins cautions us against is to think that just because some of these surface elements (dress, music) have changed, that the Christian message has really transformed a culture.

Nor is inculturation inevitable. Communities may adopt the Christian faith in its Brazilian Pentecostal or its Coptic Orthodox embodiment, not only adopting the message but the cultural practices of the messengers proclaiming it. It is also possible for a community to adopt the surface structures of the Christian religion—churches, saints, masses, feast days—while not being deeply transformed by the Christian message. This concern led Gittins[9] to conclude that the ultimate proof of the presence and reality of deep inculturation is a moral transformation which is manifested in the believers producing the fruit of the Spirit: love, joy, peace, patience, kindness, goodness, faithfulness, gentleness, self-control.[10] Inculturation may affect the visible signs and symbols of a community, but without a moral transformation the process, according to Gittins, lacks a fundamental pneumatological[11] quality.

Utilizing Gittins's evaluation would require that I make a moral evaluation of each of the believers I met and try to discern to what extent (if any) they had progressed in the qualities listed in Galatians 5. Such a project may well be viable, but it is beyond the scope of this research. This does not mean that we cannot benefit from Gittins's insight at all, though, for we can examine what the believers *say* about these qualities and the God that grants them. To say something about God, and about God's interaction with his Creation, is to engage in theology. What then can we say about the actual content of the theology? What does it claim to say about God? What knowledge does it seek to communicate? That is the central concern of this book.

Theology-making construed within the model of contextualization advanced by Coe works well as part of the larger event of inculturation, for it provides us with a specific process (albeit a flexible one) that describes how theology-making might take place.

---

9. Gittins, "Deep Structures."

10. Gal 5:22–23

11. That is, related to the activity and person of the Holy Spirit, who according to Paul's doctrine in Galatians engenders this ethical transformation.

Contextualization as Theology-making

Within the multifaceted, gradual process of inculturation, one of the projects that may sooner or later arise is that of theology-making. In chapter 1, two understandings of "contextualization" were presented. One was a form of contextualization popularized and espoused mostly by American evangelicals that I called directed contextualization. This was to differentiate it from the older and original use of the word. That model was birthed within the WCC in relation to theological education and was popularized by Taiwanese educator-pastor Shoki Coe. This ecumenical model of contextualization I called organic contextualization. The American evangelical model of contextualization was labeled "directed" because it came from outside, most specifically from missionaries who were directing the complex process of trying to make the gospel relevant, intelligible and attractive to—in our case—Muslims. My choice of the word "organic" for the ecumenical contextualization espoused by Coe and his colleagues in the WCC stems from the fact that this model of contextualization understands and accepts that it is a step in a lengthy process of maturation which *cannot be abbreviated or directed from the outside.* Like the maturation of most living beings, it is gradual, hence "organic."

Chapter 1 proposed that the most appropriate (if still imperfect) model for contextual theology-making for this study was that of Coe, which was later developed by Schreiter. Turning to directed contextualization, genealogies of the predominantly American model of directed contextualization exist.[12] The popularization of directed contextualization was due in large part to books like Parshall's *New Paths in Muslim Evangelism* and *The Gospel and Islam.*[13] Before such publications American evangelicals appeared to be working in continuity with the ecumenical model, and Bruce Nicholls produced the brief but dense 1979 book *Contextualization: a theology of gospel and culture* (IVP). That book, however, is mostly focused on biblical theology,[14] making it too narrow for this book. It is perhaps the best book by an evangelical scholar on *organic* contextualization in reference to biblical theology. By the 1980s, directed contextualization had become the

---

12. Wolfe, "Insider Movements"; Sleeman, "Insider Movement Debate."

13. Edited by Don McCurry.

14. Biblical theology is " . . . any theology which draws its materials from the Bible . . . " ("Biblical Theology" in Harrison, *Dictionary of Theology*, 95) and " . . . concerned to do justice to the theological dimension of the Bible. . ." ("Biblical Theology Movement" in Elwell, *Dictionary of Theology*, 149). The use of the Bible by CMBs has been mentioned in this thesis, but in answering the research question other possible sources of theology have been examined, namely rituals, liturgy, and texts by CMBs.

default meaning of the word "contextualization" and the existence of the older, original meaning seems to have been forgotten, excepting footnotes crediting Coe with coining the term. Coe's version of contextualization envisions the indigenous believers as the active contextualizers, and represents theology *by*, and insofar as Christians from other churches are concerned, *theology with*.

Recall from chapter 1 that according to Coe the process whereby contextualization takes place is the local believers first discerning their contextuality, and then engaging in contextualization. He also described this as wrestling with God's world and discerning his desire and activity in that world, and then in the light of that, wrestling with God's Word, and then proposing and applying a way for the church to be involved in making that vision of God's desire for the world into a reality. Coe's is the original vision of contextualization, and thus the oldest one, but because it describes *theology by*, and does not limit itself to one specific sort of theology-making, or a narrow vision of the theological artifact, I have opted to use it rather than newer models.

THE CONTENT OF THE THEOLOGIES: SALVATION, CHURCH, AND INITIATION

Specific Theological Trends

Social change places traditional structures under pressure. Symbols and traditions and meanings are re-evaluated. Some people resort to a *rejection* of the modern and re-emphasize the old symbols. Others try to *adapt* the old and new symbols so they can try to form something new that will draw on both the old and the new. Others reject some of the old symbols and *search for new* symbols, meanings, and practices. Converts from Islam to Christianity have in general resorted to the two latter practices. We have studied here the Iranians encountering forms of evangelicalism in the context of the USA and the UK, and Kitmans encountering the evangelicalism of the Juduur Christians. The Christian message can reaffirm some aspects of a culture, accommodate others, and challenge others. In Kitma, for instance, the Christian message was interpreted as challenging the separation of males from females during worship and the tradition of a male-only leadership. The old practice was discarded for something new. The ICs I studied have found much to affirm in their own traditions as the Christian message encountered Iranian culture. Thus elements like poetry, music and Nowruz were retained. It is true that these surface elements can be changed in a people without them having a deep interaction with the Christian message as Gittins argued, and it is necessary to be aware of this possibility.

With the caveats that these are generalizations, that one would expect to find different theologies being made by different groups of CMBs, and that even among ICs one might find different claims, there are a number of theological trends and emphases which I have identified in the theologies being made by the ex-Muslim Christians studied for this research, insofar as I have correctly interpreted their texts, worship, teaching and writings.[15] I am trying to interpret, summarize and order some key points which I have observed or noted in their theology-making, which itself is one aspect or part of the overarching meeting of a culture and the gospel (inculturation).

Soteriology

Soteriology: The Salvation of Cultures

Soteriology is the study of salvation, and is considered by many Christians to be central to the Christian faith. Two of the key terms that are used in the Bible and by many CMBs to describe this salvation are reconciliation[16] and atonement.[17]

In reference to questions of reconciliation with God and the atonement, the groups I studied largely adhered to commonly held evangelical views and continued to preach and teach and believe what had been handed down to them: that salvation is a gift of God, appropriated through faith, that said salvation should result in moral transformation (called sanctification), and is made available to humanity through the atoning death of the Messiah. There are, however, at least two points in which CMBs may differ from the wider evangelical context in their theology-making.

The first is that salvation in some cases is understood to spread throughout society: God's salvation is not individualistic, but it requires that churches and believers take action to see it spread, and not only on a spiritual level, in terms of calling people to conversion (though that is not precluded). The salvation achieved by God in Christ is a salvation that saves not only people (as individuals) but entire cultures. This soteriological commitment leads to several questions: what does it look like for Persian, Arab, or Turkish cultures to experience salvation in Christ? The activity and

15. In chapters 4, 5 and 6.

16. For instance Rom 5:11, 11:15, 2 Cor 5:18–19, Eph 2:16, Col 1:20–22.

17. For instance Rom 3:25, Heb 2:17, 1 John 2:2 and 4:10. In the Hebrew Scriptures the theme of atonement is central to Exodus, Leviticus, and Ezekiel.

discourse of the ICs was very intentional about bringing together Persian culture, language, traditions, food, dress and poetry while intentionally trying to excise many aspects of Islam perceived as Arab intrusions.

Texts pleading for greater religious freedom and tolerance are instances of this theological trend. For instance, Fatima, the Saudi Arabian martyr, prayed that Jesus "changes your notions and set right the scales of justice // And spread love among you oh Muslims."[18] Or as Timothy Abraham commented, "We are done with Islam and good riddance to bad rubbish, and the question that remains is, how do we fight for our rights and not yield to that Eastern fatalism in resignation to persecution?" Turkish convert Ziya Meral has brought to light the plight of ex-Muslim Christians throughout the Muslim world in *No Place to Call Home: Experiences of Apostates from Islam, Failures of the International Community*,[19] wherein he calls for concrete steps towards securing basic human rights for converts in Islamic contexts. These are a few examples of how some CMBs understand salvation not solely on an individualistic level, but as something that extends to the transformation of entire communities or cultures.

Soteriology: The Doctrine of the Atonement

Atonement is generally considered to be part of Christian faith—whether one is Catholic, Orthodox, or Protestant. Atonement is "the reconciliation of two parties . . . the restoration of the broken relationship between God and man that was accomplished in the life and death of Jesus Christ."[20] Particular emphasis came to be placed on the shedding of the Messiah's blood on the Cross as the apogee or focus of this reconciling act. Moreover, this atonement is vicarious, meaning that it is not executed personally by one's self, but vicariously, through a representative. The atonement is a dominant theme throughout the New Testament, and according to Orthodox scholar John McGuckin, "Atonement was the Apostle Paul's great theological theme in all of his writings."[21]

That God has reconciled humans to him in the life and death of the Messiah is a dogma, a central belief. The dogma itself offers no precise

18. *Way of Fatima*, 9.

19. Meral, *No Place to Call Home*.

20. Harvey, *Handbook*, 33.

21. McGuckin, *Orthodox Church*, 199. On the same page he explains that Orthodoxy affirms completely the doctrine of atonement, that, "The Orthodox know the significance of the Lord's work of atonement as the bestowing of the profound gift of reconciliation with the Father mediated through the Son's gift of the Spirit to his church."

account of *how* it becomes true, rather it claims to be an assertion of historical and theological fact. The question of *how* this is true, the mechanics, is a matter of theory and different ones have been postulated at different times: the one commonly taught among Western evangelicals is penal substitution, based on the earlier work of the Italian missionary Anselm[22] who was bishop over the Church of the Angles in England.

Evangelicals: Satisfaction of Punishment

Here I will explain how some evangelicals (including many in the USA and the UK) interpret the atonement. Then I will show how some CMBs are branching out in a different direction in relation to their understanding of the atonement.

A dominant evangelical theory to explain how the atonement is effective is called penal substitution. This proposes that Jesus received the just *pena* (Latin for punishment, hence the word *penal*) that we deserved. God thus could remain both merciful (humans are forgiven) and just (his wrath had been satisfied). This is the mechanism whereby the dogma of atonement is efficacious. Wayne Grudem, in his oft-used evangelical text book on systematic theology, says of penal substitution, "This has been the orthodox understanding of the atonement held by evangelical theologians, in contrast to other views that attempt to explain the atonement apart from the idea of the wrath of God or payment of the penalty of sin."[23] Furthermore, many evangelical proponents of Penal Substitution would claim that the Bible clearly teaches this.[24] But CMBs I have met and whose books I have read, on the whole, seem to have little use for the theory of penal substitution.

MBBs and the Atonement

Emir Rishawi, an Egyptian CMB, is a thinker and author who comes close to what would be considered speculative theology interspersed with apologetics and poetry. Consider his explicit rejection of the theory that

22. Circa 1033–1109. It is worth noting that Anselm himself did not propose penal substitution, which is to say that Jesus's death satisfied God's wrath. Rather, he proposed that Jesus's death was a satisfaction of *honor*.

23. Grudem, *Systematic Theology*, 579, chapter 27.C.c.4.

24. For a differing evangelical point of view on the Atonement see Wright, "The Cross and the Caricatures," n.p.: " . . . when Jesus himself wanted to explain to his disciples what his forthcoming death was all about, he didn't give them a theory, he gave them a meal."

the atonement derives its efficacy from Jesus being punished on humanity's behalf:

> I have read some explanations on the death of our Redeemer and Saviour that represent it as a work that Christ did to appease the wrath of God . . . But I believe that the wrath of God upon sinners and their bondage to Satan are moral images that aim at manifesting the true dimension and the deep contradiction between sin and God. The animal sacrifices that the Children of Israel offered to God expressed man's realisation of the distance that sin creates between him and God, and his conviction that death only can atone for sin, since sin is an uttermost offence against God.[25]

Penal Substitution understands Jesus taking humanity's punishment as the crux of salvific activity. While Rishawi does not dispense entirely with the image of Christ "appeas[ing] the wrath of God," he does relativize that language, seeing it as a "moral image" illustrating the "true dimension" of the gravity of sin. He then proposes that the gravity of sin, "an uttermost offence against God," requires some sort of sacrifice.

In other sections of his writing it appears that he finds the Orthodox tradition of *theosis* (or something resembling it) to be the most compelling soteriological model:

> There was found in Jesus Christ perfect and genuine human nature. The salvation of man is, above all, a salvation of being. This salvation of being is brought to fulfillment through unity with the personal being of Christ, so that it becomes "a new creation" (1 Corinthians 5:17) being united with God in substance.[26]

Also, he dislikes that "[s]ome preachers . . . " speak only of Christ's death when they are speaking of "redemption and salvation," finding this view to be "very narrow." Rather, he proposes, the incarnation itself was salvific: "Through the incarnation of the Word, human nature obtained salvation, and became united with the person of the Son of the holy God, thereby becoming 'renewed' and 'deified' (2 Pet 1:4)" (*ibid.*). Thus the fundamental problem to be resolved is not that God must punish humans with damnation, yet loves them and desires to be merciful, and that his justice demands satisfaction, which is found in the penal substitution of Jesus on the Cross. Rather, for Rishawi, the fundamental problem is that human nature has become estranged from the divine nature; God, in becoming human, opens up

25. Rishawi, *Struggle that led to Conversion*, §III.2
26. Rishawi, *Struggle that led to Conversion*, §III.3

salvation to human nature. Thus it is not *only* the Cross that is salvific, but every aspect of Messiah's advent—from Annunciation through Ascension. All of those reconcile human nature to divine nature and are thus salvific, even if the Cross is identified as the apogee of that Advent.

This is not conventional evangelical theology. It does resemble the Orthodox concept of *theosis* which reasons that "because Jesus Christ has taken to himself a true human nature, all people are truly received in him and become potential participants in his deified human nature . . . In *theosis*, believers can share, by grace and participation, in that which God is by nature."[27] It appears that Rishawi is drawing on an Orthodox theory of salvation (*theosis*) and discarding the dominant evangelical theory of penal substitution, even though he knows it and understands it.

Rishawi is one of the very few authors who explores this theological question in depth. Statements that "Jesus died for me/us/you" or that "he took my/your/our sins away on the Cross" are common, but they resist any detailed analysis. In seeking to explore this topic more thoroughly, I asked Timothy Abraham to explain, "how does Jesus's death on the Cross lead to our sins being forgiven?" His complete answer follows:

> Jesus died on the Cross. His death was one of selfless, uncondi-
> tional love. He loved me and laid down his life for me. He did it
> for me. I was on his mind. I have always been on the mind of the
> Word of God. Such love is communicated sacrificially to me and
> I am the primary beneficiary of such love. It cleanses me of all
> the ills of my soul. Such love makes me clean, pure. Cleanness
> and purity are what might be termed, in part, as forgiveness.
> Forgiveness means I am freed as well as released.[28]

Here it is the love of God that is salvific. Forgiveness of sins is under-stood as only part of salvation, though an important part of it. The Cross functions as a portal whereby that love can be "communicated" to humans. Abraham is Baptist, and is deeply familiar with evangelical theology includ-ing penal substitution; but while he knows about it, he does not find it to be useful. Unlike Rishawi though, he does not draw on the Orthodox concept of *theosis*.

Abdul Saleeb, an Iranian CMB, responded to the same question, writ-ing, "The quick answer is, we don't know." That is, while traditional Chris-tian dogma affirms the reality and efficacy of the atonement, we don't really understand precisely *how* it functions or is efficacious, though we have a wide array of *metaphors* or *narratives* that help us to understand the reality

27. "Theosis" in Fahlbusch, *Encyclopedia of Christianity*, volume 5, 453.

28. Correspondence with author, 2012.

of the dogma. I inquired a bit further about penal substitution specifically, and he responded:

> . . . penal substitution doesn't register much at all on the radar of the Iranian Christian community (not in our testimonies, hymns, writings or preaching). In our Iranian world we hardly ever think about the mechanics of atonement. Our focus is the love of Christ on the cross.[29]

This diversity stretches beyond Arabs and Iranians. A colleague (who cannot be named) carried out research among groups of Muslim-background believers in Bangladesh. Unlike the believers I studied, these people have not openly joined any of the Christian churches there, though they came to their understanding of faith through evangelical links. Nor have they remained Muslims, at least in their theological understanding. The researcher, who focused on their Christology and understanding of atonement, found that these believers saw in Jesus a mediator and patron who was more honorable and powerful than Muhammad in that he had been born of a virgin, performed miracles, and was still alive with God. Their understanding of how this salvation/reconciliation was wrought was by seeing themselves as intricately linked with Jesus, being "in him," and thereby sharing in both his death and resurrection. It is worth noting that how these MBBs conceive of and describe salvation is again very different than the norm among evangelicals.[30]

I am not saying there is some commonly identifiable CMB theory of the atonement. There are, however, enough clues here to suggest the need for further research in this area. It does appear that an evangelical orthodoxy is being revisited, altered, discarded, refuted or perhaps simply ignored.

In sum, the Atonement is a Christian dogma, and claims to assert a spiritual and historical fact. As to *how* the atonement is efficacious, penal substitution is historically the dominant soteriological theory among evangelicals, and the one that CMBs would very likely learn. While they appear to know of and understand penal substitution they do not agree with it, and respond in a number of ways. One CMB drew on an alternative Orthodox soteriology called *theosis*. Another was content to leave the question unanswered, while not doubting the dogma itself (that it is in fact efficacious). Uniting all the responses, though, was a pervading and intense concentration on the sacrificial, paternal love of God. I suspect that the idea of the

29. Correspondence with author, 2012.

30. This doctoral dissertation is embargoed for some time due to security issues; therefore it cannot be further discussed. This paragraph was edited by the researcher before it was included in this chapter.

Father actively punishing the Son (even if it is for the sake of the salvation of the world) appears to be irreconcilable with their image of a loving God.

Ecclesiology

Ecclesiology is the study of and reflection on the nature of the Christian church. Among evangelicals, it is not often a theological topic of great interest,[31] though there are some exceptions.[32] Nonetheless, ecclesiology does not generally receive the same priority in theological education as, say, theology of the incarnation or salvation. Critics of evangelicalism accuse evangelicals of neglecting this discipline.[33] I therefore was surprised that the nature and life of the church was a locus of urgent reflection and activity among CMBs.

Activity Surrounding Leadership Formation

One main factor that led me to the conclusion that ecclesiology is very important to the believers I spent time with was the intense activity surrounding leadership formation in both Kitma and among the Iranians. That the community itself, the church, was of the utmost importance was clear to me, for not only did many of the leaders speak about the issue, but devoted much time to it. Almost all of the leaders I interviewed were intensely involved in leadership formation of some sort. In Kitma the plan for empowering and forming Kitman leaders was a key concern, and likewise among the Iranians multiple projects were being pursued.

"Americans Don't Do Fellowship . . ."

One reason these CMBs find the church so important may be that they, both Iranians and Arabs, come from less individualistic communities; therefore salvation is not experienced on a purely personal level. For instance, Iranian Mina Nevisa tells the Muslim seeker/convert that "Regular sessions of [Christian] fellowship are the lifeblood for all believers . . . God has designed the Body of Christ in a manner that partially makes us interdependent upon

31. Packer, "Stunted Ecclesiology."

32. Harper and Metzger, *Exploring Ecclesiology*; De Young and Cluck, *Why we love the Church*.

33. McDermott, *Oxford Handbook*, 396; Mouw, "Problem of Authority," 130–31.

one another . . ."[34] Pastor Hisham from Plateau City recalled the days before he joined the Iranian fellowship, when his family attended a typical evangelical church, lamenting that "Americans don't do fellowship. You can go on Sunday and never meet anyone at all . . . They don't talk [to each other] during the week."[35]

"A New Home": The Church and a New Identity

A second reason the church may also be a central concern is because some CMBs sacrificed a great deal in terms of safety, health or wealth in order to be part of that community. This relates back to the soteriological facet, since establishing an indigenous church is one of the key means of evangelizing and transforming a community. One leader mentioned that the Iranian government is quite aware of this, noting, "in Iran persecution is keeping believers from gathering, for the government knows lone Christians are weak and do not do much for the growth of the faith."

Thus the success and completion of conversion relies largely on the existence of a church to welcome seekers and new believers. Converts often are estranged from their family and community, so it is important that a new community be in place to assist with the socialization and identity-formation of the new believers.[36] Without such a community/family in place, the slow and difficult "turning" may well be stymied. But as we saw with the examples of Ayya and John, finding a local church which will take up this role can be quite difficult. Here is the experience of one Jordanian CMB:

> Aslan*, one of the first Muslims to convert to Christianity in Jordan, stated . . . that when he became a Christian, no Jordanian Christian believed he was sincere, and no church reached out to help him, except for a few foreign missionaries . . .
>
> While Aslan recognises the growing sense of community in the increasing numbers of CMBs, the issue of the integration of converts into ethnic Christian communities in the Middle East remains problematic. He said that in the church he attends in Jordan there are now four other converts, but no other church members spoke to them and they were often left to talk to each other in a corner of the meeting hall where they served drinks.

34. Nevisa, *Miracle*, 223.

35. Interview, 2011.

36. Syrjänen, *Meaning and Identity*.

> Aslan's observations and experiences were echoed in interviews
> undertaken . . . in Egypt, Iran, Jordan and Kuwait.[37]

This tepid welcome, if not outright rejection, of converts has been noted before. Temple Gairdner, one of the most astute analysts of Muslim-Christian relations and witness, enunciated this point clearly as early as 1928, writing that churches in the Muslim world must shed their suspicion of Muslim seekers and present " . . . a real welcome to the Muslim convert, a welcome which would make him feel that he had found his real home . . ." and,

> The brotherhood of Islam, however imperfect, means much to those within. Since this is so, it is obvious that unless we can receive them with a brotherhood that is higher, better, more spiritual, warmer, and in a word, *truer*, they will marvel how we have the face to preach to them at all.[38]

Recalling our discussions of liminality, identity formation and stabilization (also called socialization) generally require a completion of the stage of liminality through reasssimiliation. Their Muslim community usually will not or cannot reassimilate these persons after their conversion, but a church can. This is essentially Gairdner's point above, which has, it seems, been ignored by scholars and practitioners of mission since 1928. The context/experience of conversion leads to and implies and unfolds itself in this sort of ecclesiology—the church as a new home, a new family. John (from chapter 4), reflecting on the importance of being involved in a local church, made a similar point. Speaking to a hypothetical MBB who asks, *I have Jesus and the Bible, why do I need the Church?* he answered

> . . . by yourself you're weak, and as a human being emotional. You could easily get confused and spiritually attacked. You can't do stuff you have to do as a Christian by yourself (such as baptism, Communion, tithing or the laying on of hands). By yourself you're not accountable, without anyone to encourage you, and basically vulnerable.[39]

Saiid Rabiipour, an Iranian believer and long-time Christian, questioned the very possibility of being called a Christian without a commitment to a church. I posed him the same question as John and he responded with a few questions—is this person really even a Christian in the evangelical

---

37. Meral, *No Place to Call Home*, 69.
38. Gairdner, "Home for Christ's Converts," 282.
39. Email, 2013.

sense of being born again? The question led him to reflect on baptism: "By [baptism], we identify ourselves with Christ. It symbolized death, burial and resurrection and is a very important ordinance unless we are ashamed of that identity." Here the three concepts of identity, church and baptism are intertwined, and the implication is that each re-enforces the other and guarantees the integrity of the other elements. No baptism means no accountability from a church, and points to not really experiencing the new identity of being born again. Raising the issue of baptism also implies that if such a believer has been baptized, that the baptizing church has responsibility for him. Considering this hypothetical MBB who believes in Jesus and the Spirit, but wonders about the importance of the church, the respondent concluded his answer by saying,

> Often, many people like to keep one foot in Christianity and another in their past religion. This way they can appease both. He may be at the point of searching but without real commitment at this point of his life. Loving people like him and giving them space maybe the thing they need at such a time of their life, while at the same time he needs support and encouragement to seek the right things.[40]

In other words, perhaps the person has a weak faith or has not yet received enough teaching. He is perhaps just at the beginning of his transformation and his turning away from the old and turning to the new, and in such a situation a loving, patient church is all the more necessary.

A Practical and Functional Critique of the American-British Evangelical Practice

With the issue of soteriology there was what appeared to be a break with American-influenced evangelicalism. Here there is a disagreement about the *practical* and functional nature of the church. There is no claim that evangelical *theology* as such is wrong, but rather that churches in the USA and the UK which they had known often do not *function* according to the theological *theory* of the church they espouse: they are not sufficiently robust, deep or genuine to carry the heavy burden which the profundity and scandal and danger of religious conversion from Islam to Christianity requires of converts.

Regarding soteriology one CMB seemed attracted to the ancient Eastern Orthodox thought of his Egyptian homeland, rather than to the

---

40. Correspondence, 2013.

framework of Penal Substitution. However, no one suggested adopting Eastern Orthodox practices or theologies related to a monarchial episcopate wherein the supreme ecclesial authority is an ecumenical council of bishops, and wherein each nation's church is both autocephalous but in communion with other such churches.[41] But there are claims that it is possible to follow Messiah in a genuine and fruitful manner without belonging to the church, and a brief examination of the topic is appropriate.

"Theology by" and Insider Movements

In January of 2013 the influential evangelical magazine *Christianity Today* had the headline "Worshiping Jesus in the Mosque." An article on the featured topic states that there is an "ongoing debate" and frames the issue thus:

> Insider movements raise important questions about the nature of faith in Christ. Can a Hindu or a Muslim accept Jesus Christ as Lord and Savior but not join some expression of the visible local church, yet still be a "true" Christian? Is it important for followers of Christ to use or accept the label Christian in order to belong to him? What does baptism signify? Is it fundamentally a public profession of personal faith, or does it also require participating in a visible worshiping community?[42]

In other words: Can someone say "yes" to Jesus and "no" to the existing, local expressions of the church?

Tennent notes that "scholars debate the relationship of personal salvation to identifying with the larger church and other Christians," and it is hard to read this and avoid the sense that theology is being done *for* someone else, regardless of where the scholars' positions may fall. IM is indeed an open debate among American evangelical "scholars," but among the CMBs I met, it is of no interest. Rather there is a clear consensus that belonging to a local church, being baptized and, with only *possible* exceptions when faced with danger, using the label *Christian* and rejecting the label *Muslim* are indeed what God and the Bible require. That is *their* point of view—theology done *by* the ex-Muslim Christians. The centrality of the church in this theology is not up for debate because for them, apparently, the church is seen as *part* of the Good News of God revealed in his Messiah. That Jesus died for one's sins and opened a way to be an individual child of God is not

41. For a more detailed exposition on Orthodox ecclesiology and its historical development see McGuckin, *Orthodox Church*, 238–61.

42. Tennent, "Hidden History," n.p. Available online at http://www.ctlibrary.com/ct/2013/january-february/hidden-history-of-insider-movements.html.

the entirety or end of the gospel in these theologies—but that there is this new family and home for the convert, the church, which provides accountability, encouragement, fellowship and the sacraments, is also part of the Good News.

Thus their ecclesiology can be described as a practical, applied theology, and often manifested itself with a concern for leadership formation. According to this reading the ecclesiology itself grows out of the soteriology because for the CMB, believing, growing as a believer, and maintaining the identity of believer, *require* belonging to a believing community. The success or failure of the entire conversion career may well hinge on finding a welcoming church with capable leaders—who are often the teachers and baptizers. The explicit claims relating baptism and ecclesiology in some of the statements above logically lead to a more in depth exploration of the rite of initiation into that body.

Sacramentality

The theology of baptism advanced by many of the CMBs I met and studied displays a more acute emphasis on the power and efficacy of rituals than is present in many other evangelical traditions. One reason is because for Muslims who become Christians, baptism may literally be a matter of life or death. While baptism is not itself seen as salvific, literally cleansing one's sins away from their body and soul, it is *part* of salvation—intimately linked to it, something to be done *in public* if possible and with trepidation and prayer.[43] If it does not represent the actual moment of salvation, it does often represent a key moment in the birthing of a new identity and the burial of an old one.

In terms of religious conversion, turning to the new and authentic and leaving behind the old and wrong, it *is* the birth of the new identity. In the words of IC Mina Nevisa, "It is a signal that everything of one's old life is buried. It has a special significance for Muslims because it drowns the bondages of Islam and the *Sharia* laws with finality," and, "It gives one a sense of full identification with Jesus in His death, burial and resurrection."[44] Baptism helps to forge a new identity, not only through incorporation into the church, but also by burning the bridges to the past. This does not mean that

---

43. Recall the Iranians in Plateau City who invited Muslim family members to their baptisms. Several CMBs in their autobiographies mention that they had refused to be baptized in secret (Avetaranian, *Muslim who became a Christian*; Masood, *Into the Light*).

44. Nevisa, *Miracle*, 59, 116.

the baptized person *wants* to be alienated from family and country—usually quite the opposite—but baptism is perceived as commanded by Jesus, and not some optional addition to salvation by faith through grace, which one might well want to postpone because it is not safe. Baptism is what makes you a member of the new community, the new family.

Because many churches are suspicious of the convert, the convert is usually disappointed with the lukewarm welcome given to them after they make a confession of faith and are baptized, and may well have suffered some sort of persecution.[45] This lack of prepared churches that are willing and able to welcome and incorporate the believer leads back to the urgent, practical ecclesiology mentioned above, one which is often concerned with leadership formation. That it is often elders or pastors of some kind who are responsible for both the pre-baptismal training as well as actually baptizing the initiate relates this concern quite closely with the issue of leadership selection and formation (itself a facet of practical ecclesiology) which was such a great concern for the Juduur and Iranian leaders, and often consumed a quite significant amount of their time and energy.

Christocentric Tendencies

The discourse, writings and liturgies of the CMBs I studied tend to be *Christocentric*, meaning "those types of theology in which the person and work of Christ are the bases for all theological and ethical propositions."[46] There is a strong tendency in these theologies to find all understanding about who and what God is like as seen through the person of Jesus. One of the consequences of the Christocentric tendencies I observed is that Muhammad entirely loses his status as the "ideal man."[47] He may be looked on with disgust as a violent and immoral man (possibly with some sort of psychological sickness, possibly possessed by Satan) or he may simply be dismissed as an unimportant and largely irrelevant figure. Or as Daniel Ali, a Kurdish convert put it, ". . . a frail and bitter human being."[48] I do not recall a single instance of any CMB ever telling me they had learned anything about ethics or God from Muhammad.

We recall from chapter 2 that Jesus—his person, example and message—is one of the main reasons that Muslims convert to Christianity.

45. Recall that this was the experience of John and Ayya. Syrjänen and Kraft both mention this as a recurrent complaint of the converts they interviewed.

46. Harvey, *Handbook*, 48.

47. *Al insaan al kaamil*, in Arabic. It is a common title for Muhammad in Islam.

48. Ali, *Out of Islam*, 68.

Unlike Muhammad, Jesus can be addressed using divine titles, as was the case with the Iranian Communion confession—"Jesus Christ God"—or with Fatima al Mutayri's reference to him as "Lord of the Worlds," an Islamic title used *only* to refer to Allah himself. In these theologies, the example of Jesus trumps all other biblical material. For instance, the conquest of Canaan that was carried out by the sword in Joshua is not relevant because Jesus said, "All those who take up the sword shall perish by the sword."[49] Another example: the degrading status of women in portions of the Old Testament is irrelevant, for Jesus had women as his followers[50] and friends[51] and treated them with respect and dignity, even when such interaction placed his own reputation at risk.[52] This commitment affects hermeneutics as well—the theological lynchpin of Scripture is neither Romans nor Galatians, common among many evangelicals, but Matthew 5–7, the Sermon on the Mount, which is often quoted in prayers, sermons, evangelism, and conversion testimonies. Indeed, the single-most quoted verse I heard from converts was "Love your enemies and pray for those who persecute you."[53]

An Inherited Division: The Work of the Spirit

And what of the Spirit? This is a contested issue, for as with global evangelicalism in general there is a debate regarding the presence of certain gifts of the Spirit, namely speaking in tongues and prophecy, as to whether they are active in the churches today, and, if they are, how they should be used but not abused. These issues were seen in the tumult of the church in Southern City, and the topic was also debated at the day of teaching in Castle City. There does, however, seem to be a consensus that the Spirit is active in mission. As the teacher from the Church of England said at the teaching day in Castle City when asked about the presence and role of the gifts of the Spirit, the greatest sign of the Spirit today is the conversion of Muslims around the world. In other words, the question was not answered, but activities like speaking in tongues and prophecy were relativized. All in all, though, a theology of the Spirit appears to have been largely received from various traditions within global evangelicalism *en toto*, including the disputes present in that larger community.

49. Matt 26:52.
50. Luke 8:1–3.
51. Luke 10:38–42.
52. John 4, 7:53—8:11.
53. Matt 5:44.

Nonetheless, Evangelical

Some significant divergences from the predominant, American-influenced evangelicalism have been noted here. This causes one to ask if these believers are ultimately evangelicals at all. The answer to this question is, at this point in time, yes. First, while the evangelicalism that these believers have for the most part met is influenced by the American traditions, there are many other forms or influences within world evangelicalism—from the many variations birthed from Africa to India to Messianic Judaism to Korea. That the focus in this book has been on American traditions is not to say that these are better or superior, of course, but that they are well-established and on the balance influence other contexts more than they are influenced by those other traditions. It may well be the case that this is starting to change—that American evangelicals are starting to be more influenced by other evangelicals. An example from my own context as an Anglican is that the traditional, liberal Episcopal Church of the USA (of which I am a member) has been challenged by a rival—an evangelical church sponsored by African, Asian and South American Anglicans called the Anglican Church in North America (ACNA).

There is no supreme authority in evangelical Christianity, nor is there one hierarchical structure that is able to define who is and who is not evangelical. There is, however, a loose consensus that evangelicals are the type of Christians who emphasize and center their spirituality around four characteristics: being Biblicist, cross-centered, conversionist, and evangelistic.[54] Without exploring in detail each of these terms, the CMBs I researched clearly embrace this form of Christianity.

It could be argued that it is ultimately for other evangelicals to say who is and who is not an evangelical. It is a community itself that delineates and changes and discerns, perhaps on an *ad hoc* basis, who is in and who is out. Notwithstanding the trends I have listed above that are critical of aspects of the dominant, American tradition within evangelicalism, many evangelical communities around the world have welcomed the ex-Muslim Christians I studied as fellow evangelical Christians.

---

54. Packer, "Stunted Ecclesiology."

A CENTRAL METAPHOR: LOVE : POWER :: POWER : LOVE

> *The message of Jesus—love your enemies—is what finally set me free. It no longer mattered who my friends were or who my enemies were; I was supposed to love them all.*
>
> *And I could have a loving relationship with a God who would help me love others. Having that kind of relationship with God is not only the source of my freedom but also the key to my new life.*[55]

These theology-makers, without exception, teach and emphasize that God is love. This is not a question of novelty, but of emphasis. So many of the believers I met and spoke with and studied claimed that God is love, that Jesus is loving, that God revealed his love in Christ, and moreover that the god of Islam was not loving. As mentioned above, this was often central to their soteriology. For many, this is why they had converted.[56]

I wanted to investigate this further, though, because Islam does have a tradition emphasizing the loving God, especially in such Sufi figures as Omar ibn al Faarid, Mansur al Hallaj, and Jalal ad Diin Rumi.[57] The Qur'an itself has verses on the love of God and love for God:

> Say, [O Muhammad], "If you should love Allah, then follow me, [so] Allah will love you and forgive you your sins. And Allah is Forgiving and Merciful." (3:31)

> O you who have believed, whoever of you should revert from his religion—Allah will bring forth [in place of them] a people He will love and who will love Him [who are] humble toward the believers, powerful against the disbelievers; they strive in the cause of Allah and do not fear the blame of a critic. That is the favor of Allah; He bestows it upon whom He wills. And Allah is all-Encompassing and Knowing. (5:54)

Were the converts simply unaware of this tradition within Islam? I asked Gloria, a young Iranian-American believer, what would she say to someone who said they can experience the love of God in Islam? And her answer was simple: "I would say they cannot." When I asked Timothy Abraham if he had ever heard the verses on love in the Qur'an before his conversion he answered, "In Islam, it goes like this: we are loved insofar as

55. Yousef, *Son of Hamas*, 139.

56. As both of the studies in chapter 2 mentioned.

57. Burckhardt, Sufi *Doctrine*, 31.

WE love. If you don't love, then you are not loved." This view appears to be based on verses in the Qur'an which explicitly state that there are groups of people whom Allah *does not* love.[58] Moreover, these groups are different from those whom Allah *does* love.[59]

Abraham wrote an article on the topic in 2011, "When my lover became triune," wherein he argues that Ibn al Arab does not go far enough in understanding the love of God, that his doctrine of love must by necessity lead to the Triune loving God of Christianity who within God's self is a loving community, apart from creatures whom he has made in order to love, as he feels is the case in Islam. Far from demonstrating a lack of awareness of this tradition, he argued that the lack of a Trinitarian oneness in the deity precluded the sort of all-giving, sacrificial love he encountered in the Triune God. He concludes his contrast by saying, "In Christianity, it has nothing to do whatsoever with what we do. It is all God's initiative and is immutable, as immutable as God's own character, which is love in the end."[60]

Abdul Saleeb commented on his own experience, saying that "I grew up in a Sufi home. Love of God and intimacy with God were part of the fabric of my life and faith. There are many verses in the Qur'an about God's love. The Qur'an differs from the Bible regarding the nature of that love. . ." and then he states that love as portrayed in the Bible is "unconditional" whereas in the Qur'an it is "conditional."[61]

Remah, an Iranian-American Christian, born to Muslim parents but whose mother had converted when she was a child, and who herself was raised in the church and converted as a teenager, developed this contrast of Trinitarian oneness v. monadic oneness in relation to love:

> I believe that an important consideration is that Allah metaphysically cannot be love because he is a Monad God, not a Trinity. For Allah to be self-sufficient and perfect in his love he must have an object of love detached from creation. Because he is a Monad, he had no object of love prior to creation and hence

---

58. The groups are *al mufsidiin* (the corrupters), *al mu3tadiin* (the transgressors), *al kaafiriin/kuffaar* (unbelievers), *al dhaalimiin* (sinners or wrongdoers), *al musrifiin* (wastrels, boasters, traitors), *man kaana athiiman* (habitual sinners). See Qur'an 2:205, 276, 190; 3:32, 57, 140; 4:36, 107, 148; 5:67, 90; 6:141; 7:31, 55; 8:58; 16:23; 28:76, 77; 30:45; 31:18; 42:40; 57:23.

59. These groups include those who do right, the pure, the righteous, the just, those who depend upon God, the patient, those who love him, Moses, and those who fight in his cause (*yuqaatiluuna fi sabiilihi*). See Qur'an 2:195, 222; 3:31, 76, 134, 146, 148, 159; 5:14, 45, 57, 96; 9:4, 7, 108; 19:96; 20:39; 49:9; 60:8; 61:4.

60. Personal correspondence, 2012.

61. Personal correspondence, 2012, 2013.

was incapable of loving, which makes him imperfect and unable to love in his nature without humanity. St. Augustine explains how this dilemma is solved in his illustration of the Trinity;[62] The Father is the lover, the Son is the beloved and the Holy Spirit is the spirit of love between the Father and the Son. Hence the Christian God is self-sufficient in His love apart from creation and only in Christianity can it truly be said "God is Love."[63]

In Sufi Islam, the love of the deity leads to his creative act, so that he will have creatures to love and who can love him.[64] The Augustinian, Trinitarian critique of that point of view argues that the monadic God cannot be, essentially, love, because apart from Creation (which he can love) he is not complete. In other words, monadic monotheism either compromises the self-sufficiency of God or the love of God, while Trinitarian monotheism preserves both.[65]

Mustafa, an Egyptian MBB who studied and then taught Islamic History at Al Azhar in Egypt, remembered how foreign converts would come to Al Azhar and say they had converted to Islam because of their sense that Allah was a God of love and that Islam was a "loving, peaceful and merciful religion," but then he goes on to refute this claim writing, " . . . what if those students were from Iraq, Iran, Yemen, Egypt, Afghanistan or Lebanon . . . No-one can forget these streams of blood which have been running through the Islamic history when Muslims starts [sic] killing Muslims for reasons such as Jihad, struggle for the Caliphate, sectarian strife, Apostasy war[66] and tribal disputes, etc."[67] This historical critique represents yet another vantage of criticism of the concept of Allah being a loving deity.

I asked John[68] if during his years as a Muslim he had been familiar with verses about love in the Qur'an, specifically 5:54, which speaks of a people whom Allah will love and who will love Allah. I asked, "Do you think it [5:54] contradicts people who say that God in Islam is not loving?" He responded that he had known about the love verses in the Qur'an since

62. *On the Trinity*, especially Book IX.

63. Personal correspondence, 2012.

64. Chittick, "Friendship and Love"; "Role of Love"; and *Sufi Path*.

65. This is, essentially, the same argument put forth by Ramon Llull in his *Book of the Gentile*.

66. Presumably a reference to the Wars of Apostasy (*huruub al ridda*). Soon after the Prophet died many of the Arab tribes left Islam, whereupon Caliph Abu Bakr warred against them and was victorious in forcing them to submit to his authority and return to Islam.

67. Mustafa, *Against the Tides*, 32.

68. Correspondence in 2012, by email.

his childhood, which is not unlikely, saying, "I don't think actually this verse speaks about God's love at all. It seems to me more of a threat to the Muslims. If the hearers ever decided to leave Muhammad, God will send armies upon them of strong people who have no compassion." The implication is that the combination of "love" with coercive threat is illogical or inferior to the Christian doctrine of love.

All in all, the objection that these CMBs were not aware of the Qur'anic and even more developed Sufi doctrines of the love of Allah appears to be unfounded. Rather, they appear to have known about it and found it wanting, as they have also found the theory of penal substitution to be wanting in some way.

The theologies of these ex-Muslim Christians are focused on the *proximity* of God, and emphasize his intimacy and closeness. This is related to the other factors listed above because it is precisely this intimacy, closeness and love of God that give the believer power to endure persecution, prison and exile. Mina Nevisa, an Iranian CMB, provides a good example of this. A Christian friend of hers was martyred in Iran, and she was forced to flee through the mountains to Turkey which resulted in a miscarriage. She spoke with her father on the phone and he declared that he never had a daughter and that no one may mention her name in his household. The exercise of power to stem the pollution of the Christian message in Iran had worked by forcing her and her husband and two other apostates into exile. But Nevisa experienced another source of power precisely in that she was able to forgive "all of those who had wronged me," and, regarding her father who had disowned her, "I was able to love him . . . ."[69] The implication is that she is really the powerful one, in that she can graciously forgive those who have not even realized the wrong they have committed, the act of forgiveness being a declaration that one is more powerful than the one being forgiven.

The love of God is the unifying principle that makes sense of everything else in the world—it is the key to wisdom and the motive for liberating praxis. It is the love of God the Father revealed in his Son that proves what is "wrong" in Islam. For them, power is shone in sacrificial love, as was the case with Jesus himself. True power is not to be found in the ability to compel, for such compulsion (power) can *only* lead to obedience, and not love. The deity of the CMBs takes risks and is daring, he is willing to risk disobedience of his creatures in the interest of the possibility of real love existing. IC Saiid Rabiipour reflects on this new vision of the personality of God, and compares his new faith to the unquestioning Islam he had learned in Iran, telling his Muslims readers, "It is okay to question Allah if you don't

69. Nevisa, *Miracle*, 115–16.

understand [something]. In fact I believe Allah loves it when his people question him."[70]

As was seen with the Berbers and ICs, God's love for humans is also shown in his honor for their many cultures, which is why he wants to save each culture. He acknowledges their languages and many of their customs, not forcing the language of God (Arabic) on them. He is a God who wants humans to know him, submitting his Scripture to the risky procedure of translation and personal interpretation by fallible humans. This theology of love is also a theology of wisdom, ordering the entirety of the universe, and strengthening the seeker or convert in the midst of the difficult period of liminality wherein a new identity is being formed. Conversion narratives almost always combine tales of hardship and persecution with a constant affirmation of God's hidden love and protection.

This knowledge about God is unapologetically filial in its Christology, privileging the title of Son of God on many occasions above other titles or roles. This is not a question of discarding one role or another, but of emphasis. The filial role of Christ is seen to fulfill and complete his loving person in his relation to God as Father. That God would have a Son must mean that God is loving, for even the worst humans love their children. The title "Son of God" is also the most objectionable to Muslims whom CMBs leave behind, and thus serves to accentuate the leaving of the old and the embracing of the new. The crucifixion is seen as subordinated to the love of God: God's love for his Son, and the Son's loving obedience to the Father, and the overflowing of their love which reaches into a fallen world—this loving relation is unfolded in the drama of annunciation, nativity, ministry, crucifixion, resurrection and ascension. The baptismal ritual at Plateau City, wherein initiates narrated, in the presence of Muslim family members, how they came to believe that Jesus is the Son of God (and not merely savior) is one instance of this.

Inseparable from this concept of a sacrificial love which empowers people (and entire communities) to embrace it and calls others to itself, is the concept of a loving power, rather than what had been experienced before in Islam. The "old" concept of power is found supremely in the law of apostasy, which is coercive and sometimes violent.[71] This was perceived to be the fault of the Qur'anic verse about "a people who love Allah and whom Allah will love": it was a threat and a warning. Allah's love is conditional in Islam, God's love is unconditional in Christianity, and the proof of this

---

70. Rabiipour, *Farewell to Islam*, 302–3.

71. The "old" and "wrong" concept of power is also located in the perceived deficiencies of what the Prophet and the Qur'an teach regarding the treatment of women and non-Muslims (chapter 2).

is Jesus himself. Because of this, the sort of love the Qur'an speaks of is interpreted by CMBs with whom I spoke and who have contributed to the literature as being inferior to the love seen in Jesus' advent.

In these theologies of ex-Muslim Christians this theory of power is understood to be exclusive to the Christian faith and Scripture, and is not encountered, according to them, anywhere in Islam. Moreover, sacrificial love and the Christian vision of power are impossible to separate from each other. One might be tempted to say that they are viewed as two different ways of talking about the same thing—metaphorically, that the power of God *is* his humility and self-sacrifice.

Their intuition that Christianity and Islam have two mutually exclusive constructions of love/power has been encountered at various times throughout this book, as with the theory of *tanziil* (descent) v. the theory of inspiration; or the inability of the Qur'an to be translated v. the translatability of the Bible; or the Islamic hermeneutic in Kitma of non-critical obedience v. the critical and practical study of the Bible; or in the Christian custom of addressing God as "Father" v. the Islamic insistence that this is to compromise the majesty of God; or in the doctrine of the incarnation v. the doctrine of the unknowability of the essence of God common in Islam; or in Jesus's claim that God's Spirit comes to dwell in the believer as a teacher and comforter v. the doctrine that the spirit of God is merely a title for one of the angels; or in the doctrine of a Triune God who within the divine essence is communal and loving, apart from Creation v. the Sufi teaching that the love of God had no outlet without Creation; or in Jesus's teaching regarding blessing your enemies v. the Islamic injunction to slay the apostate and humiliate the People of the Book.[72]

The two concepts of power are seen as being very different, and turning from the "old" concept of power to the "new" was particularly difficult among the believers I studied, both in Kitma and the Iranian diaspora. How strong a hold the old version of power has on ICs can be seen in the many church splits that take place (after I completed my research, I learned that the Iranian church in Bay City had split, for instance).[73] Nonetheless, in these theologies, this vision of love/power is present.

72. Qur'an 9:29. There are verses in the Qur'an that speak positively of Christians as well (notably 5:82 and 29:46). The CMBs I spoke with seemed to believe that these verses had been abrogated by later, violent verses, and that the violent verses represent the truth of Islam.

73. Roy Oksnevad, who completed his doctoral research on the sources of tension among leaders in Iranian churches, has similarly noted that "emerging Iranian fellowships struggle with internal conflicts which often end in church splits" ("BMB Discipleship," 399).

In spite of this, or perhaps because of it, the unifying metaphor of love and power is, even more than the specific theological trends mentioned in the previous section, found in almost all of the texts, discourse and liturgies of the these CMBs. It is worth noting that there is nothing particularly evangelical about this love-power theological axis. Nor, as far as I could tell, does it come from the doctrine of the ancient churches (as with the adoption of *theosis* by Rishawi above). A historical parallel might be the mysticism of Ramon Llull or St John of the Cross, but with the single exception of Timothy Abraham, nobody referenced these mystics by name. The source of this love-power metaphor appears to be nothing other than their own experiences of persecution and conversion in the light of what they have learned from the Bible and the fellowship of the church.

THE FINAL CAUSE OF THE THEOLOGIES: CREATION AND ACCEPTANCE OF A NEW IDENTITY

Do these converts engage in the activity of making their own theologies? And if so, what sort of theologies are they making? What is the content of their theologies? At this point that central research question of this book has been answered: Yes, some ex-Muslim Christians are engaged in the process of theology-making. Specific trends can be identified in the areas of theology of salvation, the church and baptism. The dominant metaphor of much of this theology-making is that the power of God *is* his humble, self-sacrificial love, and that his true power is found in this capacity for humility and *kenosis*, rather than the ability to coerce.

But there is another way to answer the question *what*? It is what Aristotle called the final cause. What is its purpose (*telos*)? Or, why is the theology-making being carried out? Some answers to this question have already been presented—the Iranians carry out this process in order to redeem their community and people, and some of the authors from chapter 5 carry this out in order to subvert unjust social structures. Some go about this theology-making in order to invite Muslims to consider the option of following Jesus, others for the sake of alerting people in the West to what they perceive as the threat of Islamization.[74]

---

74. A large number of the CMBs I interviewed commented on how, in their view, Westerns were naïve and gullible in thinking that Islam was a "religion of peace" or that terrorists were not genuine, devout Muslims. These observations were often volunteered even when I did not ask about the topic.

But there appears to be a goal, a final cause, which underlies and unites many of these activities and aims: the formation of a secure and stable new identity. And where there are social structures that make this impossible, the goal is the creation of a context wherein such a new, stable identity can be formed and lived, yet still evolve as any identity does. For instance, baptism initiates, clearly and at one point in time, through a distinct ritual universal to Christianity and recognized by Muslims as a boundary line, and the new identity gains a clarity and solidity and permanence it did not have before. Due to a confluence of traditions and shari'a, however, that identity is not recognized as valid. This was the case for the believers in Kitma and Iranian converts in Iran. The new identity and membership in a new society (the church) is hope-giving and redemptive for the new believer, but for her family, mosque, and perhaps nation, it is probably bad news, pollution, the transgression of a boundary and taboo.

The soteriological commitment to seeing cultures saved (and not just individuals) is a challenge to this state of affairs. The situation is neither just nor fair. Converts from Islam " . . . who remain in the church struggle with lifelong battles with shame, depression, and isolation, caused by the loss of their ties to their families, communities, and nations."[75] Ex-Muslim Christians think it is not the will of God that society be like this, and that it is imperative to see the love of God revealed in his Messiah spread to the rest of society: most of the converts I interviewed were adamant in explicitly supporting the evangelization of Muslims and engaged in that activity themselves. This is to secure the conversion of Muslims to Christianity (and thus their individual salvation) but also to see the entire society redeemed, for to know about God is to transform society into what he wants it to be like. That is why this theology is also, in some cases, a theology of liberation and it understands God-knowledge as being inseparable from liberating praxis.

Bilquis Sheikh ends her book *I Dared to Call Him Father* by cherishing Pakistan: she looks out at her home country from the departing airplane and says she will always love it. The people of Pakistan had rejected her. They had not allowed for her to have a communal identity as a Christian and a communal identity as a Pakistani at the same time. This is not just, for she is both. Iranians and Arabs and many other believers have made the same claim—like Fatima al Mutayri who wrote, "we truly love our homeland and we are not traitors // We take pride that we are Saudi citizens. . . ."[76] It is as if the Islamic societies of many of these Christian ex-Muslims assumed that in

75. Meral, "Silence of God," 2.
76. Sheikh, *Call Him* Father, 8.

turning away from Islam and turning to Christ, they have also turned away from being a member of their community, family and/or nation because there is indeed no division between the state and the faith.[77]

We can also phrase this by using Tim Green's identity theory: one simultaneously belongs to and has numerous communal identities, and many of these believers want to change (or have changed, or are changing) their communal identity in relation to, say, the local mosque and the Umma, but continue to belong to their nation or state as loyal citizens, and to their family. The new configuration of communal identities, at best, confuses many Muslims, and at worse, elicits persecution. This situation calls for *praxis* and action. Regarding the former, explaining one's narrative and experience may help the Muslim community to tolerate (at least) the validity of the new configuration of identities, and perhaps even convert them to such a new identity. Regarding the latter, the entire structure of the shari'a must be replaced; "the system must break," as Iskander said.

But the program of liberation in the service of *identity* advocacy and the *salvation* of entire cultures is a gradual and difficult process. Therefore, in the meantime, until their people accept them for who they are, there is the church. As problematic as it is, sooner or later (if one perseveres, and one must, in their thinking), one will find the congregation that will accept them with their new identity of Iranian or Kitman (or what have you) *and* Christian. Until the day when God's just reign has saved their cultures, these theology-makers will be active in ushering in that salvation in different ways. The hermeneutical primacy of the Sermon on the Mount prepares the believer for persecution, marginalization, exile, joblessness, poverty, homelessness, hunger, and imprisonment, each topic being addressed in that brief text.

The difficult and lengthy process of turning away from the old and turning to the new—which is an aspect of identity formation—is acknowledged by all of the theology-makers. This is why the liberation theme is often complemented with wisdom theology. For some of these theology-makers, a key goal is guiding the seeker or new believer to see the underlying and hidden unity in the loving plan of God even in the midst of the practical difficulties of being estranged from family, or viewed with suspicion by the local church, or upon losing one's job, or in relation to the common theme of (forced) migration. The completion of the turning and achievement of a stable identity in these theologies is understood to be dependent on relating to a larger community of believers, a church. The church, a source of deep

---

77. Meral, "Silence of God," 61. This is not to say that Islamic societies are unique in closely identifying nationality and religion, or ethnicity and religion.

frustration and sorrow for so many CMBs, is also fundamental and essential in this process of identity-formation. This reality—that churches so often fail to be what they should be (a new home and family for CMBs), leads to intense and urgent reflection on the topic, that is at once theological and practical. The dual status of the church—disappointing but also essential— leads to reflection on initiation into the church, baptism, and an intense focus on the formation of dependable, mature leaders. There are practical, theological resources for every stage in the life of the potential convert in this theology. In sum, the *telos* or final cause of the theology-making is inseparably intertwined with its content and context.

CONCLUSION: RETURNING TO COE

Throughout this chapter I have reformulated the *content, central metaphor,* and *purpose* of the theologies of the ex-Muslim Christians I researched. It is important not to overstate the scope of this research, nor to generalize. I have studied a handful of ex-Muslim Christians and their communities and their writings, and one might find different sorts of theologies being made among other Iranians and Arabophones, not to mention groups from other ethno-linguistic contexts altogether.

Coe wrote that contextualization is a continuation of the process of indigenization. It is the mark of maturation of a Christian community. He explained the process of contextualization as a double-wrestle: the community wrestles with what he called God's world, in reading its own contextuality, and then the community wrestles with God's Word, discerning a response and path forward. This "wrestling with God's Word' involves interacting with Scripture (and tradition) in order to propose and try out a course of action—this is called contextualization.

These theology-makers are mostly operating within the evangelical tradition, but they are nonetheless branching out and exploring different issues in different ways, some of which appear new to or different from the existing global evangelical communities. According to Coe's model, it would appear that in wrestling with "God's world" that the theology-makers identified a key issue: how can they become who they sense they should be in the light of God's self-revelation of love and power in Jesus? To become what they feel they should become, to live according to this revelation of love-power, there must be a community and family to welcome them, teach them, and initiate them; and it is God's just will that there be a society that will tolerate them; there must be a movement to spread that message; and there must be guidance and wisdom for others who may decide to turn from the old and wrong to the new and the right.

In turning away from the Umma and Muhammad and the Qur'an, they have turned away from a loveless power they perceived there to Jesus, his church and the Bible and a deity whose power is perfected in weakness and whose love is stronger than death. And from this experience of the deity's love-power some have endeavored to build a new identity from the breakage among which they have lived. These are things that some Christians who used to be Muslims claim to know about God, his revelation of himself in Jesus, and how humans can relate to him; it is their God-knowledge, their theology.

Conclusion

I started this book with the research question, do ex-Muslim Christians engage in theology-making? And if so, what is the content of their theology? Since CMBs do not compose texts traditionally considered to be "theological texts," it was necessary to ask further questions related to theology-making, and theology-makers, and what theology-making might look like.

I looked for answers to these questions in the work of Shoki Coe and Robert Schreiter. Coe offered an account of what theology-making might look like as it takes place in a given context. Schreiter added detail to Coe's dialectic of contextuality-contextualization, elucidating what theological output might look like, and who theology-makers are, and the variety of ways that different people in different communities might formulate what they perceive to be their knowledge about God.

With these tools I was prepared to begin to test my initial hypothesis, that CMBs were engaged in theology-making. I knew that theology-making could be detected in artifacts other than books and journals and was related to action and not only reflection. I was ready to look for it in their prayers, liturgies, confessions, conversations, apologetics, and testimonies. Coe and Schreiter agree that understanding the context of the potential theology-maker is of the utmost importance, so context was explored in reference to history, missionary strategy, and religious conversion theory.

I researched three loci of activity that could potentially be theology-making. The first was a group of Arabophone evangelical believers who had (somewhat inadvertently) planted a church consisting almost entirely of CMBs. I was limited in my access to the CMBs, but had access to many leaders and laity. My research suggests to me that the church planters (from Juduur) and the new believers (from Kitma) were engaging in inculturation, but that the Juduur leaders had met with difficulty in forming new Kitman leaders. This resulted in a state of patronage that was undesirable to the leaders, who were actively trying to remedy it. I concluded that I did not observe any theology-making happening in Kitma, though there were several areas ripe for the activity if the leadership plan of resolving the patronage relationship of the Juduur leaders is eventually successful.

I also examined the texts written by CMBs to try to test my hypothesis. I focused on a common type of text: conversion and persecution narratives written by CMBs. I argued that these texts often represent theology-making which can be best described as liberation and wisdom theologies. I then explained how these two components complement each other in the context of persecution/marginalization encountered by these converts.

Chapter 6 was about a number of Iranian diaspora congregations in the USA and Scotland. By observing their worship, prayers, and sermons, by reading their texts and interviewing them, I concluded that contextual theology-making was taking place. The theology-making I observed was intent on preserving and restoring what they viewed as genuine Persian-ness, purged of what were seen as Arabo-Islamic contaminations. Emphasis was placed on Iranian language, food, and Nowruz. Unequivocal empha-sis on Jesus as Son of God, seen specifically in the rites of baptism and Communion, helped to distance the new ICs from Islam. As with Kitma, leadership formation appeared to be a key concern. As with the believers in Kitma-Juduur, the contextuality had been discerned: IC churches need mature, reliable leaders. Several leaders had taken up the task, and were in the process of proposing and trying out ways to train leaders. As of the end of the research period though, as with Kitma, it did not seem that a satisfac-tory way of meeting this pastoral need had been identified.

The final chapter was concerned with identifying commonalities in the theology-making of these disparate CMBs. One common theme was an apparent dissatisfaction of some converts with the soteriological theory of penal substitution. I also identified a concern with questions related to the nature and function of the church (ecclesiology), evidenced in the intense activity surrounding leadership formation, and I suggested that this was related to the contextuality of the CMBs and the fact that without a mature and welcoming church (something CMBs rarely find), assimilation into a new community and the maturation and development of a convert iden-tity is unlikely to take place. In other words, without a church there can be no end to the stage of liminality, in that one cannot be reincorporated into any other community. This leads to a focus on the ritual of baptism, which is a key moment in identity-formation for many CMBs, ending the phase of liminality by ritually incorporating the convert into a new community, which is not a church of the type converts might initially have expected to join when they first considered conversion.

CMBs would like to be accepted by their Muslim families and coun-tries, but this rarely takes place because Islam sees apostasy as a form of pollution and seeks to eliminate it. This state of things is not considered by converts (or some Muslims) as being in accord with the just will of God, so some converts engage in liberating praxis in order to call for greater religious freedom and an end to discrimination against apostates. This liberating project is, however, gradual and it is not clear that it will succeed, so in the meanwhile converts explain how a benevolent and loving God can be present (in a hidden manner, quite often) in the context of persecution and danger—this itself is wisdom theology. The liberation project seeks to see the salvation brought by Jesus spread through entire societies, and does not come to a conclusion with a person's conversion.

A main goal of this theology-making is identity-formation—trying to understand who they are in the midst of the context of rapid social change which can submit existing identity to stress, as they are "living among the breakage" of today. Some theology-makers move to advocacy—calling for toleration and justice and the recognition that they are who they say there are: genuine Christians who are loyal citizens and members of their communities and families. In meeting the coercive power of persecution and marginalization they draw upon the weapons of the weak: especially the reversal of power structures found in Jesus's own life. This love is sacrificial and salvific. When one is persecuted by her family or government or another finds himself homeless and hungry because of his faith, it is this love that gives them power to persevere.

I have argued that there is a key metaphor that is common to these theologies: that the nature of God's *power* and how we relate to it cannot be understood outside of an understanding and indeed experience of God's *love*—a love that is centered and communicated primarily in the person of Jesus Christ who in his words and life demonstrates that sacrificial love *is* the ultimate form of divine power. God as he is revealed in Christ communicates that sacrificial love *is* the supreme form of true and real power, and this power is demonstrated in acts of love, not coercion. This conviction appears as an axis whereupon the theology-making turns. This has many implications but it is present in every single facet of theology-making explored in this book, from liberation to wisdom to the salvation of Persian-ness to strategies for confronting persecution.

Moreover, this metaphor is understood as fundamentally undermining the validity of Islam, where the converts perceived that the love of Allah was conditional and arbitrary, and that the power of Allah was essentially coercive. Theologically this was also related to Trinitarian one-ness, wherein God is loving within the Trinitarian community, as opposed to monadic one-ness, wherein God can neither love nor be loved without first creating those loving and beloved things. In relation to Scripture and the person of Jesus, this conviction was seen in the oft-mentioned verse about loving one's enemies, which was taught by Jesus and demonstrated in his passion and death.

I tried to discern from my research some recurring and important themes, but there is much more to explore.[1] Further issues for research would seek to branch out in relation to diversity, such as Kosovar Muslims converting to Catholicism, or Indonesian Muslims converting to Orthodoxy. As was made clear, many Muslims who leave Islam do not become Christians but atheists or agnostics, and sometimes these ex-Muslims form communities, like the Council of Ex-Muslims of Britain. Without research into this other major branch of apostates, the field of ex-Muslim studies will remain incomplete.

1. For more on the eschatological trends among CMBs see my chapter in Neely and Riddell, *Islam and the Last Day*.

Bibliography

Abdallah, Maher. "Six Million Muslims Leaving Islam Every Year in Africa: Interview with Sheikh Ahmad al Katani." *Al Jazeera* (2009).

Abdel Haleem, M. A. S., trans. *The Qur'an*. Oxford: Oxford University Press, 2005.

Abdo, Genieve. *No God but God: Egypt and the Triumph of Islam*. Oxford: Oxford University Press, 2000.

Abou El Fadl, Khaled. "The Place of Tolerance in Islam." In *The Place of Tolerance in Islam*, edited by Joshua Cohen and Ian Lague, 3–26. Boston: Beacon, 2002.

Abraham, Timothy. "When My Beloved Became Triune: Encountering Ibn Arabi in the Religion of Love." *SFM* 7/5 (2011) 29–35.

Abu Banaat. "Daisy Marsh: Missionary to the Kabyles." *SFM* 2/3 (2006) 1–6.

Abu Daoud. "Apostates of Islam." *SFM* 3/4 (2006) 1–8.

———. "Mission and Sacrament, Part II." *SFM* 4/3 (2008) 1–6.

———. "Mission and Sacrament, Part III: A Paleo-Orthodox Approach to Contextualization in the Muslim World." *SFM* 5/2 (2009) 1–17.

———. "Observations on Abuna Zakaria Botros (and a Book Review)." *SFM* 5/5 (2009) 93–98.

———. "Rebecca Lewis and Kevin Higgins against the Ropes: Sounding the Death Nell of the Insider Movements and the Victory of Apostolic Faith." *SFM* 9/4 (2013) 52–58.

———. "Sacrament and Mission Go Together Like Bread and Wine: Part I: Baptism, Discipleship, and the Apostles' Creed." *SFM* 4/1 (2008) 1–7.

Ajaj, Azar. "Baptism and the Muslim Convert to Christianity." *SFM* 6/4 (2010) 595–611.

Al Bukhari, Muhammad. *Sahiih al Bukhari*. Translated by M. Muhsin Khan. http://www.usc.edu/org/cmje/religious-texts/hadith/bukhari/.

Alam, Christopher. *Out of Islam*. Lake Mary, FL: Charisma, 2006.

Ali, Daniel. *Out of Islam: 'Free at Last'*. Mustang, OK: Tate, 2007.

Ali, Kecia, and Oliver Leaman. *Islam: The Key Concepts*. London: Routledge, 2008.

Amaladoss, Michael. "Double Religious Belonging and Liminality: An Anthropo-Theological Reflection." (ND) http://sedosmission.org/old/eng/amaladoss_8.htm.

An-Na'im, Abdullahi Ahmed. "The Islamic Law of Apostasy and its Modern Applicability: A Case from the Sudan." *Religion* 16 (1986) 197–224.

Andrew, Brother, and Al Janssen. *Secret Believers: What Happens When Muslims Believe Christ*. Grand Rapids: Revell, 2007.

Arab World Ministeries (AWM). "Contextualization of Ministry among Muslims: A Statement on the Appropriate Limits." *SFM* 3/1 (2007) 1–2.

Armbruster, Heidi, and Anna Lærke. eds. *Taking Sides: Ethics, Politics and Fieldwork in Anthropology*. New York: Berghahn, 2008.

Arthur, J. Bryson. "Out on a Limb: A Theological Exploration of Suffering, Risk, and Persecution." *Mary's Well Occasional Papers* 1/1 (2012) 1–47.

Ateek, Naim Stifan. *Justice, and Only Justice: A Palestinian Theology of Liberation*. Maryknoll, NY: Orbis, 1989.

Atkinson, David, and David Field, eds. *New Dictionary of Christian Ethics and Pastoral Theology*. Leicester: InterVarsity, 1995.

Audeoud, Martine. "Niamey—What Is Its Context for Christian Service? Part One." *Lausanne World Pulse* (Oct–Nov 2009) 22–4.

———. "Niamey—What is its Context for Christian Service? Part Two." *Lausanne World Pulse* (Oct–Nov 2009) 24–32.

Augustine of Hippo. *On the Trinity*. In *Nicene and Post-Nicene Fathers* Vol 3. Translated by Arthur West Haddan. Edited by Philip Schaff. Buffalo, NY: Christian Literature, 1887. Revised and edited for New Advent by Kevin Knight. http://www.newadvent.org/fathers/1301.htm/.

Avetaranian, John, and Richard Schafer. *A Muslim Who Became a Christian: The Story of John Avetaranian (born Muhammad Shukri Efendi) 1861–1919, An Autobiography*. 2nd ed. Translated by John Bechard. Sandy, UK: AuthorsOnline, 2010 [1905].

Ayub, Edward. "Observations and Reactions to Christians Involved in a New Approach to Mission." *SFM* 5/5 (2009) 21–40.

Badeau, John S. "The Arab Role in Islamic Culture." In *The Genius of Arab Civilization: Source of Renaissance*, edited by John R. Hayes, 3–14. New York: NYU Press, 1975.

Beit-Hallahmi, Benjamin. *Prolegomena to the Psychological Study of Religion*. London: Associated University Press, 1989.

Bell, Catherine. *Ritual: Perspective and Dimensions*. Oxford: Oxford University Press, 1997.

Belt, Don. "The Forgotten Faithful." *National Geographic* (June 2009).

Bender, Doug, and Steve Sims. "Short-term Trips, Bible Storying & Church Planting." *Mission Frontiers* (Jan–Feb 2012) 10–13.

Berger, Peter. *Facing up to Modernity: Excursions in Society, Politics, and Religion*. New York: Basic, 1977.

———. 1979. *The Heretical Imperative: Contemporary Possibilities of Religious Affirmation*. Garden City, New York: Anchor.

Bevans, Stephen. *Models of Contextual Theology*. Rev. and exp. ed. Maryknoll, NY: Orbis, 2002.

Blader, Steven L., and Ya-Ru Chen. "Differentiating the Effects of Status and Power: A Justice Perspective." *Journal of Personality and Social Psychology* Advance online publication. doi: 10.1037/a0026651 (2012) 1–21.

Blincoe, Robert. *Ethnic Realities and the Church: Lessons from Kurdistan*. Pasadena, CA: Presbyterian Center for Mission Studies, 1998.

Bloch, Marc. *The Historian's Craft*. Translated by Peter Putnam. New York: Vintage, 1953.

Boff, Leonardo. *Jesus Christ Liberator: a Critical Christology for our Time*. Translated by Patrick Hughes. Maryknoll, NY: Orbis, 1978.

Boff, Leonardo, and Clodovis Boff. *Introducing Liberation Theology*. Translated by Paul Burns. Maryknoll, NY: Orbis, 1987.

Bonk, Jonathan J. "The Defender of the Good News: Questioning Lamin Sanneh." *CT* (Oct 2003). http://www.christianitytoday.com/outreach/articles/defenderofthegoodnews.htm.

Bourne, Phil. "Summary of the Contextualization Debate." *SFM* 5/5 (2009) 58–80.

Bradley, Mark. *Iran: Open Hearts in a Closed Land*. Milton Keynes, UK: Authentic, 2007.

——. *Iran and Christianity: Historical Identity and Present Relevance*. London: Continuum, 2008.

Bridger, J Scott. "Raymond Lull: Medieval Theologian, Philosopher, and Missionary to Muslims." *SFM* 5/1 (2009) 1–25.

——. "Take up and Read: Kenneth Cragg's Call for Muslims to Engage the Biblical Christ." *SFM* 5/3 (2009) 37–62.

Brown, Rick. "Biblical Muslims." *IJFM* 24 (2007) 65–74.

——. "Brother Jacob and Master Isaac: How One Insider Movement Began." *IJFM* 24 (2007) 41–42.

——. "Part I: Explaining the Biblical Term 'Son(s) of God' in Muslim Contexts." *IJFM* 22 (2005) 91–96.

——. "Part II: Translating the Biblical Term 'Son(s) of God' in Muslim Contexts." *IJFM* 22 (2005) 135–45.

——. "The 'Son of God': Understanding the Messianic Titles of Jesus." *IJFM* 17 (2000) 41–52.

Burckhardt, Titus. *An Introduction to Sufi Doctrine*. Translated by D. M. Matheson. Wellingborough, UK: Thorsons, 1976.

Caffulli, Giuseppe. "A Catacomb Church? Perhaps, but One That Is Alive and Well . . . and Universal." *AsiaNews.it* (July 9, 2004). http://www.asianews.it/news-en/A-catacomb-Church-Perhaps,-but-one-that-is-alive-and-well-.-.-.-and-universal-1436.html.

Campbell, Jonathan. "Releasing the Gospel from Western Bondage." *IJFM* 16 (1999) 167–71.

Cardeillac, Louis. *Moriscos y Cristianos: Un enfrentamiento polemic (1492–1640)*. Translated by Mercedes Garcia Arenal. Madrid: Fondo de Cultura Economica, 1977.

Cassell, Joan. "Ethical Principles for Conducting Fieldwork." *American Anthropologist* 82 (1980) 28–41.

Cate, Patrick, and Dwight Singer. *A Survey of Muslim Converts in Iran*. 1980. http://duanemiller.wordpress.com/2012/06/19/a-survey-of-muslim-converts-in-iran-for-patrick-cate-by-dwight-singer-1980/.

Cavadini, John C. *The Last Christology of the West: Adoptionism in Spain and Gaul, 785–820*. Philadelphia: University of Pennsylvania Press, 1993.

Centennial of the American Press of the Board of Foreign Missions of the Presbyterian Church in the U.S.A. Beirut: American Press, 1923.

Chelkowski, Peter. "Ta'zia." In *Encylopaedia Iranica*. http://www.iranicaonline.org/articles/tazia/.

Chittick, William C. "Friendship and Love in Islamic Spirituality." 2011. http://new.oberlin.edu/dotAsset/2684649.pdf.

——. "The Role of Love in the Qur'anic Worldview." Audio lecture. Iran: 2010.

——, trans. *The Sufi Path of Love: The Spiritual Teachings of Rumi*. SUNY Series in Islamic Spirituality. Albany: State University of New York Press, 1983.

Cockroft, Lucy. "Bible moved to library top shelf over inequality fears." *The Telegraph* (Feb 18, 2009). http://www.telegraph.co.uk/news/religion/4687077/Bible-put-on-top-shelf-in-move-to-appease-Muslims.html.

Coe, Shoki. "In Search of Renewal in Theological Education." *Theological Education* 9 (1973) 233–43.

————. "Theological Education—a Worldwide Perspective." *Theological Education* 11 (1974) 5–12.

Cohen, Anthony. "Ethnographic Method in the Real Community." *Sociologia Ruralis* 18 (1978) 449–69.

Coleman, M., and P. Verster. "Contextualization of the Gospel among Muslims." *Acta Theologica* 2006:2 (2006) 95–115.

Cone, James H. *A Black Theology of Liberation.* Philadelphia: Lippincott, 1970.

"Conversion Rate: A Surprising Story of Muslim Converts to Christianity." *The Economist* (Dec 30, 2007). http://www.economist.com/node/12868180/print.

Cooper, Barbara M. *Evangelical Christians in the Muslim Sahel.* Indianapolis: Indiana University Press, 2006.

Copeland, Lynn, ed. *Into the Den of Infidels: Our Search for the Truth.* Bartlesville, OK: Living Sacrifice, 2003.

Corrie, John, Samuel Escobar, and Wilbert Shenk, eds. *Dictionary of Mission Theology.* Downers Grove, IL: InterVarsity, 2007.

Cragg, Kenneth. *The Arab Christian: A History in the Middle East.* Louisville: Westminster John Knox, 1991.

————. "Being Made Disciples—the Middle East." In *The Church Mission Society and World Christianity, 1799–1999,* edited by Kevin Ward and Brian Stanley, 120–43. Grand Rapids: Eerdmans, 2000.

————. *The Call of the Minaret.* 3rd ed. Oxford: One World, 2000.

————. "Temple Gairdner's Legacy." *IBMR* 5 (1981) 164–67.

Crisp, Oliver D. *Divinity and Humanity: The Incarnation Reconsidered.* Current Issues in Theology. Cambridge: Cambridge University Press, 2007.

Darg, Christine. *The Jesus Visions.* Orlando: Daystar International, 1995.

Dawn Bible Students Association. "Preaching the Gospel." *The Dawn* (October 2003). http://www.dawnbible.com/2003/0310-hl.htm.

De Blois, Reinier. "The Impact of Technology on Bible Translation." *Lausanne World Pulse* (Oct–Nov 2009) 4–9.

De Sam Lazaro, Fred. "Chrislam." *Religion & Ethics Newsweekly* (Feb 13, 2009). http://www.pbs.org/wnet/religionandethics/episodes/february-13-2009/chrislam/2236/.

De Young, Kevin, and Ted Kluck. *Why We Love the Church: In Praise of Institutions and Organized Religion.* Chicago: Moody, 2009.

Dibaj, Mehdi. "The Written Defense of the Rev Mehdi Dibaj Delivered to the Sari Court of Justice." Translator unknown. (1993) http://farsinet.com/persecuted/dibaj.html/.

Douglas, James, ed. *The New International Dictionary of the Christian Church.* 2nd ed. Exeter: Paternoster, 1974.

Douglas, Mary. *Purity and Danger.* London and New York: Routledge Classics, 2002 [1966].

Dutch, Bernard. "Should Muslims become 'Christians'?" *IJFM* 17 (2000) 15–24.

Eisenstadt, S. N., and L. Roniger. "Patron-Client Relationship as a Model of Structuring Social Exchange." *Comparative Studies in Society and History* 22 (1980) 42–47.

Eliot, T. S. *The Four Quartets.* New York: Harcourt, 1943.

Eltahawy, Mona. "Why Do They Hate Us? The Real War on Women is in the Middle East." *Foreign Policy* (May/June 2012). http://www.foreignpolicy.com/

articles/2012/04/23/why_do_they_hate_us?print=yes&hidecomments=yes&p%E
2%80%A6.

Elwell, Walter, ed. *Evangelical Dictionary of Theology*. Grand Rapids: Baker, 1984.

Epistle to Diognetus. In *Ante-Nicene Fathers*, Vol. 1. Edited by Alexander Roberts, James Donaldson, and A. Cleveland Coxe. Translated by Alexander Roberts and James Donaldson. Buffalo, NY: Christian Literature, 1885. Revised and edited for New Advent by Kevin Knight. http://www.newadvent.org/fathers/0101.htm.

Esther, Gulshan, and Thelma Sangster. *The Torn Veil*. 1984. Reprinted, Fort Washington, PA: CLC, 2010.

Fadle, Essam. "Baptism Brings together Muslims and Christian in Drenka Celebrations." *Daily News Egypt* Sep. (2008). http://www.thedailynewsegypt.com/article.aspx?ArticleID=16162.

Fahlbusch, Erwin, and Geoffrey W. Bromiley, eds. *The Encyclopedia of Christianity*. 5 vols. Grand Rapids: Eerdmans, 1999–2008.

Farah, Warrick. Mapping People Groups in [country name] for Informed Church Planting: A Research Project. Unpublished manuscript. 2005.

Fatah, Tarek. *Chasing a Mirage: The Tragic Illusion of an Islamic State*. Mississauga, ON: Wiley, 2008.

Francisco, Adam S. "Luther, Lutheranism, and the Challenge of Islam." *Concordia Theological Quarterly* 71 (2007) 283–300.

Friedman, Thomas. *The World is Flat*. New York: Farrar, Straus & Giroux, 2006.

Gairdner, William Henry Temple. "The Christian Church as a Home for Christ's Converts from Islam." *Moslem World* 14 (1924) 235–46.

Galinsky, Adam, et al. "From Power to Action." *Journal of Personality and Social Psychology* 85 (2003) 453–66.

Garrison, David. *Church Planting Movements*. Richmond, Virginia: International Mission Board of the Southern Baptist Convention, 1999.

———. "Church Panting Movements vs. Insider Movements: Missiological Realities vs. Mythological Speculations." *IJFM* 21 (2004) 151–54.

———. *The Nonresidential Missionary: A New Strategy and the People it Serves*. Birmingham, AL: MARC & New Hope, 1990.

Gaudeul, Jean-Marie. *Called from Islam to Christ: Why Muslims become Christians*. East Sussex: Monarch, 1999.

Gennep, Arnold van. *Les Rites de Passage*. Paris: Nourry, 1909.

Georges, Robert A., and Michael Owen Jones. *People Studying People: the Human Element in Fieldwork*. Berkeley: University of California Press, 1980.

Gilliland, Dean, ed. *The Word among Us: Contextualizing Theology for Mission Today*. 1989. Reprinted, Eugene, OR: Wipf & Stock, 2002.

Giddens, Anthony. *Central Problems in Social Theory: Action, Structure, and Contradiction in Social Analysis*. Berkley: University of California Press, 1979.

Gittins, Anthony. "Beyond Liturgical Inculturation: Transforming the Deep Structures of Faith." *Irish Theological Review* 69 (2004) 47–72.

Goddard, Hugh. *A History of Christian-Muslim Relations*. Chicago: New Amsterdam Books, 2000.

Gooren, Henri. *Religious Conversion and Disaffiliation: Tracing Patterns of Change in Faith Practices*. New York: Palgrave MacMillan, 2010.

Grafton, David D. "Mission Paradigms in the Pax Americana." *Currents in Theology and Mission* 32 (2005) 348–54.

Green, Michael. *Evangelism in the Early Church*. London: Hodder & Stoughton, 1970.

Green, Tim. "Factors Affecting Attitudes to Apostasy in Pakistan." MA thesis, University of London, 1998.

———. "Identity Issues for ex-Muslim Christians, with Particular Reference to Marriage." *SFM* 8/4 (2012) 435–81.

Greenham, Anthony Bryan. "A Study of Palestinian Muslim Conversions to Christ." *SFM* 6/1 (2010) 116–75.

Greil, Arthur L., and David Rudy. "Social Cocoons: Encapsulation and Identity Transformation Organizations." *Sociology Enquiry* 54 (1984) 260–78.

Groff, Peter S. *Islamic Philosophy A–Z*. Edinburgh: Edinburgh University Press, 2007.

Grudem, Wayne. *Systematic Theology: An Introduction to Biblical Doctrine*. Grand Rapids: Zondervan, 1994.

Guera, George. "The Church Planting Movement among the Kabyle Berbers of Algeria." Guest lecture, Nazareth Evangelical Theological Seminary, Nazareth, Israel. Dec 8, 2009.

Gustafson, K., and Common Ground Consultants. *An Insider View*. Minneapolis: Common Ground Consultants, 2007.

Guthrie, Shirley C. *Christian Doctrine*. Rev. ed. Louisville: Westminster John Knox, 1994.

Gutierrez, Gustavo. *Teología de Liberación: Perspectivas*. Salamanca: Sígueme, 1972.

———. *A Theology of Liberation: History, Politics, and Salvation*. Translated by Caridad Inda and John Eagleson. Maryknoll, NY: Orbis, 1973.

Hakimzadeh, Shirin. "Iran: a Vast Diaspora Abroad and Millions of Refugees at Home." Migration Policy Institute (Sep 1, 2006). http://www.migrationpolicy.org/article/iran-vast-diaspora-abroad-and-millions-refugees-home.

Harper, Brad, and Paul Louis Metzger. *Exploring Ecclesiology: An Evangelical and Ecumenical Introduction*. Ada, MI: Brazos, 2009.

Harrison, Everett, Geoffrey Bromiley, and Carl Henry, eds. *Baker's Dictionary of Theology*. Grand Rapids: Baker, 1960.

Harvey, Van A. *A Handbook of Theological Terms*. New York: Macmillan, 1964.

Hefner, Robert W. "Of Faith and Commitment: Christian Conversion in Muslim Java." In *Conversion to Christianity: Historical and Anthropological Perspectives on a Great Transformation*, edited by Robert W. Hefner, 99–125. Berkeley: University of California Press, 1993.

Herald, Timothy. "Making Sense of Contextualization: A Guide on Setting Parameters for Church Planters." *SFM* 5/6 (2009) 138–57.

Hesselgrave, David J. "Contextualization that is Authentic and Relevant." *IJFM* 12 (1995) 115–9.

———. "Great Commission Contextualization." *IJFM* 12 (1995) 139–45.

Hiebert, Paul. "Critical Contextualization." *IBMR* 12 (1987) 104–12.

Holder, Arthur G. "Wisdom." In *The New Westminster Dictionary of Christian Spirituality*, edited by Philip Sheldrake, 643–44. Louisville: Westminster John Knox, 2005.

Humphries, Mark. *Early Christianity*. London: Routledge, 2006.

Huntzinger, Allyn. *Persians in the Bible*. Salem, NJ: Persian World Outreach, 2001.

Ibn Ishaq. *The Life of Muhammad: A Translation of Ibn Ishaq's Sirat Rasul Allah*. Translated by A. Guillame. Oxford: Oxford University Press, 2002.

Ibn Warraq, ed. *Leaving Islam: Apostates Speak Out*. Amherst, NY: Prometheus, 2003.

Ibn-Mohammad, Mir. "A Muslim Tribal Chief is Bringing Jesus to His People." *MF* (May–June 2011) 18–9.

"Into the New Millennium: The Changing Face of Bible Translation." *LWP* (Jan 2007) 17–20.

Jackson, Bruce. *Fieldwork*. Urbana: University of Illinois Press, 1987.

Jacobsen, Karen, and Loren B. Landau. "The Dual Imperative in Refugee Research: Some Methodological and Ethical Considerations in Social Science Research on Forced Migration." *Disasters* 27 (2003) 185–206.

Jaffarian, Michael. "The Statistical State of the North American Missions Movement, from the *Mission Handbook*, 20th Edition." *IBMR* 32 (2008) 35–38.

James, William. *Varieties of Religious Experience*. Glasgow: Collins, 1977 [1902].

Janson, Marloes. "Chrislam: Forging Ties in a Multi-Religious Society." Work in Progress (2001?) http://www.egodiuchendu.com/index.php?option=com_content&view=article&id=65:chrislam-forging-ties-in-a-multi-religious-society&catid=5:papers&Itemid=11.

Jenkins, Philip. *The Lost History of Christianity: The Thousand-Year Golden Age of the Church in the Middle East, Africa, and Asia—and How It Died*. New York: HarperOne, 2008.

———. *The Next Christendom: The Coming of Global Christianity*. Oxford: Oxford University Press, 2002.

John Paul II. *Redemptoris Missio: On the Permanent Validity of the Church's Missionary Mandate*. United States Catholic Conference, Washington, DC, 1990.

Johnson, Callum. "One Under Our Father?: A Socio-anthropological Approach to Patronage, Reconciliation and Salvation in the South Asian Islamic Setting." *SFM* 4/3 (2008) 1–10.

Karecki, Madge. "Discovering the Roots of Ritual." *Missionalia* 25 (1997) 169–77.

Kedar, Leah, ed. *Power through Discourse*. Norwood, NJ: Ablex, 1987.

Khalil, Mohammad Hassan, and Mucahit Bilici. "Conversion out of Islam: A Study of Conversion Narratives of Former Muslims." *Muslim World* 97 (2007) 111–24.

Kraft, Charles. "Dynamic Equivalence Churches in Muslim Societies." In *The Gospel and Islam: A Compendium*. Abridged ed. Edited by Don M McCurry, 78–92. Monrovia, CA: MARC, 1979.

Kraft, Kathryn Ann. "Community and Identity among Arabs of a Muslim Background who Choose to Follow a Christian Faith." PhD diss., University of Bristol, 2007.

———. "Faith Is Lived out in Community: Questions of New Community for Arab Muslims Who Have Embraced a Christian Faith." *SFM* 6/6 (2010) 954–82.

Leaman, Oliver, ed. *The Qur'an: An Encyclopedia*. London: Routledge, 2006.

Lewis, Bernard. "Some Observations on the Significance of Heresy in the History of Islam." *Studia Islamica* 1 (1953) 43–63.

Lewis, Christopher. "It's Primetime in Iran / Looking for Home." *CT* (Sep 2008).

Lewis, Rebecca. "Insider Movements: Honoring God-given Identity and Community." *IJFM* 26 (2007) 16–9.

———. "The Integrity of the Gospel and Insider Movements." *IJFM* 27 (2010) 41–8.

———. "Promoting Movements to Christ within Natural Communities." *IJFM* 24 (2007) 75–6.

———. "Strategizing for Church Planting Movements in the Muslim World." *IJFM* 21 (2004) 73–7.

Livingstone, Greg. "Why Have Such a Small Percentage of the 1.6 Billion Muslims Become Christians? '34 Theses.'" *SFM* 9/3 (2013) 28–33.

Llull, Ramon. *Ars Breve*. In *Doctor Illuminatus: A Ramon Llull Reader*. Edited and translated by Anthony Bonner. Princeton: Princeton University Press, 1985.

———. *The Book of the Gentile and the Three Wise Men*. In *Doctor Illuminatus: A Ramon Llull Reader*. Edited and translated by Anthony Bonner. Princeton: Princeton University Press, 1985.

———. *The Book of the Lover and the Beloved*. Translated by E. Allison Peers. Cambridge, ON: In Parentheses Publications, 2000.

———. *Raymond's Proverbs, Pt 1: 100 Names of God*. Translated by Yanis Dambergs. http://orbita.bib.ub.es/ramon/complet.asp?2526.

Lofland, John, and Norman Skonovd. "Conversion Motifs." *Journal for the Scientific Study of Religions* 20 (1981) 373–85.

Louy, Stephen D. "The Origins of Christian Identity in the Letters of Paul." PhD diss., University of Edinburgh, 2012.

Lotfi, Nasser. *Iranian Christian*. Waco, TX: Word, 1980.

Lukes, Steven. *Power: A Radical View*. New York: MacMillan, 1974.

MacCulloch, Diarmaid. *Tudor Church Militant: Edward VI and the Protestant Reformation*. London: Allen Lane, 1999.

Madany, Bassam M. "The Missiology of Kamil Abdul Messiah, A Syrian Convert from Islam to Christianity." *SFM* 3/4 (2008).

———. "The New Christians of North Africa and the Insider Movement." *SFM* 5/5 (2009) 49–57.

———. "The Trinity and Christian Mission to Muslims." *SFM* 6/3 (2009) 444–63.

Madany, Shirley W. *Muslims Meeting Christ*. Upper Darby, PA: Middle East Resources, 2005.

Mahdi, Ali Akbar. "The Iranian Women's Movement: A Century Long Struggle." *Muslim World* 9 (2004) 427–48.

Maier, Martin. "Inculturation." *Stimmen der Zeit*, (Aug 2007) 505–6.

Makdisi, Ussama. *Artillery of Heaven: American Missionaries and the Failed Conversion of the Middle East*. Ithaca: Cornell University Press, 2008.

Mallouhi, Mazhar. "Comments on the Insider Movement." *SFM* 5/5 (2009) 3–14.

Mandryk, Jason, ed. *Operation World*. 7th ed. Colorado Springs, Colorado: Biblica, 2010.

Mansour, Ahmed Subhy. *The False Penalty of Apostasy (Killing the Apostate)*. 2008. http://ahl-alquran.com/English/show_article.php?main_id=3776.

———. *The Penalty of Apostasy*. Translator unknown. Toronto: International Publishing and Distributing, 1998.

Markarian, Krikor. "The Long March Forward: From Cyrus to Ayatollah." *Mission Frontiers* (Sep–Oct 2008) 15–17.

———. "Spiritual Vacuum." *Mission Frontiers* (Sep–Oct 2008) 10–13.

———. "Today's Iranian Revolution: How the Mullahs are Leading the Nation to Jesus." *Mission Frontiers* (Sep–Oct 2008) 6–13.

Masood, Steven. *Into the Light*. Bromley: STL, 1986.

Mattingly, Cheryl. "Toward a Vulnerable Ethics of Research Practice." *Health* 9 (2005) 453–71.

Massey, Joshua. "God's Amazing Diversity in Drawing Muslims to Christ." *IJFM* 17 (2000) 5–14.

McCurry, Don, ed. *The Gospel and Islam: A Compendium*. Abridged ed. Monrovia, CA: MARC, 1979.

McDermott, Gerald, ed. *The Oxford Handbook of Evangelical Theology*. Oxford: Oxford University Press, 2011.

McGuckin, John Anthony. *The Orthodox Church: An Introduction to Its History, Doctrine, and Spiritual Culture*. Malden, MA: Blackwell, 2008.

McLaughlin, Abraham. "In Africa, Islam and Christianity are growing—and blending." *Christian Science Monitor* (Jan 26, 2006). http://www.csmonitor.com/2006/0126/p01s04-woaf.html.

McNeal, Melani. "Contextualization or the Affirmation of Patriarchal Norms? The Case for Breaking Cultural Norms to Reach Muslim Women." *SFM* 3:2 (2007).

Meral, Ziya. 'Bearing the Silence of God." *CT* 52/3 (March 19, 2008) 41. http://www.christianitytoday.com/ct/2008/march/29.41.html?paging=off.

———. *No Place to Call Home: Experiences of Apostates from Islam, Failures of the International Community*. Surrey, UK: Christian Solidarity Worldwide, 2008. http://www.online2.church123.com/attach.asp?clientURN=christiansolidarity worldwide2&attachFileName=09ae125dba76986113441ef1463aca8e.attach &attachOriginalFileName=CSW_Briefing_Apostasy_April_2008.pdf .

Miller, Duane Alexander. "The Conversion Narrative of Samira: From Shi'a Islam to Mary, Her Church, and Her Son." *SFM* 5/5 (2009) 81–92.

———. "The Episcopal Church in Jordan: Identity, Liturgy, and Mission." *Journal of Anglican Studies* 9 (2011) 134–53.

———. "An Exploration of Christ's Converts from Islam: Reasons Given for their Conversions." *Journal of Asian Missiology* 15 (2014) 15–27.

———. "Power, Personalities, and Politics: The Growth of Iranian Christianity since 1979." *Mission Studies* 32 (2015) 66–86.

———. "Reappropriation: An Accommodationist Hermeneutic of Islamic Christianity." *SFM* 5/3 (2009) 3–36.

———. "The Secret World of God: Aesthetics, Relationships, and the Conversion of 'Frances' from Shi'a Islam to Christianity." *Global Missiology* 9/3 (2012) 1–14.

———. "Woven in the Weakness of the Changing Body: the Genesis of World Islamic Christianity." Paper presented at Coming to Faith Consultation 2, Buckinghamshire, UK, February, 2010.

Miller, Duane Alexander, and C. M. "Muslim-background Congregations in the Villages around Lucknow, India: An Interview with C**** M*****." *SFM* 8/4 (2012) 482–88.

Miller, Duane Alexander, and Patrick Johnstone. "Believers in Christ from a Muslim Background: A Global Census." *Interdisciplinary Journal of Research on Religion* 11:10 (2015) 1–19.

Miller, William McElwee. *Ten Muslims Meet Christ*. Grand Rapids: Eerdmans, 1969.

Mitchell, Bill. "Bible Translation in the New Millennium: The Changed and Changing Context." *LWP* (Jan 2007) 2–7.

Mouw, Richard. "The Problem of Authority in Evangelical Christianity." In *Church Unity and the Papal Office*, edited by Carl Braaten and Robert Jenson, 124–41. Grand Rapids: Eerdmans.

Mustafa. *Against the Tides in the Middle East*. Dorpspruit, South Africa: International Evangelical Resource Centre, 1997.

Naaman, Paul. "Maronite Society at the End of the XVI Century." http://www.lebanese-forces.org/media/articles/abbotnaaman/MaroniteSociety.htm.

Nasser, David. *Jumping through Fires*. Grand Rapids: Baker, 2009.

Neely, Brent J., and Peter G. Riddell, eds. *Islam and the Last Day: Christian Perspectives on Islamic Eschatology*. Wantirna, VIC: Melbourne School of Theology Press, 2014.

Nelson, Jeff. "Going Public with Faith in a Muslim Context: Lessons from Esther." *IJFM* 28 (2012) 191–4.

Nevisa, Mina, and Jim Croft. *Miracle of Miracles*. Fairfax, VA: Touch of Christ Ministries, 2004.

Nicholls, Bruce J. *Contextualization: A Theology of Gospel and Culture*. Downers Grove, IL: InterVarsity, 1979.

Nikides, Bill. "The Church at the Crossroads: A Global Perspective." *SFM* 2/4 (2007).

———. "The Emergence of Insider Movements." *SFM* 7/3 (2011) 46–57.

———. "Evaluating 'Insider Movements': C5 (Messianic Muslims)." *SFM* 1/4 (2006).

Nock, Arthur Darby. *Conversion; the Old and the New in Religion from Alexander the Great to Augustine of Hippo*. Oxford: Oxford University Press, 1933.

Oksnevad, Roy. "BMB Discipleship: An Investigation into the Factors Leading to Disharmony within the Iranian Church in the Diaspora." *SFM* 8/4 (2012) 397–434.

———. "Contextualization in the Islamic Context." *LWP* (April 2007). http://www.lausanneworldpulse.com/themedarticles-php/686/04-2007.

Ottenberg, S. "Thirty Years of Fieldnotes: Changing Relationships to the Text." In *Fieldnotes: The Makings of Anthropology*, edited by R. Sanjek, 139–60. Ithaca, NY: Cornell University Press, 1990.

Packer, J. I. "A Stunted Ecclesiology: The Theory and Practice of Evangelical Churchliness." *Touchstone* 15/10 (2002).

Parshall, Phil. *Divine Threads within a Human Tapestry*. Pasadena: William Carey, 2000.

———. *Muslim Evangelism: Contemporary Approaches to Contextualization*. Waynesboro, GA: Gabriel, 2003.

———. *New Paths in Muslim Evangelism: Evangelical Approaches to Contextualization*. Grand Rapids: Baker, 1980.

Patterson, George, and Richard Scoggins. *Church Multiplication Guide: Helping Churches to Reproduce Locally and Abroad*. Pasadena, CA: William Carey Library, 1993.

Paul VI. *Evangelii Nuntiandi: On Evangelization in the Modern World*. Boston: Pauline, 1976.

Pew Forum. "Event Transcript: The Coming Religious Wars? Demographics and Conflict in Islam and Christianity." Washington, DC: Pew Research Center, 2005. http://pewforum.org/events/?EventID=82.

———. *The Future of the Global Muslim Population: Projections for 2010–2030*. Washington, DC: Pew Research Center, 2011. http://www.pewforum.org/The-Future-of-the-Global-Muslim-Population.aspx.

———. "An Uncertain Road: Muslims and the Future of Europe." Washington, DC: Pew Research Center, 2005. http://pewforum.org/uploadedfiles/Topics/Religious_Affiliation/Muslim/muslims-europe-2005.pdf.

Pikkert, Peter. *Protestant Missionaries to the Middle East: Ambassadors for Christ or Culture?* Hamilton, ON: WEC Canada, 2008.

Pratt, Douglas. *The Challenge of Islam: Encounters in Interfaith Dialogue*. Aldershot, UK: Ashgate, 2005.

Rabiipour, Saiid. *Farewell to Islam*. Maitland, FL: Xulon, 2009.

Rambo, Lewis. *Understanding Religious Conversion*. New Haven: Yale University Press, 1993.

Register, Ray. *Back to Jerusalem: Church Planting Movements in the Holy Land*. Enumclaw, WA: Winepress, 2000.

———. *Dialogue and Interfaith Witness with Muslims: A Guide and Sample Ministry in the USA*. Rev. ed. Ephrata, PA: Multi-Language Media, 1979.

———. "Discipling Middle Eastern Believers." *SFM* 5/2 (2009) 1–80.

Reynolds, Gabriel Said. "Evangelizing Islam." *First Things* (January 2011).

———. "The Muslim Jesus: Dead or Alive?" *Bulletin of the School of Oriental and African Studies* 72 (2009) 237–58.

———. "Sanctifying Islam." *First Things* 194 (2009) 50–2.

Richardson, Don. *Secrets of the Koran: Revealing Insights into Islam's Holy Book*. Ventura, CA: Regal, 2003.

Ripken, Nik, and Barry Stricker. "*First Let Me Go and Bury My Father* . . . The Costly Call to Follow Christ—and a Special Challenge for Muslim Seekers." *Called to Faith Consultation 2*, Resource CD (2009),

———. "Muslim Background Believers and Baptism in Cultures of Persecution and Violence." *Called to Faith Consultation 2*, Resource CD (2006).

Rippin, Andrew. *Muslims: Their Religious Beliefs and Practices*. 3rd ed. New York: Routledge, 2005.

Rishawi, Emir. *A Struggle that Led to Conversion: Motives for a Gospel-based Faith*. Translator unknown. Villach, Austria: Light of Life, 1993.

Robinson, Stuart, and Peter Botross. *Defying Death: Zakaria Botross Apostle to Islam*. Upper Mt. Gravatt, Australia: City Harvest, 2008.

Rusin, David. "Fear Stalks Muslim Apostates in the West." *Middle East Forum* (2008). http://www.meforum.org/1966/fear-stalks-muslim-apostates-in-the-west.

Saada, Tass, and Dean Merrill. *Once an Arafat Man*. Carol Stream, IL: Tyndale House, 2008.

Saleem, Kamal, and Lynn Vincent. *The Blood of Lambs*. New York: Howard, 2009.

Sanneh, Lamin. "Muhammad, Prophet of Islam, and Jesus Christ, Image of God: A Personal Testimony." *IBMR* 8 (1984) 169–74.

———. *Whose Religion is Christianity? The Gospel beyond the West*. Grand Rapids: Eerdmans, 2003.

Schineller, Peter. *A Handbook on Inculturation*. Mahwah, NJ: Paulist, 1990.

Schmidt, John, dir. *The Jesus Film*. Mount Royal, Quebec: Madacy, 1979.

Schmidt, Mette. "An Ecumenical Miracle—An Arabic Satellite Channel Devoted to Christian Unity in a Torn Region." *International Review of Mission* 96 (2007) 288–92.

Schreiter, Robert J. *Constructing Local Theologies*. Maryknoll, NY: Orbis, 1985.

Shah, Hannah. *The Imam's Daughter*. Grand Rapids: Zondervan, 2010.

Shahbazi, A. Shapur. "Nowruz ii: In the Islamic Period." In *Encyclopaedia Iranica*. (2007) http://www.iranicaonline.org/articles/nowruz-ii/.

Shaw, R. Daniel. "Contextualizing the Power and the Glory." *IJFM* 12 (1995) 155–60.

Shaw, Rosalind, and Charles Stewart. "Introduction: Problematizing Syncretism." In *Syncretism/Anti-Syncretism: The Politics of Religious Synthesis*, edited by Charles Stewart and Rosalind Shaw, 1–26. London: Routledge, 1994.

Sheikh, Bilquis, and R. Schneider. *I Dared to Call Him Father*. Lincoln, VA: Chosen, 1978.

Sheldrake, Philip, ed. *The New SCM Dictionary of Christian Spirituality*. London: SCM, 2005.

Shenk, Calvin E. "The Demise of the Church in North Africa and Nubia and Its Survival in Egypt and Ethiopia: A Question of Contextualization?" *Missionalia* 21 (1993) 131–54.

Shorter, Aylward. *Toward a Theology of Inculturation*. 1988. Reprinted, Eugene, OR: Wipf & Stock, 1999.

Siirat al Masiih Bilisaan 3arabi Fasiih. Larnaca, Cyprus: Abdo, 1987.

Sleeman, Matthew. "The Origins, Development and Future of the C5 / Insider Movement Debate." *SFM* 8/4 (2012) 498–566.

Smith, Eli, and H. G. O. Dwight. *Missionary Researches in Armenia*. London: Wightman, 1834.

Sobrino, Jon. *Christology at the Crossroads: A Latin American Approach*. Translated by John Drury. Maryknoll, NY: Orbis, 1978.

Sollier, J. "Adoptionism." In *The Catholic Encyclopedia*. New York: Robert Appleton, 1907.

Sookhdeo, Patrick. "Persecution of Christians in the Muslim World." *LWP* (Nov 2005).

Span, John, and Anne Span. "Report on the Common Ground Consultants Meeting." *SFM* 5/4 (2009) 52–73.

Starling, Allan. "Oral Communications and the Global Recordings Network." *LWP* (Oct–Nov 2009). http://www.lausanneworldpulse.com/themedarticles-php/1217/10–2009.

Stanley, Brian. "Inculturation: Historical Background, Theological Foundations and Contemporary Questions." *Transformation* 24 (2007) 21–27.

Syrjänen, Seppo. *In Search of Meaning and Identity: Conversion to Christianity in Pakistani Muslim Culture*. Helsinki: Finnish Society for Missiology and Ecumenics, 1984.

Talman, Harley. "Comprehensive Contextualization." *IJFM* 21 (2004) 6–12.

Tennent, Timothy C. "The Hidden History of Insider Movements." *CT* 57 (2013) 28–29.

Tertullian. *Ad Nationes* in *Ante-Nicene Fathers*, Vol. 3. Translated by Peter Holmes. Edited by Alexander Roberts, James Donaldson, and A. Cleveland Coxe. Buffalo, NY: Christian Literature, 1885. Revised and edited for New Advent by Kevin Knight. http://www.newadvent.org/fathers/0306.htm/.

———. *Apology* in *Ante-Nicene Fathers*, Vol. 3. Translated by S. Thelwall. Edited by Alexander Roberts, James Donaldson, and A. Cleveland Coxe. Buffalo, NY: Christian Literature, 1885. Revised and edited for New Advent by Kevin Knight. http://www.newadvent.org/fathers/0301.htm/.

Traub, James. "Exodus: Is there a Place for Christians in the New Middle East?" *Foreign Policy* (October 21, 2011). http://www.foreignpolicy.com/articles/2011/10/21/exodus?print=yes&hidecomments=yes&page=full.

Travis, John. "The C1 to C6 Spectrum." *Evangelical Missions Quarterly* 34 (1998) 407–8.

———. "Messsianic Muslim Followers of Isa: A Closer Look at C5 Believers and Congregations." *IJFM* 17 (2000) 53–9.

Turner, Victor. *The Forest of Symbols: Aspects of Ndembu Ritual*. Ithaca, NY: Cornell University Press, 1967.

Vander Werff, Lyle L. *Christian Mission to Muslims: The Record: Anglican and Reformed Approaches in India and the Near East, 1800–1938.* Pasadena: William Carey Library, 1977.

Viswanathan, Gauri. *Outside the Fold: Conversion, Modernity, and Belief.* Princeton: Princeton University Press, 1998.

Walls, Andrew F. *The Christian Movement in Christian History: Studies in the Transmission of Faith.* Maryknoll, NY: Orbis, 1996.

The Way of Fatima: A Collection of Articles, Messages, and Poems Related to Fatima Al-Matayri who was Martyred in August 2008, in the Kingdom of Saudi Arabia, for her Faith in the Lord Jesus Christ. Translator unknown. http://www.jesus-for-all.net/christian_books/pdf_234.pdf.

Whittaker, Elvi. "Anthropological Ethics, Fieldwork and Epistemological Disjunctures." *Philosophy of Social Science* 11 (1981) 437–51.

William, J. S. "Inside/Outside: Getting to the Center of the Muslim Contextualization Debates." *SFM* 7:3 (2011) 58–95.

Willis, Avery T., Jr. *Indonesian Revival: Why Two Million Came to Christ.* Pasadena, CA: William Carey Library, 1977.

Wolfe, J. Henry. "Insider Movements: An Assessment of the Viability of Retaining Socio-religious Insider Identity in High Religious Contexts." PhD diss., Southern Baptist Theological Seminary, 2011.

Woodberry, J. Dudley. "Contextualization among Muslims: Reusing Common Pillars." *IJFM* 13 (1996) 171–86.

Woodberry, J. Dudley, and Russell G. Shubin. "Muslims tell. . . 'Why I Chose Jesus.'" *Mission Frontiers* (March 2001). http://www.missionfrontiers.org/pdf/2001/01/muslim.htm> and accessed 18 September 2013 <www.missionfrontiers.org/issue/article/muslims-tell. . .-why-i-chose-jesus.

Woodberry, J. Dudley, Russell G. Shubin, and G. Marks. "Why Muslims Follow Jesus." *CT* (Oct 2007). http://www.christianitytoday.com/ct/2007/october/42.80.html.

Wright, N. T. 2007. "The Cross and the Caricatures." *Fulcrum* (Eastertide 2007). http://www.fulcrum-anglican.org.uk/news/2007/20070423wright.cfm?doc=205.

Yousef, Mosab Hassan, with Ron Brackin. *Son of Hamas.* Carol Stream, IL: Tyndale, 2010.

Zanganeh, Hamid. "Socioeconomic Trends in Iran: Successes and Failures." *Muslim World* 94 (2004) 481–94.

Zehner, Edwin. *Unavoidably Hybrid: Thai Buddhist Conversions to Evangelical Christianity.* PhD diss., Cornell University, 2003.